Too Cold for Mermaids

Alice Rose at anchor
in a secluded Georgian Bay cove

Too Cold for Mermaids

David J. Forsyth

Rock's Mills Press
Oakville, Ontario
2017

PUBLISHED BY
ROCK'S MILLS PRESS
www.rocksmillspress.com

Copyright © 2016 by David J. Forsyth
All rights reserved. Published by arrangement with the author.

For information, contact customer.service@rocksmillspress.com.
Library and Archives Canada Cataloguing in Publication data is available from the publisher.

Love and Adventure
are the
Condiments of Life.

≈≈≈≈≈≈≈≈≈≈≈≈≈≈

To my wife Trisha,
who selflessly supported my cruising obsession,
repeatedly surprised me
with her ability to adapt to every situation,
and kept me warm
through dreary days and cold nights.

Contents

PREFACE / ix

CHAPTER ONE Palm Trees and Parrots / 1
CHAPTER TWO The Pequod Mutiny / 13
CHAPTER THREE Alice Rose and Lap Cat / 24
CHAPTER FOUR Mimico to Montreal / 32
CHAPTER FIVE Yacht Club de Quebec / 46
CHAPTER SIX North of Forty-Eight / 54
CHAPTER SEVEN Beyond the End of the Road / 66
CHAPTER EIGHT "The Rock" / 78
CHAPTER NINE The Labrador Coast / 89
CHAPTER TEN The Iceberg / 98
CHAPTER ELEVEN *Ombre Rose* / 106
CHAPTER TWELVE Farewell Penetanguishene / 116
CHAPTER THIRTEEN *Alice Rose*'s Rebirth / 127
CHAPTER FOURTEEN East by Northeast / 136
CHAPTER FIFTEEN Retreat, Regroup and Resume / 148
CHAPTER SIXTEEN The Void / 157
CHAPTER SEVENTEEN Sprint to the Finish / 169
CHAPTER EIGHTEEN The Resurrection / 174
CHAPTER NINETEEN The Circle of Light / 185
CHAPTER TWENTY New York and the Hudson / 194
CHAPTER TWENTY-ONE Goodbye, *Alice Rose* / 202

GLOSSARY OF MARINE TERMINOLOGY / 211

List of Maps

1. The Great Lakes / 7
2. Hamilton Harbour / 8
3. Georgian Bay / 10
4. Lake Ontario / 16
5. Western Lake Ontario / 34
6. Eastern Lake Ontario / 35
7. The Upper St. Lawrence River / 42
8. The Lower St. Lawrence River / 50
9. Port Menier / 63
10. Newfoundland and Labrador / 72
11. The U.S. Atlantic Coast (South) / 108
12. The U.S. Atlantic Coast (North) / 109
13. Goderich to Hamilton / 118
14. L'Anse-à-Beaufils to Halifax / 170
15. Boston to Albany / 191
16. New York City Waterways / 194
17. Erie Canal, Eastern Section / 203
18. Erie Canal, Western Section / 204

Preface

There *was* a time in my life when I wasn't in love with water. That was when I was a toddler, raised on a farm and compelled to suffer a weekly bath in a galvanized tub of tepid well-water. But by the time I was six, I had discovered the nearby creek, where wading among frogs and water-bugs seemed far superior to bathing. And then there were the one-week summer vacations that our family enjoyed at various lakeside cottages, where my brother and I always managed to acquire a boat of some description, or, at the very least, construct a crude raft. That's how it all began. After that, I can't recall a time when I didn't dream of sailing around the world.

Cruising to foreign shores under sail is one of those childhood fantasies that are seldom achieved but which one never outgrows. My obsession with the idea was possibly the result of my second or third reading of *The Coral Island*. I loved that story. My grandmother had received Robert M. Ballantyne's classic novel as an academic prize in 1906 and passed it on to me a half-century later.

Eventually, while still an aspiring artist, I dreamed of acquiring my own boat and sailing the world, earning my living as a freelance commercial artist or perhaps through the sale of my paintings. The dream, however, faded as I slipped unnoticed into the workforce, married and became a father with commensurate responsibilities.

One afternoon, in the spring of 1989, while enduring a particularly difficult day at the office, I took my first step toward my elusive dream. That initial step changed my life. It opened doors to understanding and adventure—and to writing. Within weeks, I noted changes in my behaviour that made my goals seem achievable. As time passed, I learned how to sail, how to choose the appropriate boat, and how to suitably equip it to meet the challenges of cruising. Finally, I set out to explore the world and informally document my adventures for family and friends.

At first, I sailed only in the protected waters of Hamilton harbour, then on Lake Ontario and windswept Georgian Bay. My skills accumulated in barely noticeable increments, as I waded through a maze of marine terminology and technology, studied seamanship and navigation, and developed competence. My wife,

Patricia, shared those early years of trial and terror, frequently supporting my obsession beyond my expectations, and pardoning my behaviour when, out of urgency, I raised my voice more than the situation warranted. Gradually, I accumulated the knowledge, certifications and confidence to venture farther afield.

On one occasion, I left the comfort of my home and family behind for a period of seven weeks, in order to gain valuable cruising experience as a crewmember on a passage to Newfoundland and Labrador. During that voyage, I shared experiences with my shipmates that novice sailors would envy. The following year, I flew to Fort Lauderdale with two other crewmembers to deliver a thirty-six foot Gozzard to Maine. That passage, orchestrated by a capable and affable skipper, lasted five weeks, and was, for the most part, a relaxing holiday featuring sights and events to be cherished.

On my return home, I gathered my own crew and sailed my classic little sloop, *Alice Rose*, from Georgian Bay to Hamilton, her port of registry, where she endured a three-year refit in preparation for an Atlantic crossing. With my wife and a close friend of more than forty years on board, *Alice Rose* cruised eagerly eastward, through the locks of the St. Lawrence, toward Sydney, Nova Scotia. Little did I know at the time what was in store for us at the St. Lawrence port of Matane.

The final passage, an unscheduled cruise from Nova Scotia to Hamilton by way of New York City, was not the triumphant return of which I had dreamed, but in some respects it ranked among the best sailing *Alice Rose* and I ever shared. Much of the passage was a warm and welcome change from the cold North Atlantic, and, compared to the previous year's eastward shake-down cruise, all the equipment on board functioned in accordance with the manufacturers' claims. Still, that cruise severely challenged *Alice Rose* and her crew on at least two occasions.

Years later, following the sale of my beloved *Alice Rose*, I wrote my first book, a memoir of growing up on a farm in the shadow of World War II. It was to be a gift to my grandchildren. The experience encouraged me to continue writing; the subject with which I was most familiar was cruising, so I eagerly assembled my journals, logs and correspondence, and began this book.

Though, in the end, my lofty fantasy eluded my grasp, I came tantalizingly close to achieving it, and in the interim enjoyed more than a decade of sailing on North America's Great Lakes and along its Atlantic coasts. While I hope readers will find *Too Cold for Mermaids* entertaining, it is also intended to provide inspiration to those dreamers who haven't yet taken that first step, and perhaps act as an introduction to cruising. If indeed your goal is to sail to distant ports, I wish you the best of luck, and assure you that the vast majority of those I met in the marinas and yacht clubs along my routes began as landlubbers with no more than a dream of standing on the salt-washed decks of their own yachts someday.

CHAPTER ONE
Palm Trees and Parrots

I can't remember a time when I *didn't* dream of sailing to far-off places. It was a relentless childhood fantasy that pursued me into adulthood.

My first love and I were naive, aspiring artists. We talked of buying a boat instead of a house and sailing the world together, earning our living through our combined artistic skills. The dream died with the relationship, and I slipped incrementally into the process of earning a living, maintaining a home, and raising children. As an adult with responsibilities, my dream appeared impractical and financially beyond my reach.

After a series of false starts in advertising and graphic reproduction, I accepted a more secure position with a department of the local municipal government. Within a few months, I was reassigned to the organization's in-house printing facility. My artistic skills and graphics training enabled me to significantly expand the branch's services which, in turn, led to my promotion to supervisor.

Fifteen years passed while I transformed the two-man print shop into a modern, full-service graphics facility with a staff of six. Just as my role was becoming a little too routine, I secured a challenging middle management position that put me in charge of another significant corporate project. I loved my job, and I earned a reputation among upper management for personal integrity and accountability. Well into my career and immersed in a reorganization of my department, I noted the corporate culture was changing. From my point of view, bureaucracy was getting in the way of common sense, and as time passed, I found it increasingly difficult to fit into the new corporate paradigm. One afternoon in the spring of 1989, while sitting at my desk and feeling a little more stressed than usual, I found myself wishing I could sail away to a land of palm trees and parrots.

This time, things were different; a recent corporate seminar had featured the setting and reliable accomplishment of goals. When the speaker's presentation concluded, I purchased a set of audio tapes that reiterated and reinforced his approach to reaching objectives. The tapes contained invaluable insights based on the precept, "If you want to be successful, do what successful people do!"

How could I argue with that? The concept was so simple and elegant! Success isn't about a family name, one's social status, or some unique pre-existing advantage; it's about *behaviour*.

Decades earlier I had come to the conclusion that, while many things in the world are incredibly beautiful, complex, and enigmatic, there is no magic. I had subsequently adopted the pragmatic view that I and the mathematics of chance determine my future. So what had I done toward fulfilling my dream? *Absolutely nothing!*

I hastily scribbled one more objective into my Day-Timer, and so began the fulfilment of my childhood fantasy. At the time, I failed to understand the significance of that first step though I had unknowingly embarked on one of the greatest adventures of my life.

The audio tapes recommended I make a list of the things I could do to make my dream a reality—little things. I began with:

- Read sailing magazines;
- Determine what a suitable boat costs;
- Tell friends and family about my dream;
- Search the public library for books about sailing;
- Visit marinas and chandleries to familiarize myself with equipment and gear;
- Search classified ads for boats for sale.

I knew I couldn't afford a yacht, even though I had no idea what a suitable vessel would cost. At the time, I barely knew the difference between a yawl and a ketch, but I was going sailing. The following day, on my lunch hour, I walked to a nearby bank to open a savings account, thereafter known as *the boat account*. I signed the signature card and handed the teller a ten-dollar bill. Then I began reassessing my spending habits and cutting back on unnecessary expenditures. I bought fewer coffees at work, and whenever I was tempted to buy something, I asked myself, "Do you want that more than a boat?"

That was a major factor in reaching my goal because the answer was almost always, "No."

My payday deposits increased from ten dollars to twenty. Over the next few months, I began adding larger sums, including my life insurance dividend, my income tax return, and what I earned from occasional freelance design jobs. While I waited for the boat account to grow, I spent my lunch hours at the library, researching every aspect of boating. On weekends, my wife and I wandered the docks of marinas, admiring the sailboats. I read accounts of ocean passages, circumnavigations, and feats of survival at sea.

By the summer of 1990, my loving wife Trisha had been a spouse and mother for more than half of her life. Barely out of school, she had accepted those responsibilities without taking the time to identify or develop interests of her own. She hadn't chosen a career, seen the world, nor indulged herself with activities for her own entertainment or self-fulfilment. Trisha had always put my needs and those of our children ahead of her own. Her housekeeping, parenting, and cooking skills were above reproach, and my many interests were almost always accommodated. Finally, with the kids grown to adulthood, my wife could experience life without the constant distraction and responsibility of raising children.

When I proposed that we learn to sail, Trisha embraced the idea as if it had been her own. We learned that the local sailing club was offering a thirty-hour coastal cruising course the following summer, so we enrolled. We met other couples with similar interests and began absorbing the culture. My wife may have lacked my determination, but she made every effort to accommodate my obsession.

Following the course examination on the final day of classes, we wandered among the boats in the Harbour West Marina boatyard. There, a chance encounter with an aging mariner led me down an unforeseen path. It was to be the road to my goal. His thirty-foot Alberg nestled firmly into its rough-hewn, wooden cradle, a hundred feet from the water. The name "Pequod" was emblazoned on her bows in Old-English letters. Tacked to the cradle beneath the hull was a black and red "For Sale" sign. With the traditional launch season long past and her mast, stanchions, and life-lines conspicuously absent, she appeared naked. Yet, aside from a film of fine, teak-coloured dust around her midship's deck combing, the vessel was spotless.

Though grey-haired and obviously middle-aged, I had just written the certification exam for basic keelboat cruising and had virtually no practical sailing experience; I was a novice. From the perspective of the scruffy, old troll, I was a landlubber, and through *his* weary eyes, *just a kid*. I squinted into the late morning sun at the squat silhouette near the top of the ladder.

"Is this an Alberg twenty-nine?" I inquired.

Without turning in my direction or showing any sign of civility, the grizzled skipper continued sanding the teak toe rail. Then, as I was about to repeat the question, he replied, "It's thirty-foot." I could feel the disdain in his response.

If *Pequod* was a thirty, she must have been built at least twelve years earlier and could be as much as thirty years old. Carl Alberg's more recent twenty-nine-foot design, featuring an expanded cabin and a wheel in place of its tiller, was at the top of my list of suitable sailboats. *Pequod* was equipped with a tiller; how had I overlooked that? In an attempt to impress the old man, I had embarrassed myself.

With Trisha lingering inconspicuously nearby, I explained I had just completed the sailing course and added that I would be willing to crew for him in exchange for the experience. He ignored me.

With the rhythmic sound of the man's sanding over my shoulder, I walked among the maze of idle keelboats in the boatyard. Then, as Trisha passed Pequod's stern in pursuit, the sanding stopped.

"What's your 'usband's phone number?"

Trisha had witnessed the stranger's rude treatment of her husband, and her response reflected her disapproval.

"Same as mine," she quipped with uncharacteristic cheek.

I didn't observe the exchange, but once I came to know Mr Markey, I had little doubt that my wife's response had triggered a restrained smile and perhaps an inaudible chuckle.

When Trisha caught up to me, she described what had transpired. I wrote my name and phone number on a scrap of paper and delivered it to Pequod's skipper. He took a break from his task, turned toward me and entered into a conversation about his boat, his situation, and the lateness of the season. Living in the shadow of a heart condition and crewless—no doubt due to his disposition—the retired ship's carpenter was preparing his vessel for potential buyers. I thought it unlikely that anyone would pay his price and wondered if, in his opinion, anyone else would be worthy of commanding *Pequod*. I sensed that he doubted my value as a deckhand, but in the end, perhaps out of desperation, he accepted my offer subject to certain conditions. Apparently in the boating tradition, crew members are crew members—on the water and in the boatyard. Even if *Pequod* wasn't launched that season, I was expected to show up for work every weekend and evening to do whatever Mr Markey determined was necessary. If I worked late at the office or had a social commitment, I was likely to be met the following day with, "Where were you yesterday?"

The "For Sale" sign quietly vanished within a few days, and for much of the summer, I helped Mr Markey prepare his thirty-year-old blue-water cruiser for the 1991 sailing season. Though he never thanked me and likely undervalued my contribution, I could see how much he needed and, on occasion, appreciated my help. When time and funds permitted, I booked three-hour rentals of twenty-four-foot Sharks to test my recently acquired sailing knowledge. The Sharks were easy-to-sail, sloop-rigged keelboats, and with Trisha as my crew, I practiced "coming about" in the shelter of the Hamilton Harbour.

Over the next few weeks I scraped, scrubbed, sanded, and sweated whenever I could find the time while the old slave-driver imparted his water-wise wisdom in bits and pieces. Between tasks, he recounted tales of serving aboard the ships of the Blue Funnel Line and described his surveying of Ontario's lakes while in the employ of the Canadian Hydrographic Service. His incredible repertoire included passing references to a boxing career in England, service as a Labour Member in the British Parliament, and hard-hat diving in the Suez Canal in the late 1950s. How closely his fantastic stories represented truth is unimportant. They were entertaining and passed the time, and, if I listened intently, a gem of seamanship could always be found hidden somewhere within his tale. The crusty old man's eyes sparkled with excitement as he relived his adventures; so much so that just listening to him felt like giving him a gift.

One of my favourite anecdotes was Mr Markey's description of a northward passage from South Africa. His ship, laden with bananas, was bound for England, and as ship's carpenter, he was responsible for maintaining conditions favourable to the preservation of the cargo. That meant controlling humidity and temperatures below decks by ensuring adequate airflow. During each watch, he made his rounds of the compartments that held the stalks of fruit, opening and closing bulkhead hatches as needed.

> *Sometimes, when you opened an 'atch, a rush of air would 'it you from the other side. The trouble was that the bloody banana spiders would spin a web across the 'atchway. Some of 'm were the size of dinner plates. I 'ated 'em with a passion!*

It wasn't immediately obvious to me that the old merchant seaman was teaching his pupil about ingenuity and resourcefulness, but he eventually made his point.

> *When we put in at Sierra Leone, I went ashore and bought a plastic water-gun on the market. I filled it with ammonia, and whenever I saw one of the little bastards, I let 'm 'ave it. We were in the Bay of Biscay off the coast of France when the skipper sent a deck'and to fetch me. I went to the bridge and 'e said, "Chippy, come wi' me. I want to show you some'ing."*
>
> *We went below and 'e pointed out stalks of bananas covered in little black spots. "Ever seen anything like 'at before?" 'e asked.*
>
> *"No Cap'n. Never," I said.*

Mr Markey's eyes twinkled as he chuckled boisterously, clearly pleased that the ship's captain hadn't connected the cargo damage to his ingenious conquest of the repulsive spiders.

By the end of the summer, I had logged fifteen hours of daylight sailing on club rentals. As time passed and my sailing experience accumulated, my appreciation of Trisha's contributions grew. While I pursued my dream over the next fifteen years, her support endured—with a couple of caveats. My wife adamantly refused to participate in a trans-Atlantic crossing though she agreed to fly to Europe and share with me the exploration of its coasts. Neither would she agree to join me in the Intermediate Cruising Course scheduled for the summer of 1991.

The following season, in response to the increasing costs of winter storage and summer berthing, Mr Markey launched his little yacht, sailed her across the bay, and tied her to a rented mooring buoy at LaSalle Park Marina. Thereafter, every time we worked on the boat or sailed her, we dragged *Pequod*'s unstable, wooden dinghy into the water and paddled out to the bobbing Alberg. With the cockpit deck three feet above the waterline, climbing aboard *Pequod* without capsizing the tipsy tender was always a challenge.

I spent most of my weekends aboard *Pequod* in Hamilton Har-

Map 1. The Great Lakes

bour though we sometimes motored through the canal beneath the lift bridge into Lake Ontario. On one of those occasions, a strong northeast wind drove unusually large waves onto the lake's western shores. Just beyond the lift bridge, *Pequod*'s bow began rearing up like a wild horse. She leapt over successive swells, plunging heavily into the troughs beyond their crests. Sheets of spray blew back toward the cockpit, drenching the decks and cabin-top. The air was filled with the intermittent sounds of wind and spray and the steady drone of *Pequod*'s four-cylinder, Atomic engine. Another sailboat and a large powerboat shared the scheduled ten o'clock lift, but as they neared the canal's east end, they abruptly put about, retreating toward the protected harbour. The skipper eyed them disdainfully and roared, "If you're not willing to go out in this, you're never going to cross the Atlantic."

We continued on into the lake.

To my surprise, once we raised the sails and shut down the engine, the impact of the waves ceased, and *Pequod* rose up as each successive wave slid gently beneath us. We became one with the wind and waves. It occurred to me at that moment that the operator of the other sailboat had missed an opportunity to expand his seamanship skills and would most likely be forever confined to the harbour on windy days.

In July, I enjoyed a week-long training experience on a CS 33 in Lake Huron's Georgian Bay. I was one of four adult students aboard the thirty-three foot sloop, each eager to soak up every aspect of cruising under sail. Paul, our youthful trainer, was fit and knew his stuff. His relaxed, confident approach to instruction made learning effortless. Warren, Don, and Judy were attentive novices with aspirations similar to my own, so everyone pulled their weight and got

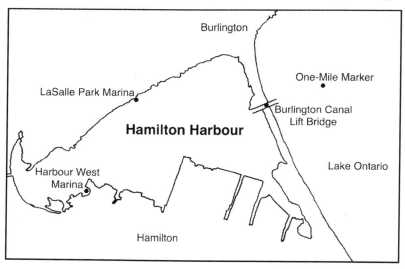

Map 2. Hamilton Harbour

along well. The course was primarily practical, with a minimum of paperwork expected. Each day we immersed ourselves in two or three aspects of cruising. We hove-to in deep water, anchored in various bottom conditions, and plotted courses and positions until we became familiar with the processes.

One warm afternoon, as we lingered over the last remnants of lunch in the cockpit, we faced an unexpected challenge. We were sailing lazily in open water at about five knots, having spent the morning covering the man-overboard procedure. Suddenly, our instructor burst out of the companionway in a wet-suit and leapt over the stern, screaming, "Man overboard!"

For a second we froze in astonishment while Paul's head grew smaller in the boat's wake, but we quickly recovered and sprang into action, each of us assuming a role in the rescue process. Warren threw the man-overboard pole into the water to mark Paul's location. Then, he took up a standing position on the starboard quarter, pointing directly at the now distant figure. He continued to point throughout the rescue exercise to ensure that we didn't lose track of our instructor among the sun-splashed waves.

I was on the helm and muttered "Oh shit!" as I tried to remember the details of the morning's lesson. As precious seconds ticked away, I began dropping off the wind to port, putting the boat on a beam reach. My mind raced in an attempt to recall the steps we had rehearsed earlier in the day. A few seconds passed.

Perhaps a little too authoritatively, I shouted, "Prepare to come about!"

The crew responded in the prescribed fashion with, "Ready!"

Don hauled in the mainsheet, took up the starboard jib sheet, unlocked the rope clutch, and watched me for a sign that I was about to turn upwind.

"Helm's alee!" I shouted as I spun the wheel to windward.

Don released the starboard jib sheet while Judy took up the slack on the port sheet. A few seconds later, we were on a downwind run with Paul waving confidently off the port bow. I held our course until he was directly up wind before turning into the light breeze and closing the figure-eight course that was key to the retrieval routine. We approached our fearless leader with the sails flapping erratically. For a moment, I thought we would stall before reaching him, but amazingly, one third of the hull passed by our quarry before our forward momentum petered out. We hauled Paul aboard triumphantly.

The following day, I was privileged to witness a phenomenon that few will experience. Midway between Hope Island and Thornbury harbour, located at the mouth of the Beaver River, the growls of distant thunder drew our attention to an approaching squall.

Paul estimated that we had fifteen minutes to prepare and directed us to put on our rain gear and reduce sail. We quickly complied and waited as the blue-black cloud line sped toward us.

The entire crew awaited the squall with confidence, and when the initial torrent of wind-driven rain hit us, we were ready for the vessel's response. I was sitting on the port cockpit seat, watching the first heavy raindrops slam into the water's mercury surface beyond the starboard rail. Paul sat facing me on the starboard cockpit seat while Don was on the helm, looking straight ahead beyond the bow. Without warning, what appeared to be a cylindrical bolt of lightning, with a diameter like that of a small farm silo, struck the water about fifty yards off the starboard beam. I was

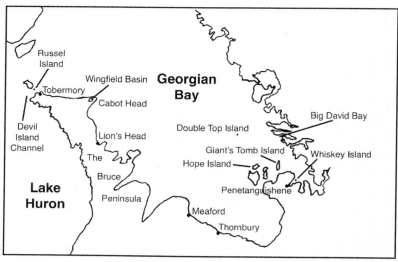

Map 3. Georgian Bay

momentarily blinded and deafened by the strike's proximity, and for a split second, I thought I felt radiated heat on my face though the event was over before I could fully comprehend what had happened. To our amazement, Paul and Don reported seeing exactly the same phenomena at the same instant though they were looking in different directions. It seemed a bolt of lightning had descended from directly above the vessel and branched into three tentacles, striking the water all around us.

I'd heard stories of sailboat masts being struck by lightning, but they were always unverified, third-person accounts. The most commonly described outcome was the sudden appearance of one or more holes in the hull, where the electrical charge escaped into the surrounding water. In one reported case, the holes were tiny and numbered in the hundreds, and the fibreglass boat sank at the dock since its crew were unable to determine how the water was entering its hull. In spite of the countless sailboat masts poking into the sky in all the harbours, lakes, and oceans of the world, accounts of mast strikes are rare.

When I skippered my own boat a few years later, I carefully maintained the ground strap that connected the mast and rigging to a bronze ground plate in the hull, yet even this direct path to ground never attracted a lightning strike.

While a child, I was warned of the dangers of being in a bathtub during a thunderstorm, yet not one incident involving lightning and a bathtub has ever come to my attention. It appears my mother's fear, though well-meaning, was unjustified. Similarly, a novice sailor would be well-advised to worry more about falling overboard than being struck by lightning.

Toward the end of our training, Paul asked for a volunteer to go up the yacht's mast in a bosun's chair. In spite of my fear of heights, I realized I would have to be capable of ascending the mast of my own boat one day, so I volunteered. Though being hoisted skyward by my fellow trainees stimulated a release of adrenaline, I was surprised to discover that I could control my anxiety and function almost normally while dangling at the end of the main halyard. Perhaps my confidence was inspired by the fact that both the main and the jib halyard which had been attached to my harness as a back-up were each capable of lifting hundreds of pounds. Besides, I was distracted by the fantastic panorama of shallow, turquoise water that surrounded the boat. With a little encouragement, I pushed off the mast and swung out over the water, slamming clumsily into the mast again on my return. With my feet planted firmly on the deck a few minutes later, I knew I would be able ascend a mast to clear a jammed halyard or replace a burned out masthead light if the need arose in the future.

At the end of the week-long course, we wrote our certification exam, and Paul signed each student's logbook before we packed up our gear, shook hands with one another, and returned with newfound confidence to our individual sailing adventures.

CHAPTER TWO
The *Pequod* Mutiny

Sailing with the unpredictable Mr Markey was indeed an adventure. One summer afternoon in the west end of Lake Ontario, I stood in *Pequod*'s cockpit facing a cool breeze and adjusting the tiller in response to its gusts. I was alone on deck, shifting my weight from one foot to the other as the vessel rolled and yawed among passing, broken rows of waves. The skipper was below, making a pot of tea.

A few hours earlier, I witnessed the sloop's owner lugging provisions aboard and noted, with little interest, a one-gallon can of Coleman fuel. I gave no thought to its intended purpose, and I certainly didn't expect he would pour its contents into the galley's alcohol stove. Old Gordie knew more about seamanship than I was likely to learn in a lifetime, but his vast, accumulated knowledge obviously excluded any insights into fuels and their appropriate uses.

At the instant that the explosive fireball belched from the companionway, I couldn't have guessed what had occurred. In a split second, the distance between me and the hazy shoreline became my sole interest. I wondered how long I could tread water.

Then, almost before the fireball had ascended to the height of the spreaders, a galvanized pail flew like a wounded duck out of the flames. In a reflex motion to avoid injury to my face, I caught the pail with my left hand.

From within the flames, I heard a shout.

"Get some water!"

Abandoning the helm, I grasped the bucket's handle and reached over the rail toward a wave-top that was sliding by at six knots. Perhaps even before the wave entered the pail, I recognized that the laws of physics were about to convict my stupidity. The force of the water, somewhat more powerful than my leg muscles, dragged me part way out of the cockpit and threatened to wrench me out of the boat into the cold water. I envisioned poor Gordie sailing away with no pail to douse the flames while I swam about with a pail of lake-water and no flames to douse. Somehow, I managed to hold on and wrestled the precious liquid into the cockpit. I took a deep breath and reached into the dense black smoke that had replaced the flames in the interim. I heard clanking, then splashing and the hissing of cold water on hot stainless steel. With the fire extinguished, the shaken skipper, black-faced with soot, explained that Coleman fuel was a fraction of the cost of alcohol.

The smoky cabin was littered with bits of charred rag, apparently the remains of the tea towel with which Gordie had tried to beat out the flames while awaiting the water. What a mess!

"Why didn't you use the damned fire extinguisher?" I queried.

In the heat of the moment—pun intended—neither of us had thought to retrieve the fire extinguisher, passively clamped in its bracket beside the companionway.

The rest of the summer sped by. Then, in late October, the season's sailing opportunities came to an end when *Pequod* was hoisted into her cradle for the coming winter.

In the spring of 1992, Mr Markey, another crew member, and I delivered the aging Alberg to her new home port over a hundred miles away. I had already sailed aboard her for several months though always within view of familiar shores in daylight. Under those circumstances, my local knowledge rendered navigation unnecessary. In fact, we never had occasion to use the ship's compass. Even so, it seemed odd that the instrument had remained in the skipper's Burlington apartment while we sailed in Hamilton Harbour and Lake Ontario. I had studied most aspects of marine navigation in a classroom but had made no concerted effort to practice even the fundamentals on the water.

The skipper, a veteran of numerous ocean passages aboard British freighters, was tough, impatient, and abrasive though a chuckle often bubbled just beneath his most recent, abusive outburst. There were times when I thought about chucking his withered, old carcass overboard, but inexplicably, I liked him.

It mattered not that I was the butt of his criticism. After all, I was sailing *his* Alberg long before I had the means to buy my own, and I was benefiting from *his* experience. He was a constant source of seamanship wisdom and humorous tales of life at sea though his small yacht sailing skills were at times embarrassing. In the beginning, accidental jibes and poorly trimmed sails were routine, but with time and diplomacy, I managed to pass on what I had learned in the classroom. Even so, my role remained subordinate. Mr Markey expected his orders to be carried out immediately and without discussion. Any hint of a challenge to his command brought colour to his weathered cheeks and a threatening tone to his tongue. Eventually though, he allowed me to sail the vintage Alberg on my own while he pottered about the deck and cabin, enjoying the wind and the slap of the water against her hull.

Local marina fees were getting expensive by Mr Markey's standards, so he decided to move his little yacht to a slip in Picton. There, about 140 miles northeast of Hamilton, he planned to live in the marina aboard *Pequod*. The boat was lifted into the water on the morning of April 30 and almost sank alongside the pier while old Gordie and I prepared the mast for stepping. Prior to launching her, the skipper had undertaken a repair to the engine's cooling system and had overlooked tightening five screws that held the impeller's cover in place. It was pure luck that I was sent to retrieve a wrench from below deck where I discovered hatch covers floating in several inches of water. I sounded the alarm and pumped her dry while Gordie identified the water's source and sheepishly secured the impeller's cover. With our departure somewhat delayed, we returned to the task of preparing *Pequod* for her passage. The aforementioned compass was unceremoniously hung by a yellow polypropylene line from a cleat on the cockpit bulkhead. Finally, in the early evening, we loaded provisions aboard for the passage to Picton.

Hamilton's lights twinkled in our wake as the lift bridge rose quietly above the Burlington Ship Canal. We cleared the harbour at 8 p.m. and, just ahead of a bulky freighter, sailed into Lake Ontario on a light westerly breeze.

Within minutes, the wind dropped and a shroud of cold, black drizzle engulfed us in the vicinity of the one-mile marker. At the captain's direction, I called the freighter on the VHF to confirm that its crew was aware of our position. We started the engine, lowered the sails, and listened intently for the discarnate ship's throaty rumble somewhere off our stern. The noise of our four-cylinder engine overwhelmed all other sound as it pushed *Pequod*'s five-and-a-half-ton bulk easterly through the swells.

An explosion of brilliant, white light hit me—and then it was gone. At the expense of my night vision, the ship's officer had assured himself of our position, no doubt precisely where his radar had indicated. I was impressed. The laker, visible only as a disembodied constellation of electric lights, turned southeast across our wake and, within minutes, vanished in the cold, spring rain.

With no radar or electronic navigation equipment, we relied entirely on our senses and mathematical calculations to guide *Pequod* toward her destination. By midnight, with visibility less than 300 yards, I felt uneasy.

Mr Markey's heart condition confined him to the shelter of the cabin, and Ted, the other member of the crew, had no cruising experience whatsoever. I resigned myself to remaining in the cold cockpit throughout the night. While I endorsed the skipper's policy of "two on deck after dark," I wasn't looking forward to a

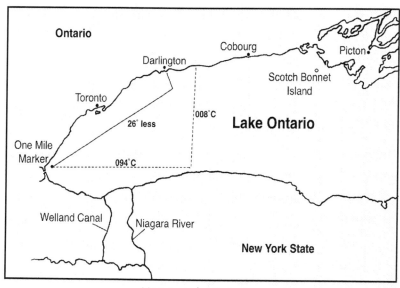

Map 4. Lake Ontario

sleepless night after a full day of rigging and provisioning.

Our hurried departure left several basic tasks incomplete, including connecting the compass light. Subsequently, we played a

16 *Too Cold for Mermaids*

flashlight on the compass card periodically to confirm our course of zero-nine-four degrees, slightly south of east.

Hour after hour, the rain invaded my clothing and robbed my body of heat. I shivered uncomfortably. Ted and I hadn't previously met, but he was pleasant company and willingly took his turn at the tiller. By morning, I would come to doubt his reliability as a helmsman though, in the end, my suspicions were discredited.

Allowing for the effects of wind and current, a vessel's position can be calculated if one knows its starting position, its speed, and its direction of travel over a specific period of time. Of course, determining a vessel's direction depends on a magnetic compass which is subject to external influences known as variation and deviation. I had been taught the principles of variation and deviation in a classroom, but I lacked practical experience. More importantly, I hadn't had an opportunity to verify the compass's accuracy due to our hurried departure.

Though I found my inability to fix our position stressful, blindly maintaining the assigned heading appeared to be my only option. My anxiety grew throughout the night as we plunged headlong into the darkness.

It's worth noting at this point that a moving vessel's direction can be described in many ways. Three of them involve the division of a circle into 360 degrees and are, by convention, expressed as three digits: for example, zero-nine-four degrees. The first is the vessel's heading in relation to the geographic North Pole which is always located in the same place at the top of the world. It's referred to as zero-nine-four degrees *true* and is the course drawn onto a chart. The second is based on the position of the magnetic north pole which moves about slowly over time in the high Arctic. It is specified as zero-nine-four degrees *magnetic*. The difference between these two directions is known as *variation*. Each chart contains a unique notation which enables mariners to convert the magnetic heading, indicated by the compass, to a true heading.

Though all compasses point to the magnetic north pole in theory, they are often influenced by metals used in marine engines and nearby deck fittings. This deflection of the compass needle is known as *deviation*, and the resulting heading is denoted as zero-nine-four degrees *compass*. The discrepancies between these three directions, true, magnetic and compass, become critical in areas where shallow bottoms, rocky shores, or other vessels pose a danger. Failure to properly calculate variation and deviation could put the vessel and crew at risk.

By dawn, the rain had turned to impenetrable fog, and I began experiencing the preliminary symptoms of hypothermia. I was mentally exhausted, and my judgment was undoubtedly impaired. Ted reached his limit and crawled into the V-berth for some sleep around 9 a.m. Two hours later, Mr Markey had me change course northward to zero-zero-eight degrees.

The skipper was bent over the chart table, fixing our position on the chart when he called me below to review his calculations. I engaged the auto helm, briefly peered into the murky fog beyond the bow, and went below. Mr Markey had also been awake throughout the night and likely felt a need for reassurance. I approached the chart table and saw that he had put us just north of the American shore on the southern edge of Lake Ontario—*thirty nautical miles from the Canadian coast.*

As I struggled to concentrate on the old mariner's calculations, a yellow spar buoy slid past the bronze portlight above the chart table. It appeared to be making about five knots. For a split-second, my brain screamed in protest, and then I understood. I almost knocked the bewildered skipper over as I charged up the companionway, disengaged the auto helm, and swung the tiller hard over. A vertical stone breakwall towered above the bow just a few yards away. The impact might have killed our snoring crewman who had, for reasons known only to the landlubber, gone to sleep with his head toward the bow.

Beyond the breakwall on the *north* shore of the lake stood the Darlington Nuclear Generating Station. Somehow, during a virtually windless night, our sloop had veered approximately *twenty-six degrees* to port of our intended course. Surely, variation and deviation could not account for such a substantial course error. It was easier to believe that Ted had not accurately maintained the assigned course during his turns on the helm.

Standing off the shore as far as we dared without losing sight of it in the fog, *Pequod* eased toward Cobourg throughout the afternoon. By the time we entered the harbour at about 4 p.m., the fog had cleared. We replenished our fuel and enjoyed a dinner of fish and chips, purchased from a local shop. An hour later, we again got underway, but the lack of wind forced us once more to employ the engine. The skipper assigned the heading and promptly retired to his berth.

Within minutes, it became apparent that shallow water off a headland lay across *Pequod*'s course. Ted remained on the helm while I went below to review the chart. The air was still, the swells were long and gentle, and the old gasoline engine throbbed monotonously. Mr Markey had laid down a true course from Cobourg harbour that easily cleared the headland. I calculated the variation and arrived at the same compass heading he had given us. Then, I drew a line on the chart from the harbour to the tip of the headland, transferring it to the chart's compass rose with parallel rules. *The difference between the two lines was exactly twenty-six degrees.*

The captain was irritable when I woke him. Though we had been underway less than an hour, he quickly assumed his crew hadn't maintained the assigned heading. Straying that far off course in daylight would have taken considerable effort, even for an incompetent novice. I pointed out the coincidence of the twenty-six degree error.

Mr Markey's cheeks burned red. He seized on the word "error," interpreting it as a personal attack on his navigation skills.

"Error?" he shouted.

Of course I had meant no such thing. I'd simply used the word as shorthand for compass error, a term widely used among mariners to describe the difference between a true heading and a compass heading. Further discussion was impossible, and with the fury of a full gale, Captain Markey reminded me of my lack of social standing before impatiently ordering me to round the peninsula and resume the assigned course.

Huddled against the chill of the night air, Ted and I speculated on the cause of the discrepancy while Mr Markey snored confidently in his berth. Slipping below to study the chart, I subtracted twenty-six degrees from the true course and plotted the result on the chart from our position off the headland. If *Pequod* actually was sailing twenty-six degrees to port of our intended course, and we maintained the assigned heading, she would crash headlong onto the rock-strewn shore of Scotch Bonnet Island a few minutes after midnight. With a clear understanding of the danger we faced, I studied Mr Markey's shadowy shape in the dim light of the cabin, searching my mind for a solution.

The values of integrity and respect for authority are sacred to me. They were entrenched in my character by my father who, coincidentally, resembled the sleeping captain in many ways. I could imagine only one solution, and it made me extremely uncomfortable.

The sky was clear, and though the air was cool, it was tolerable in the absence of any perceivable wind. The Canadian shore's sparkling lights flickered over the port quarter.

Ted was exhausted from the long watch of the previous night, so at 10 p.m., I managed to convince him that weather conditions didn't warrant two people on deck; I wanted no witnesses.

"Here," I said, "take your life jacket with you, just in case."

Gratefully, he went below to sleep.

Alone in the cockpit, I struggled with my conviction that we were on a collision course with Scotch Bonnet's jagged rocks. Was it a worse crime to deliberately alter course in defiance of the captain's orders or hold the assigned course, knowing that we might perish in the frigid water because of it? Deliberately altering our heading without permission might seem trivial on land in the light of day, but it's a serious breach of marine law, a deceit that most mariners consider indefensible.

In the distance, a creeping cluster of lights betrayed the shipping lanes indicated by the chart. Several silent apparitions moved steadily eastward and westward off our starboard bow throughout the inky night. Altering course to starboard would put us closer to the shipping lanes, perhaps even in the path of a freighter.

What if I was mistaken? Could I defend my actions if something unexpected occurred? I switched my flashlight on to look at my watch. Our anticipated encounter with Scotch Bonnet's ragged rocks was little more than ninety minutes in our future. Any further delay might render a small course change ineffective.

At 10:22 p.m., I altered course to starboard.

Had I made the course change six hours earlier, we would have been on a known, safe heading all evening. Now, well to port of our intended course and suffering from sleep-deprivation, I couldn't begin to calculate a safe heading. I'd been awake for thirty-eight hours, and I wasn't able to concentrate for more than a few seconds at a time.

I recall thinking "It will just have to do"—*and it was done.*

I listened intently for the telltale sound of waves surging against rocks in the darkness and checked my watch every few minutes for the next three hours. Then, satisfied that we were well beyond danger, I began to relax.

Mr Markey stirred about five in the morning and started fumbling about in the gloom of the cabin. Ever so gently, I eased the rudder to port, bringing the bow steadily back onto the assigned heading. We were likely fifteen miles beyond the rocks. At our current speed, *Pequod* would cruise safely in deep water until well after sunrise.

"Where's Ted?" Mr Markey bellowed accusingly over the engine noise.

"I sent him below a little while ago," I lied. "I guess he's asleep in the V-berth."

"I'll take her for a while. You need to get some rest too," he replied uncharacteristically.

I don't remember anything after that until the engine's RPM increased an hour later. The sudden change awakened me abruptly, and I stumbled partway up the companionway.

"What's wrong?" I asked, looking toward the north shore about two miles distant.

"Nothing. We just seem to be farther out than I had expected." he complained.

I fell back onto my berth, certain now that the mutiny had succeeded undetected.

Mr Markey passed away a few years later. Shortly after his death, while at the wheel of my own Alberg in Georgian Bay, I heard the distant thunder of a summer storm. For no apparent reason, the events of that memorable passage flooded into my consciousness. Surely that wasn't the old captain still grumbling at my defiance of his orders.

I never saw *Pequod* again, though I once heard a rumour that she had been seen hundreds of miles away in Halifax harbour. Gradually, stories emerged about the old carpenter's passage to New York City via the Erie Canal and the Hudson River. From there, he was said to have soloed to Halifax where *Pequod* eventually changed hands.

During 1993, I studied coastal navigation and began crewing for a friend and neighbour on his Columbia 25. Over the next few months, I enrolled in a basic sail-making course and acquired VHF radio operator certification. Throughout this period, I quietly and persistently increased my weekly deposits to the growing boat account and read dozens of books containing personal accounts of challenge, endurance and survival. While the books' authors were often motivated by a need to be the first or the fastest, my drive was far less competitive in nature. It wasn't necessary that no one had done it before; it was significant only that *I* hadn't yet done it.

By July of 1995, my original target date for the acquisition of a boat, I had yet to accumulate enough cash to buy the vessel of my dreams. The second boat that I had considered, back in the summer of 1991, was an Alberg 29. Though I looked at numerous vessels while accumulating the necessary funding, I always returned to Carl Alberg's twenty-nine-foot, blue-water, masthead sloop. She had four of the five features most important to me. Her full keel provided directional stability and rudder protection. Her keel stepped mast added strength to her rigging while at the same time eliminating excessive load on the coach roof. The vessel's ballast to displacement ratio was forty-four per cent, a very comforting feature in heavy weather. Also, I considered the diesel auxiliary safer than the gasoline-powered Atomic 4 used in earlier Albergs like *Pequod*. The design was a foot short of my arbitrarily set thirty-foot minimum, but it had a wheel instead of a tiller and, by eliminating the lazaret incorporated into earlier designs, its architect had increased the cabin size substantially. Bronze fittings made it compatible with salt water, and its fine bow and deep forefoot were romantically classic and seaworthy.

Trisha's approval grew along with our boat account, and we began looking at sailboats in spite of our inadequate resources. We drove hundreds of miles to attend boat shows and made appointments with intractable owners and indifferent yacht brokers to view potential vessels. I considered Island Packets, Contessas, Bayfields and Albergs until finally, in February of 1996, I submitted a conservative offer on a reasonably priced Alberg 29 named *Odyssey*. Trisha and I had viewed the blue-water sloop one warm, rainy morning the previous summer. After two weeks of silence, just hours before the offer expired, the telephone rang and I learned that the seller had accepted my terms. We took possession of *Odyssey* in a muddy boatyard in Penetanguishene, Ontario, on the second of May. I handed her owner a certified cheque for $33,000 and scribbled abbreviated notes while he outlined the winterizing process and familiarized me with the vessel's electrical, plumbing, and rigging systems. I was bursting with excitement and a little overwhelmed by the realization that I was investing a year's net income in my fantasy.

It had taken a seminar and a set of audio tapes to awaken me to the fact that, until then, I had contributed *nothing* toward my dream. My once impossible fantasy began to materialize the moment I opened the boat account. That simple act separated me from tens of thousands of others who *still* dream of having a sailboat, a vacation cottage, or an engineering degree. Signing up for sailing courses and reading about boating intensified my focus. As other interests became subordinate, they consumed less of my income, and the funding of my goal became easier. I spent hours researching design characteristics and equipment needs where, previously, I had squandered my time merely *wishing* I had a boat.

I was finally the skipper of my own modest though very capable little yacht, but it was clear that I needed to prepare myself and my boat to fulfil the rest of my dream. I really hoped to wake up one day in some foreign port, surrounded by parrots and palm trees.

With no comprehension of the countless tasks still ahead, I announced my purchase to our family and friends. My life filled with activity as I compiled lists and hurried from one project to another. First, I had to arrange a marine survey in order to insure my investment. Then I had to ready her for the spring launch and prepare her for our first sail together.

Trisha assembled her own list of minor changes and essential accessories. We had come a long way together, but neither of us understood at the time how much more there was to cruising than paying for a boat.

CHAPTER THREE
Alice Rose and *Lap Cat*

Unlike those countless powerboats tied to cottage docks on the fringes of every inland lake, the inherent complexities of a live-aboard sailboat demand a detailed understanding of points of sail, standing rigging, mechanical advantage, coastal navigation, and obscure characteristics like hull speed and centre of effort. Little did I realize that the training and experience I had accumulated over the previous six years was just the beginning of my marine education. Neither did I comprehend the expenses that sailboat owners regularly face nor the hours of labour they endure in exchange for access to distant shores.

Odyssey was a masthead sloop, a design that maximized the potential size of her foresail. She was fitted with a forty-two-foot aluminium mast though six feet of it, once installed through the coach roof, were seen only within the cabin. With her mainsail and 120 per cent genoa raised, she carried 460 square feet of canvas. Thanks to a 4,000-pound encapsulated lead ballast and a centre of gravity located just fifteen inches above the bottom of her keel, she stood close to upright in most weather. Her deck was officially twenty-nine feet, three inches long, and her beam (width) was nine feet, two inches. Her full-length keel hung four and a half feet below the waterline, and the classic lines of her white, fibreglass hull attracted admirers and questions in anchorages and ports everywhere we went.

Below, a holly and teak cabin sole and mahogany-finished lockers and bulkheads gave her cabin a cosy feel. Sleeping accommodations included two main salon berths, a double V-berth, and a port quarter-berth. The spacious cabin also featured a closet-style head, a navigation station, and a hanging wet-locker. Thirty-three other lockers provided ample storage for clothing, equipment and provisions. A small galley, occupying the starboard-aft portion of the main salon, included a sink, a twelve-volt refrigerator, and a two-burner propane stove.

Trisha and I introduced ourselves to the marina staff, made friends in the boatyard, and arranged our launch date. We walked the maze of floating docks to determine exactly where *Odyssey*'s berth was located. My heart pounded in my chest when she was lifted from her cradle by two massive slings and slowly carried to the launch slip in the grip of the marina's travel-lift. Every aspect of the launching process was stressful, since I imagined everything that could go wrong. I was relieved when neither of the slings broke and my little yacht did not crash to the ground. I was ecstatic when she didn't sink after being lowered into the water.

The initial rigging of *Odyssey* that first season was a confusing and daunting task, not unlike solving a complex puzzle for the first time. The process was accomplished a step at a time, very slowly, though eventually the assembled components appeared to correspond to those of the other boats in the marina, and everything seemed to function as intended.

Again, my heart pounded and adrenaline flowed as I motored the short distance from the launch slip to our berth alongside an outer finger of the floating docks. I inched the bulk of my seven-ton vessel through the marina with great care, shifting between forward and neutral and trying desperately to precisely time my turns to keep *Odyssey* midway between obstacles. I made the final turn into our impossibly tight slip for the first time, terrified that I would scrape the side of the Beneteau 34 in the adjoining slip or crash *Odyssey*'s bow headlong into the dock. Though determined to remain calm, my inexperience and lack of confidence must have been obvious to everyone within hearing when my directions to my crew became desperately urgent and unnecessarily loud.

Of course, in the end I succeeded with the help of my crew and other boaters on the dock. With our dock lines secured, I took a deep breath and relaxed. I don't actually remember, but we most likely sat in the cockpit and enjoyed a drink after shutting down the engine. In any case, drinks in the cockpit became a traditional end to our days once our lines were secured or our anchor had a firm grip on the bottom.

During our first sailing season, we sometimes remained in our slip for the entire weekend, cleaning or repairing *Odyssey*'s minor shortcomings. We fully understood how little we knew about cruising and never strayed more than twenty miles from the dock during that first summer. Nevertheless, we discovered the absolute peace of anchoring in sandy bays under blue skies for days at a time. We slept soundly, awoke refreshed, and thoroughly enjoyed sharing our little piece of paradise at the end of our anchor rode.

Engrossed in a minor maintenance task atop the cabin one warm afternoon, I consciously experienced a long forgotten feeling. I couldn't describe it in words then or now, though I remember feeling it in my distant past—when I was a child. That day, with little of importance to do and nothing significant to worry about, I found myself completely free of anxiety and stress. Sailing provided me with several such moments over the next decade.

Our first summer in Georgian Bay passed quickly. Not long before our scheduled haul-out, I gave way to an overtaking vessel as Trisha and I sailed south of Whiskey Island on our approach to Penetanguishene harbour. I wasn't required by tradition or marine law to do so, but we were sailing at slightly more than four knots, and the overtaking powerboat was moving at close to twenty. At the time, it seemed the courteous thing to do. When our keel struck a rock on the edge of the channel, it became clear that my first responsibility was to the safety of my vessel. Had I maintained my course, well within the deep channel, the powerboat, with its minimal draft, could have safely altered course in accordance with marine law. With somewhat more water than usual in her bilge, we hauled *Odyssey* prematurely to inspect the keel.

The damage was relatively minor, though it had breached the hull sufficiently to sink her had she been left in the water for several days. Though our first season ended on a low note, we had sailed a total of 275 nautical miles, gained valuable experience, and thoroughly enjoyed the summer. I undertook the repair myself, but the injury to my confidence never healed. Thereafter, an awareness of the fragility of my vessel tenaciously haunted my subconscious.

Mid way through the following January, I made a slushy sojourn to the boatyard to clear accumulated snow from the thirty-by-forty-foot plastic tarpaulin that protected my little sloop from Old Man Winter. By mid-afternoon, piles of lumpy snow reached halfway up the hull, obscuring the cradle from view. With the snow-free, bright blue tarp drying in the sun, I snugged the maze of lines that held it in place and trudged through the boatyard's deep drifts to the car. Though exhausted by the effort and the long drive in mid-winter conditions, I was relieved that for the time being my investment was secure.

In April, Trisha and I lived aboard for a few days while we prepared *Odyssey* for the spring launch. Initially, we had to access the cabin by climbing a purpose-built ladder and crawling through the tented cockpit, though we soon unwrapped *Odyssey* to admit light and occasional sunshine to her cabin. On our late night and early morning treks to the marina washrooms and showers, we braved frost and sticky boatyard mud. It was a miserable contrast to the warm barefoot sailing that we had enjoyed a few months earlier.

During our second sailing season, we investigated the narrow channels among the windswept islands of Georgian Bay with new-found confidence. The rewards were spectacular. Over the next four summers, Trisha and I explored many of the islands, inlets, and secluded bays within a hundred or so miles of the marina, sometimes with family and friends but more often alone. We particularly enjoyed anchoring in isolated bays, sharing quiet moments in the cockpit with steaming cups of tea or coffee just after sunrise, and taking refreshing swims in the heat of mid-day. We nibbled lunches in the cockpit to the squeaks and groans of our anchor rode straining against the bronze chock in the deck combing. Together, we watched the setting sun paint the sky and clouds in shades of mauve and gold. The distant cries of loons in the evening stillness and the endless patter of drizzle on dreary days erased the accumulated urban clatter from our souls. We endured oppressive, windless heat and pesky swarms of voracious mosquitoes, and on warm afternoons, as our little yacht rocked gently in one of the countless secluded bays along the eastern shore, we made love.

Throughout our five seasons in Georgian Bay, I continued to ready myself and my vessel for crossing the Atlantic. I wasn't prepared to undertake the passage alone, and even before I had found a suitable boat, I invited Bob, a close friend, to share the adventure.

Bob and I first met in the summer of 1960. I had just completed my first year at high school when I moved with my mother and brother to Fife Street, a block-long residential street in central Hamilton. Bob lived in the house next door, and it was natural that we would become friends. After all, we were about the same age and shared similar interests—*cars and girls*. At the time, he drove a 1953 Meteor, and a year or so later, he risked putting me behind the wheel to teach me to drive. Three and a half decades later, I taught him to sail.

Bob and I spent hours working on cars together without realizing how far into the future our friendship would endure. In 1964, when he was driving a rather sleek-looking '56 Mercury hard-top, and I was still riding city buses, he agreed to a blind date so I could take a young lady on our first date in style. The four of us went to a drive-in movie and later to a drive-in restaurant. He and his date didn't hit it off, but my date eventually became my wife.

For decades, Bob and his wife and Trisha and I shared life's trials and triumphs. Our families were so connected that he and I were each known to the other's children as "uncle." Bob often sailed with Trisha and me and, even more frequently, helped to maintain and renovate *Odyssey* in preparation for the long-anticipated crossing of the Atlantic.

In January of 1999, Bob accompanied me to the Toronto Boat Show. I had been attending shows since establishing the boat account a decade earlier. We talked to vendors and learned about the equipment we would need to accomplish our goal. In the spring, we completed an offshore first aid course, designed to prepare us for those days at sea when medical care was out of reach. I continued to make lists of essential equipment, most of it more expensive than I had ever imagined and often beyond my means for some time. Nevertheless, I continued to save and inched my way toward my objective.

By the time we began our third summer in Georgian Bay, our granddaughter, Jaclyn, was almost five years old. For the pure fun of it, I constructed a rather genuine looking pirates' chest over the winter and filled it with pennies, a few foreign coins and an assortment of costume jewellery. In early August, I went ashore on Giant's Tomb Island to bury the treasure well above the high water mark. I easily recognized the poison ivy growing in the vicinity though I had no idea that the roots through which I was digging with my bare hands were connected to the nearby plants. It wasn't long before I began to suffer from what my doctor later described as "the worst case of toxicological dermatitis I've ever seen."

The remainder of my week's holiday was almost entirely occupied with my efforts to relieve the burning and itching on my hands and wrists and between my fingers. I found that hanging over the side of the boat with my hands and forearms in the water was the most effective treatment.

In September of the same year, we returned to Giant's Tomb Island with Jaclyn and an artificially aged treasure map that I claimed to have acquired during a trip to the Caribbean. My son and son-in-law accompanied us in the dinghy to look for the pirate's treasure. I paced off the location according to the map's instructions and donned my raingear and gloves to prevent further contact with the poison ivy. With Jaclyn looking on from a safe distance, I dug up the chest and carried it to the shore for a thorough scrubbing in the surf. Once cleansed of the nasty ivy's poison, we opened the hasp of the heavy chest and revealed its contents. Jaclyn's excited reaction made my efforts, and even my ruined week of holidays, worthwhile. For months afterward, she enthusiastically described the discovery of her treasure to anyone who would listen.

Long before setting eyes on *Odyssey*, I pledged to name my dream boat *Alice Rose* in honour of my late grandmother, and since it was my intention to sail to and through the waters of other nations, I deemed it appropriate to register my provincially licensed vessel as a federally registered Canadian "ship." Subsequently, in the fall of our third sailing season in Georgian Bay, I undertook the expensive, bureaucratic process of federal registration. With the pertinent information and appropriate payment properly submitted to Transport Canada's Registrar of Ships, I awaited his response. Finally, on May 21, 1999, Odyssey was officially declared *Alice Rose*, hull number 821210, a Canadian ship with a registered tonnage of seven tons and an impressive bronze "ship's carving" mounted on the port bulkhead. I removed the provincial registration number from her bows and proudly applied her new name as required under the Canada Shipping Act. On her stern, beneath her name, appeared the word "HAMILTON," designating her port of registry.

Trisha and I read in *GAM* magazine about the Toronto-based World Cruising Club. We soon became members and often tolerated treacherous winter driving conditions to meet and talk with fellow dreamers. The club's monthly gatherings provided us with opportunities to share our aspirations with other sailors and learn from their cruising experiences. Meetings generally featured a presentation addressing technical issues or a first-person account of a sailing adventure. Initially, I felt a little awkward because most members had been sailing for many years. They had numerous stories to relate, and a wealth of experience to share. Collectively, they exposed me to potential equipment options, and recommended sources of specialty items and expert craftsmanship. I eagerly soaked up the lessons that others had already learned. Their slideshows, films, and narratives lured me ever closer to my dream of sailing the world.

Through the World Cruising Club, I learned of an opportunity to gain valuable experience by crewing aboard someone else's boat. A small group of privately owned vessels was bound for the northern tip of Newfoundland. The eclectic assortment of boats had been organized to celebrate the one-thousand-year anniversary of the Vikings' landing at L'Anse aux Meadows. The modest fleet of a dozen or so boats, known collectively as Flotilla 2000, was patterned after a similar assembly of yachts that sailed to Newfoundland in 1997 to mark the landing of explorer John Cabot in 1497.

I recognized that *Alice Rose* was far from ready to face the complexities of the St. Lawrence Seaway, the remote shores of Labrador and the Atlantic Ocean. Neither had I been sufficiently prepared by my sweet-water sailing experiences to skipper a vessel on such a voyage. I was, however, confident that I could provide valuable assistance to another skipper in need of a crew.

I posted my personal information and sailing experience on the flotilla's website and waited hopefully. Not long afterward, Adrian, the owner of *Lap Cat*, contacted me and invited me to meet with him regarding a crewing position aboard his thirty-foot Nonsuch. Trisha came through again, agreeing within a year of my retirement to stay home and deal with whatever happened while I went sailing with strangers for seven weeks.

My initial impression of Adrian, a local entrepreneur, was that he was mechanically competent, and while he was a somewhat inexperienced sailor, he was cautious and thoughtful. He must have found my personality agreeable and my knowledge of sailing adequate because he agreed to take me aboard for the one-way passage to L'Anse aux Meadows.

Throughout late April and May, I helped Adrian prepare *Lap Cat* for departure. While my assistance was minute compared to the overall preparations, working together helped us get to know one another, and it gave me a better understanding of the equipment essential to offshore sailing in northern latitudes.

Lap Cat was a beamy, fibreglass, cat-rigged design known as a Nonsuch. She was characterized by a single sail mounted on a tapered, un-stayed fifty-two-foot mast at her bow. Unlike the vast majority of small sailboats, the bow of her cabin was not fitted with a V-berth. Instead, it was primarily occupied by the enormous base of her mast. The Nonsuch design featured double quarter berths for the skipper and his wife as well as a pair of single mid-ship berths, ideal for crew. A full galley was located aft of the port side mid-ship berth and adjacent to it, on the starboard side, was a head with a shower. The feature most appreciated by everyone on board was her beige canvas cockpit enclosure fitted with clear plastic windows. It kept us dry in rough weather and provided protection from the cold winds that we encountered, particularly off the coast of Labrador.

CHAPTER FOUR
Mimico to Montreal

In early June of the year 2000, *Lap Cat* and a dozen or so other vessels set out from Mimico Cruising Club and sailed eastward into Lake Ontario. So began my first saltwater cruise which, in addition to being a sailing holiday, served as a school of practical seamanship and navigation.

The following account, initially compiled from a meagre collection of journal entries, post cards, and letters to my wife, has been supplemented with recollections of those memorable days. The journey was, at the very least, a great adventure for most of us and, unfortunately, outside the experience of most people. Perhaps this description of my time aboard Lap Cat will serve as a minor reference to those planning similar voyages.

The risks to participants were minimal, and no great hardships were endured, though most crews and vessels faced challenges well beyond their previous experience. Lap Cat was my home for forty-three of the forty-eight days and nights that I was away from my wife and family. I shared her cramped quarters with her captain, Adrian Kloet, his wife, Wilma, and the only other member of her crew, Ian Bruce. Ian was primarily responsible for provisioning, meal preparation and galley maintenance though he willingly took his turn on the helm and on deck as well. Ian and I got along nicely and became friends during the passage, sharing the workload, the challenges, and on occasion, a little rum.

In recognition of Ian's culinary expertise, I began referring to him as Cooky. Adrian, generally addressed as Skipper, carried the weight of responsibility for the vessel and all on board, a burden only another skipper can fully appreciate.

My responsibilities began in earnest on the ninth of June at a floating dock belonging to the Mimico Cruising Club in Etobicoke, Ontario. Trisha and I were about to be parted for seven weeks, and neither of us delighted in that aspect of the venture. I was apprehensive about abandoning her for so long, and I pledged to send her a postcard from Kingston, our first port of call. Trisha remained supportive throughout our preparations, gracefully accepting my quest for adventure. I hoped to find a way to make it up to her on my return. We kissed goodbye, and I watched as she left the club with tears in her eyes.

Having attached all of the ship's flags and burgees to *Lap Cat*'s flag halyard in the fading glow of dusk, I modified a stainless bolt, converting it into an anchor retention pin. Muffled laughter and music emanated from the clubhouse as members of the flotilla celebrated our impending departure. In Trisha's absence, I felt little inclination to party and had returned to *Lap Cat* after dinner to attend to a few last-minute preparations. As I worked, I became aware of a nebulous sense of isolation. It was 8:30 p.m., and I was poised on the brink of the unknown. Taking care of last minute business, procuring and assembling my kit, packing, unpacking and stowing everything in my assigned lockers had worn me out. I decided to write a few lines to Trisha, turn in early, and defer my shower until first light.

The air was crisp when I rose at 5:15 a.m. and made my way to the club's shower facilities. Skippers and crews gathered in the dining room for breakfast, readied their vessels for departure, and cast off their dock lines within minutes of one another. The boats assembled according to size and exited the harbour in single file, saluted by a municipal fireboat. Its graceful arcs of white spray sparkled in the morning sun like streams of diamonds.

The adventure had begun!

Some time prior to our departure, someone had intimated that as many as thirty boats were expected to participate in the sail to Newfoundland, so I found the twelve or so vessels that formed our fleet a little disappointing. Several boats appeared to have dropped out prior to departure, perhaps because they were unable to complete their preparations in time.

The weather was warm and clear throughout the day, and with two guests aboard during the run to Kingston, the skipper assigned one hour shifts on the helm which resulted in rather easy duty. Determined to develop safe habits and good seamanship, I wore my inflatable PFD with the safety tether attached though rolled up and stuffed into my pocket. It would be convenient, I reasoned, to clip on quickly if the need arose. The habit proved a useful one in the weeks that followed.

I was barely aware of the vessel's motion until I noticed that one of the skipper's guests had turned grey. Eventually, unable to sup-

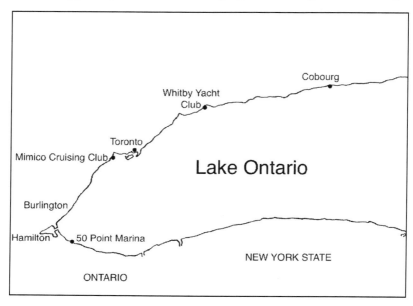

Map 5. Western Lake Ontario

press his gag reflex any longer, the poor wretch lost the nutritional benefit of his breakfast.

Ian demonstrated his culinary competence that first day. While *Lap Cat* rolled rhythmically on a broad reach, we thoroughly enjoyed his debut dinner, a delicious curried coconut-chicken dish. The robust Scot proved to be meticulously efficient and organized in the execution of his duties. Within a few minutes, he prepared and served the meal, cleared up the dishes, and restored the galley to order.

Though Ian, the skipper, and I had each owned hand-held global positioning systems for several weeks, the practical application of GPS technology was still relatively new to sailing and particularly to us. For the most part, we had used them only in our living rooms with operating manuals in hand. From our position, six to seven hours from our first waypoint off Point Petre, I could barely make out the U.S. and Canadian shores. We sailed eastward along an imaginary line at six knots in the wakes of the flotilla's flagship, *Burin Star*, and two other sizable yachts, *Moonshadow* and *Stand Sure*. Since the length of a hull's waterline has a significant effect on a sailboat's maximum speed, the larger vessels tended to lead while the smaller ones gradually fell behind. At this point in the passage, the remaining vessels maintained more or less stable positions abeam and astern.

I had been assigned the starboard salon berth and developed a curious fondness for that tiny portion of the boat. It became my refuge, the one place that was *mine*, a space within which I could escape the brisk Atlantic air and, to some extent, the noisome social interaction of my shipmates. It wasn't that I came aboard with anti-social tendencies, but after hours, then days and ultimately weeks of living with three other people in the confinement

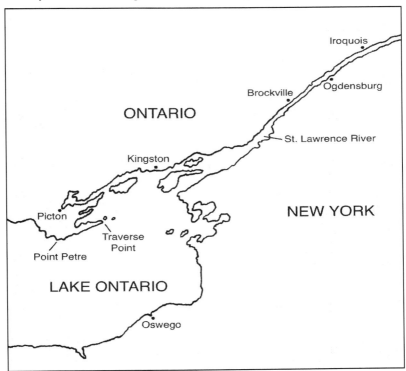

Map 6. Eastern Lake Ontario

of *Lap Cat*'s cabin and cockpit, I cherished that little space. There, I could hide beneath a blanket and slip into unconsciousness. That first night, I quickly dashed off a few lines to Trisha before climbing into my berth to recharge my physical and mental batteries. I was scheduled to begin a three-hour watch at midnight.By late evening, cold, blustery winds drove us through unfamiliar coal-coloured waters toward a series of electronically designated points on the lake's surface. I had known the skipper only a few weeks, and I wasn't yet ready to trust him with my life among the shoals of eastern Lake Ontario. While I understood that a degree of blind faith would at some point be necessary, I didn't yet entirely trust my GPS either. I studied the chart, frequently plotting our position as indicated by the GPS to reassure myself. Oddly, our physical location in the black emptiness of the night became less mysterious when it was recorded on a marine chart in the glare of the chart light.

At the end of my watch, we double reefed and continued to sail in excess of seven knots for most of the early morning. Reluctant to forfeit what little control I had over my destiny, I remained on deck with the skipper until we rounded Point Petre and entered a narrow fourteen-mile strait to Traverse Point. Ultimately, my unwarranted lack of confidence in the skipper was overwhelmed by fatigue, and I retired to my berth and slept fitfully until my next watch at 9 a.m.

Engulfed in a chilly, morning mist, we tied up just after eleven o'clock on the eleventh of June. It seemed the night had drained all colour from the city of Kingston, infusing the sky, the water, and the wooden docks with multiple shades grey. It was as though I was trapped within a vintage black and white photograph.

Having fulfilled my duties for the present, I followed the maze of fog-soaked docks toward the shore. Boaters adjusted lines and fiddled with equipment as I passed. One mariner hung from a halyard beneath his masthead, tinkering with the navigation lights. At the time, many members of our fleet remained nameless with faces only vaguely familiar. I nodded and exchanged small talk as I walked. When I reached an on-shore community information kiosk, I asked for directions to the showers. The steaming spray was a welcome contrast to the cold, grey morning. Like my berth aboard *Lap Cat*, marina showers took on a greater significance as we travelled northeast over the next few weeks.

Twenty-five skippers and crew members dined at Kingston's

Prince George Hotel that night. Suppressing a fleeting tendency toward consideration for others, I claimed a seat by the fireplace in an effort to warm my bones for the first time since my morning shower. Still an outsider among many who were already friends with one another, I loitered on the fringes of the conversation.

The flotilla disembarked early Monday morning and arrived in Brockville about 1:30 p.m. *Lap Cat* edged her way cautiously into a snug, shore-side slip at the yacht club where we secured her for the night. During the tricky docking manoeuvre, I noted the skipper's skills reflected a competence that until then had eluded me. Relieved of duty, I strolled casually to a nearby park, sat at a picnic table, and addressed a post card to Trisha.

Burin Star passed by on the river. She was an impressive forty-six-foot Egyptian-blue ketch, skippered by John Dunford, the flotilla's commodore. In contrast to powerboats, the purring engines of sailing vessels are seldom heard from shore, preserving the illusion of their elegant progress even when their sails are stowed. *Burin Star* was no exception and slid down river with no visible or audible means of propulsion—as if by magic.

In the evening, the Brockville Yacht Club hosted a dinner to welcome the flotilla and wish us a safe and enjoyable trip. Such was the custom throughout the cruise to L'Anse aux Meadows. Each of our ports of call were aware of our scheduled arrival and welcomed our small infusion of economic stimulation. At various times throughout the trip, the fleet numbered twelve to fifteen vessels, since individual boats joined or left the flotilla at various points along the route. The majority of participating vessels carried three or four individuals who often dined and shopped in the tiny riverside and coastal communities. While most welcome dinners cost from seven to fifteen dollars, all were more than worth the price of a ticket, and some were worth double the amount.

As we approached the bridge at Ogdensburg, New York the following day, I heard *Burin Star*'s radio operator report that she had grounded beyond the southern boundary of the channel, and her crew were unable to free her of the mud bottom without assistance. Inexplicably, she appeared to be several hundred feet beyond the green channel marker. I watched her through binoculars as we passed, knowing that the depth of *Lap Cat*'s keel summarily excluded us from participating in the ketch's rescue. *Scotia Blue*, a trawler with much less draft, returned from down river, and after several unsuccessful attempts, towed *Burin Star* into deeper water. By then, she had been grounded for several hours without suffering any apparent damage.

Lap Cat approached the first of the St. Lawrence Seaway locks at Iroquois along with other members of the fleet. Together, we watched an up-bound freighter's bridge rise gradually above the lock's distant gate. A cluster of lights blinked and changed colour, signalling the lock's status. We waited while the freighter exited the lock and slid past our poised, little fleet. With the appearance of a green light, the larger yachts entered in single file and secured their lines to vertical cables spaced along the lock wall. Smaller vessels eased into position and rafted alongside until some rafts grew to be four boats wide. An unseen seaway operator pushed a button or pulled a lever, and the water level in the huge concrete box began receding. The crews of the larger yachts spent their entire descent holding their vessels off the wall with boathooks and broom handles, adjusting lines and eyeing their protective fender boards. Aside from a liberal coating of brown-green slime, the walls of the lock looked as I imagine course sandpaper must appear to an insect. Slowly, the hulls and, eventually, the mastheads of our vessels descended below the lock's rim until we were at the bottom of a gigantic rectangular well. Soundlessly, the massive gates at the far end of the lock swung inward, and crews began letting their rafting lines go.

On leaving the lock, *Lap Cat* turned north around the second marker as directed by the fleet's commodore. Beyond a serpentine buoyed entrance, several flotilla boats were already tying up in an abandoned, nineteenth century lock which had been converted to a marina. Most of the channel markers were the traditional red and green, but a couple of yellow ones momentarily confused us until shouts from shore alerted us to our error.

The little community of Iroquois had erected a number of carnival tents and food concessions alongside the marina and had apparently invited all the Newfoundlanders in the area to attend our reception. It seemed that everyone we met there was an outgoing expatriate of our island destination.

When *Burin Star* arrived at Iroquois, I approached Hugh, a member of her crew, to discover what had happened at Ogdensburg. He readily admitted that he was responsible for navigation at the time of the grounding and volunteered that the incident was due to overconfidence and inattention. Concerned that the conversation might be uncomfortable for him, I casually changed the subject. Hugh's candid admission and humility were admirable, and his recent experience was a practical lesson for us all.

It suddenly became apparent that our informal approach to the assignment of duties aboard *Lap Cat* was fraught with ambiguity. I recalled numerous occasions when the responsibility of navigation was shared or presumed. It was often unclear exactly who was actually assigned to ensure the vessel's safe progress. I resolved to suggest the skipper formalize the assignment of duties a little. While I was prepared to be accountable for my actions, it was essential that I know when I was assigned and when I was relieved of a specific duty.

I walked a mile of winding country road into the village of Iroquois to mail a letter and buy additional batteries for my GPS. Not since my childhood had walking played such a substantial role in my daily life. On the down side, walking was ponderously slow, but on the up side, *it was ponderously slow*. I hadn't anticipated the benefit of walking everywhere. It gave me time to think! Life was slowing down, and I was seeing each minute in greater detail.

On my return, I sat down at a picnic table in a sheltered corner of a canvas marquee. There, I composed a message on the back of yet another post card while I awaited a cold lager and a hot sausage on a bun. The volunteer cook had run out of sausage and was anticipating a delivery from town. A featureless sky and cold drizzle dampened my spirits in spite of the lively down-home music emanating from the next tent.

When the sausage finally arrived, it was tepid, closer to raw than cooked, and pale pink inside—almost white. I was shivering and craved hot food. With a conscious effort, I suppressed my concerns about undercooked pork and potential food poisoning, washing each disgusting bite down with a mouthful of icy beer.

Before returning to the security of my dry berth on *Lap Cat*, I chatted for some time with a retired police officer about police administration and politics. Once aware of my thirty-three year career with the Hamilton Police, he enthusiastically shared his views and experiences. The conversation provided a refreshing highlight to an otherwise miserable day, and I was a little surprised how my feelings of isolation were relieved, at least temporarily, by a simple encounter with a stranger whose interests were similar to mine.

During the first few days of our voyage, every task was new and required conscious thought, but only four days into the first week, the rhythm of life on the water was becoming routine. I snuggled into my berth to conserve body heat and slept soundly until morning.

Lap Cat sat passively in the cool, damp morning air on a black, glass-like surface. We took on fresh water and pumped out the waste tank before untying her dock lines. She eased gently by several other boats that were still secured alongside the narrow lock until she reached a small basin at its end. There, we were able to come about and retrace our path toward the marina entrance. As we exited the channel on June 14 and re-entered the St. Lawrence, *Lap Cat*'s diesel throbbed monotonously at 2,000 RPM.

Moments later, the dull morning's routine was shattered by a shrill, high-frequency alarm—the engine's high-temperature indicator. Adrian shut down the overheated four-cylinder Volvo immediately. *Lap Cat*, now drifting at the same speed as the river's current, lost directional stability and turned broadside to the current. The velocity of the river's seaward rush became apparent as a counter eddy swept us toward the river's bank. I sprinted forward, released the anchor pin, and stood by while the skipper waited for the depth-sounder to indicate the appropriate moment. At thirty feet he ordered, "Let it go!"

The chain rattled out of the hawse pipe. *Lap Cat* swung around, jerked the anchor rode rigid, and came to a stop facing upriver. The sense of relief was almost tangible.

One characteristic of sailing in a temperate climate can be fully appreciated only through experience. At our latitude, apart from a few days in July and August, escape from the penetrating cold and dampness was, at best, elusive. For days at a time, we endured an environment created by winter melt-water and cold spring rains.

Though *Lap Cat*'s cabin provided shelter from the wind, the temperature inside varied only marginally from a refrigerator because, below the waterline, it lost what little warmth it had to the river. My sleeping bag became my cherished and only refuge from the chill.

Ironically, it was our aversion to cold that had caused the engine to overheat. A brief analysis of the cooling system suggested that the recently installed hot water heater was the likely cause. We had connected it before departure to help us cope with the cool Labrador nights, but because the heater was located in the bow, a forty-foot loop of hose had been added to the cooling system. The skipper speculated that the water pump was, for the most part, re-circulating and reheating the same water and drawing in very little cold river water. Resourceful and always quick to invent a solution, he clamped the heater hose between the jaws of a pair of vice grips and restarted the engine. In seconds, the engine sucked icy seawater into the system, and with the alarm silenced, we resumed our passage.

We cleared the American Eisenhower and Snell locks before midday without incident.

The afternoon sky was still overcast as the fleet waited for an up-bound ship to clear the Upper Beauharnois Lock. Adrian held the wheel loosely, motoring in lazy circles above the lock. Finally, leaving the wheel hard over, he came below to attend to some trivial task. Seconds ticked by as he became mired in the distraction while *Lap Cat* circled lazily. I was sitting on my berth, immersed in Frank McCourt's *Angela's Ashes*, when the sound of crunching gravel interrupted the author in mid-sentence. In unison, Cooky and I exploded off our respective berths and burst out of the companionway, spilling clumsily into the cockpit to confirm our shared assumption. We had landed on a U.S. beach—*without clearing customs*.

The skipper quickly reversed off the gravel, looking around to see if anyone in the fleet had noticed. Satisfied that it was our little secret, we checked the bilge to confirm that the hull hadn't been breached. It was a very soft grounding at idle speed, but it took little effort to check—just in case. Once secure in the knowledge that no harm had been done, we began assaulting the skipper with lighthearted comments, threatening to expose the incident to the rest of the fleet and assuring him that tradition demanded he buy the crew a beer. The crew was bonding through shared experiences, and we seemed to be getting along very well together.

A few minutes later, we entered the first of the two Beauharnois locks.

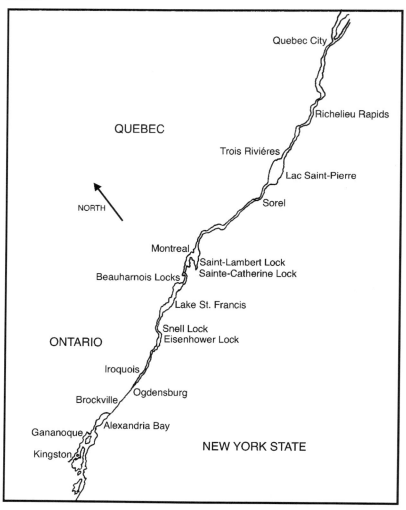

Map 7. The Upper St. Lawrence River

One of the vessels in the flotilla, a thirty-seven-foot Alberg named *Ciaccona* (pronounced "She-a-cone-a"), was the home of Bob and Jana Johnston and their daughters, Emma and Kai. Bob and Jana had given up their jobs and their house, and had taken the children out of school to cruise. The family planned to sail to Ste Anne des Monts with the fleet before turning south around the Gaspé and cruising to the Azores, off the coast of Portugal. That same route became my intended course four years later.

After *Lap Cat* was securely rafted to *Ciaccona* in the lock, I stepped onto her deck and took up a position on the bow to help fend her off the lock's abrasive wall. As the water began draining from the lock, five-year-old Kai pointed to the radar antenna mounted on *Lap Cat*'s mast and asked, "What's that?"

Jana provided a brief explanation of its purpose, and Kai quickly responded with "Is that like echo location?"

I couldn't believe those words had come from the mouth of a five-year-old. It turned out that she had learned how bats locate their prey with sound and was able to relate the concept to Jana's

Flotilla vessels in one of the St. Lawrence Seaway locks

description of radar. Moments later, when her mother reminded her to stay on the cabin top out of everyone's way, Kai asked, "What are your concerns, Mom?"

Kai's vocabulary and articulation were completely incongruous with her age and tiny voice. Her communication skills dispelled any concerns I might have previously harboured about home schooling. Not only were these little girls experiencing the world in a way that few people could ever hope to, but judging by Kai's questions, they were being provided with an exemplary education as well.

The previous day, while moored at Iroquois, we had snuggled into our berths by 9:30 p.m. and slept until 5:15 a.m., but negotiating the Beauharnois locks substantially disrupted our schedule. Though Ian had begun preparing spaghetti around five in the evening, it appeared that *Lap Cat* was about to lock through Lower Beauharnois, so dinner was postponed until the transit was complete. In the end, we faced several delays due to up-bound traffic, and hours slipped by before we exited the lock in fading light. Then, we spent considerable time locating a suitable anchorage in the dark. Finally, *Lap Cat*'s anchor gripped the steeply sloped bottom somewhere southeast of the lock. When we sat down to dinner it was 11:45 p.m. We wolfed our meals down and, being thoroughly exhausted, slipped appreciatively into our berths.

It was still early morning when we reached the floating dock of the penultimate down-bound lock. We secured our lines and chatted with other members of the fleet while we waited for the Sainte-Catherine lock to turn. Ultimately, a flashing yellow light indicated the massive gates were about to open. I was releasing dock lines when I was unexpectedly assigned to the helm. The idea of piloting a boat of *Lap Cat*'s size for the first time in a congested lock rattled me. Her displacement was at least twenty-five per cent in excess of *Alice Rose*'s, and every one of her dimensions was greater. The fleet circled a few times like a flock of gulls, each skipper manoeuvring to secure his preferred position. While it was understood that the larger vessels would assemble along the wall of the lock, they showed little enthusiasm for hugging the rough concrete. Most other skippers favoured rafting alongside vessels known to have experienced, competent crews. Gradually, each member of the fleet settled into single file.

On our approach to the lock entrance, I noted a rather strong following wind. I could feel the cockpit enclosure acting like a sail, something I would not have noticed if I hadn't been on the helm. There were already eight yachts inside, and we would have to raft to one of them while being driven forward by that wind. Many of the vessels weren't yet secured, and even in neutral, I was moving toward them at an alarming speed. I shifted into reverse to slow *Lap Cat*'s forward motion to a knot or so in order to come alongside the forty-six-foot, nineteen-ton *Marguerite*. At that speed, steering became unreliable, and the manoeuvre quickly escalated from stressful to terrifying. In spite of my discomfort, and due more to luck than skill, *Lap Cat* came alongside and stopped within a foot of *Marguerite*'s rail while the crews of the two vessels traded greetings and lines. A wave of relief washed over me. I was beginning to gain confidence both in the Nonsuch and in my own seamanship.

CHAPTER FIVE
Yacht Club de Quebec

A downpour engulfed *Lap Cat* as we approached Sorel. I donned my brand-new bright yellow Wetskins, matching sou'wester, and yellow Helly Hansen deck boots. With my shoulders hunched and bent a little at the waist, I must have looked like a giant, ripe banana. I went forward to attach a docking line to the T-cleat on the bow. It rained so heavily that we had difficulty discerning the channel markers as we picked our way into the marina. Once secured to the dock, I returned to the shelter of the cockpit enclosure where I was amazed to discover that I was as dry as I had been before I set out. There is simply no substitute for good quality equipment.

Patient Nancy, a home-built trimaran, hit bottom on her way into the docks but reported no damage. It was her second grounding, the first being at Iroquois where her skipper had to repair her removable dagger board before continuing.

We registered at the marina office, and I obtained a shower key in exchange for a deposit of ten dollars. Having anchored offshore the previous night, we were all anxious to shower and change into clean clothes. After dinner, I went looking for a mailbox which, according to one of the Francophone marina staff, was "just outside of the gate to the right."

I thought perhaps the young man had misunderstood my question since I was unable to speak any French at all. I did, after all, turn right at the entrance to the marina property, and I didn't see a mailbox anywhere along my route. A light rain persisted, and a series of streetlights intermittently illuminated the sidewalk as far as I could see. I continued walking toward the town centre on the treed avenue until I came to a hospital. When I approached its double glass doors, I saw a traditional red Canada Post box just inside. According to a sign mounted on the door, visiting hours had ended five minutes earlier. I tested the doors to confirm that they were locked and waited for an opportunity to slip inside when someone came out. After a few minutes, I surrendered and turned to walk away. Almost immediately, I heard the door open and spun around just in time to see it close as a woman walked purposefully toward the parking lot.

Defeated, I returned to the marina and spied the elusive mailbox a hundred feet to the right of the gate—*as I approached it*. The young man had described its location as he saw it on his arrival at work rather than from my perspective within the marina.

The following morning, after breakfast, I repaired a locker door on the starboard side of the cabin, the hinges of which had torn away. Did that make me the ship's carpenter? Almost immediately, I found myself engaged in yet another field of expertise when, in a slightly less prestigious role, I lugged Ian's laundry, along with my own, to the marina's laundromat.

We sailed out of Sorel at midday on June 16 in significantly better weather. Not surprisingly, navigation was quickly becoming second nature. I was able to enter waypoints into the GPS and plot positions on charts faster and with greater confidence than I had at the beginning of the journey.

The afternoon was hot and humid throughout our transit of Lac Saint-Pierre though we were reasonably comfortable in the shade of *Lap Cat*'s cockpit enclosure. We arrived in Trois Riviére at 4:30 p.m. Having secured *Lap Cat* in her assigned slip, I quickly found my way to the marina bar where I looked forward to quenching my thirst with a cold draft beer.

"Biére a füt! Merci."

My feeble attempt to order a draft beer resulted in the barman looking at me as though I was speaking Klingon. I later learned that I had said something along the lines of "Thanks, a beer barrel."

No wonder the poor fellow reacted strangely.

I've since been advised that a request for an ice cold draft in Quebec should approximate "biére pression, s'il vous plait," though I'm reluctant to try saying it aloud—in case I've got it wrong again. In the end, the barman responded with just enough English to make the sale. I sat on the patio, enjoying a light breeze in the shadow of an umbrella sprinkled with Heineken logos. All around me, francophone sailors chatted casually over their drinks. I felt totally relaxed—a far too infrequent experience for me. What a life!

Refreshed, though still uncomfortably warm, I returned to *Lap*

Cat in the glare of the hot sun, went below, and changed into my bathing suit. The skipper and first mate removed their bikes from the port rail and went riding together. In the galley, Ian prepared pork chops for dinner while I played Barbara Streisand's *Memories* on *Lap Cat*'s stereo system. I lounged in the cockpit, soaking up the sun's warmth as if I could save it for the cold days yet to come. Feeling every bit like the stereotypical sailing bum, far from home and free of responsibility, I penned a letter to my wife.

A week had passed since I embarked at Mimico, and time was passing quickly. In fact, it was already June 17, my eldest daughter's thirty-fourth birthday. It occurred to me that I had been twenty-one years old when she was born—*time was indeed passing quickly*.

My alarm was set for 5 a.m. We were scheduled to get underway at six because seventy miles of river still separated us from Quebec City, our next destination. That meant a passage of about ten hours, subject to tides and river currents. At the Quebec suburb of Sillery, I would be able to enjoy a couple of days to myself since the flotilla planned to remain at Yacht Club de Quebec for three nights. By the time we cast off our dock lines the next morning, we were already forty minutes behind schedule.

About midday, near Portneuf above the Richelieu Rapids, we were enveloped in the familiar melody of our national anthem. The volume and clarity of the music amazed us as we sought to identify its source. Once discovered, Adrian passed the binoculars around, so each of us could see the riverside resident responsible for the music. He stood by his flagpole, high atop the cliffs overlooking the river's south shore. A few feet away from the distant figure, there were two black speaker boxes, each of which compared in size with a garden shed. When *O Canada* ended, the patriot dipped the Canadian flag and played *The Maple Leaf Forever*. We later learned that he repeated the ceremony for the benefit of each vessel in the flotilla as it passed beneath the cliff. Cooky informed us that the Canadian patriot had similarly honoured the 1997 flotilla, but to the best of our knowledge, no one in our flotilla knew who he was or how the tradition had begun.

Living on a small boat with others requires both tolerance and consideration. I was at the wheel until shortly after lunch when I retired to my berth for a short nap. With each successive sunrise, sleep was becoming more precious. As I began slipping into oblivion, Wilma's cell phone rang less than three feet from my head. I groaned in frustration, and when the preliminary small talk evolved into a lengthy conversation, I reluctantly abandoned my nap without a word.

The Yacht Club de Quebec's cannon saluted each vessel as it passed between the federally funded breakwalls at the marina entrance. It was a nice touch. Twenty-knot winds and powerful tidal currents challenged the flotilla's helmsmen at the basin's inlet. The skipper followed the dock crew's directions to our assigned slip and expertly manoeuvred *Lap Cat* into it. We secured our lines to T-cleats and watched as other vessels wound their way among the maze of tightly packed floating docks. Several were blown dangerously close to other boats, and one skipper desperately backed away from an imminent collision only to crunch onto the rocks of the break wall. Urgent shouts and the sounds of running deck shoes were heard intermittently until the last yacht had arrived.

After dark, I went once more in search of a mailbox and a shop where I could buy postcards. The first part of my walk led up the steep escarpment to the Plains of Abraham via Côte Gilmour. At the summit, I stumbled on an expansive park, its fringes illuminated by a mere handful of street lights. The park's interior was lit only by the full moon when the glowing orb wasn't obscured by passing clouds. I was somewhat surprised to find so many people casually strolling through the darkened park and along the dimly lit side streets beyond it. Pedestrians were everywhere in numbers that suggested few Quebecers spent their evenings at home. When a woman passed me on the sidewalk, the momentary scent of her perfume invoked thoughts of Trisha. We had only been separated for eight days, but I missed her already.

On my return to the boat, I walked briskly through a particularly dark area of the park and barely avoided stepping on a couple lying quietly together on a blanket. By the time I set foot on the yacht club's docks, I had walked about four miles, and I was more than ready to climb into my berth for the remainder of the night.

I was up at 5 a.m. on the 18th and off to the showers before anyone else stirred. To accommodate the area's near-twenty-foot tides, a hinged bridge provided a flexible link between the floating docks and the shore. I climbed the aluminium, dew-covered ramp, swung open the gate, and plodded sleepily toward the clubhouse. Finding the main door locked, I turned and carelessly stepped from the low porch onto uneven ground. My ankle collapsed to one side, and I fell heavily onto my knees. My left knee burned as blood oozed through my green cotton pants. Within a few minutes, I had showered, returned to *Lap Cat*, and converted my torn pants to a pair of cut-off shorts. I gave it little thought at the time since I had two additional pairs of pants in my kit, but a few days later, I suddenly found myself at sea with only one pair remaining.

Later in the morning, I learned that *Moonshadow* had jibed unexpectedly on her way to Quebec City, fracturing the gooseneck on the forward end of her boom. She and her skipper would be compelled to remain at the yacht club to await the delivery of a replacement part. As our progress toward Newfoundland continued, it was becoming abundantly apparent that cruising is hard on both

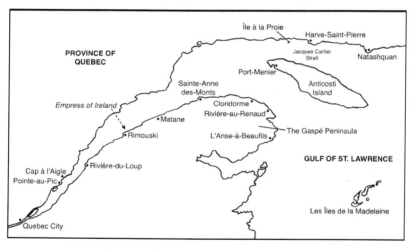

Map 8. The Lower St. Lawrence River

vessels and their crews. Injuries and damage to boats appeared to be a rather frequent occurrence.

Anxious to see something beyond the waterfront, I joined Cooky and Al Dimetric, skipper of a thirty-six-foot Nauticat named *Pampero*, on a re-provisioning expedition. A member of the yacht club offered to drive us to a suitable grocery store. He let us out at a large mall, but we were unable to locate the supermarket. After a few minutes of aimless wandering, we began approaching other shoppers, asking "Parlez-vous anglais?" Eventually, having been directed to another part of the mall on the far side of an expansive parking lot, we found our provisions on their shelves, patiently awaiting our selection.

It was our ninth day of living in *Lap Cat*'s belly. Adjusting to one another's habits and idiosyncrasies was a greater challenge for some than for others, and some friction was to be expected under the circumstances. Nevertheless, Cooky both surprised and amused me when I reminded him that the skipper's wife had asked that we add peppermint tea to our list of required provisions. As my shipmate strode indifferently past the largest herbal tea display that I had ever seen, he quietly replied, "I don't see any."

Naively, I scanned the dozens of colourful packages and called out "Here it is!" as, list in hand, he continued toward the end of the aisle.

"I don't see any," he repeated without turning.

I made a mental note to always endear myself to the ship's cook.

The cashier called a taxi on our behalf, and with several shopping carts piled high with supplies, the three of us waited near the door. When a Volkswagen Rabbit pulled up, we impatiently pointed out to the driver that we required a larger vehicle. The driver argued that we needed two taxis, but Cooky held his ground until the cabby drove off in a huff. We made a second call to arrange a larger vehicle, and shortly thereafter, a van arrived. We loaded our groceries quickly and began boarding just as a third cab stopped. The driver jumped out and complained loudly in a barely intelligible mixture of French and English that he, and not the van, had come in response to our call. The van driver had scooped his fare because we had assumed he was responding to our second call. Though sympathetic, we had tired of the delays and were not sufficiently concerned to transfer our bags—or contend with the van driver's reaction.

I spent much of the next day poring over charts and working out courses and waypoints for Tuesday's cruise to Cap à l'Aigle. After dinner, I walked briskly along the moonlit waterfront in search of a mailbox. The night was clear and the air was cool. A mile upriver, I met a woman who was obviously walking for exercise. I inquired, in a combination of English and clumsy French, where I might find a mailbox. Despite the language barrier, she was able to convey to me that it was at the top of the escarpment, directly in front of her house. So, in response to her offer, I let her post it for me. On my walk back to the yacht club, I wondered briefly if, before pushing it through the box's slot, she could resist reading the intimate message I had written to my wife.

When Tuesday arrived, I found myself oddly restless after two days and three nights in the same port. Perhaps I was developing an addiction to the nomadic life of cruising. I was eager to continue our exploration of the river and looked forward to the twelve-hour passage to Cap à l'Aigle and the scheduled fourteen-hour sail to Rimouski the following day.

The entire crew was below, preparing for *Lap Cat*'s imminent departure when I heard the desperate shriek of an obviously distraught woman.

"Oh God! No!"

As I rushed up on deck, my mind replayed an earlier sound which I had until then disregarded. It was an indistinct crunching and grinding of metal that had immediately preceded the woman's cry. Once on deck, I quickly discerned what had happened. During her turn toward the yacht club's exit, *Threshold*'s sweeping port quarter had struck the stern of *Kiaora II*, a 42 Niagara still moored in her slip. Both vessels were flotilla participants. The Niagara's inflatable tender hung limply from twisted davits like a lifeless, grey seal. With a tenuous grip on the deflated dinghy's transom, a nearly submerged outboard motor bobbed among glittering wavelets.

Both boats remained in Quebec pending repairs and settlement of the insurance claim. I never saw either vessel again.

Lap Cat left Yacht Club de Quebec at ten-to-nine, thirty-five minutes prior to high tide, thus taking advantage of the ebbing tide's two-and-a-half-knot current. We were bound for a one-night stay at Cap à l'Aigle, just beyond Pointe au Pic on the north shore. The skipper's wife wasn't aboard for this leg of the cruise because she had gone to meet her art class which, coincidentally, was on a field trip elsewhere in Quebec. Wilma planned to meet up with us at Rimouski in a couple of days.

I worried that my recent fall might have an adverse impact on the performance of my duties, but my knee was already healing well, its movement only slightly restricted by a crusty scab where there once was skin. We sailed downwind and downriver beneath a sky cluttered with puffy, cumulous clouds and passed the popular ski resort of Mont-Sainte-Anne at nine-point-four knots over the bottom. Of course, *Lap Cat*'s progress was to some extent due to the outgoing tide, but at that point in our passage, it was an unprecedented speed.

Just prior to sunset, we arrived at Cap à l'Aigle, a federally funded port of refuge in a section of the St. Lawrence River that offered no alternative harbour or suitable anchorage. It was a remote area where the lack of commercial and municipal facilities would otherwise have meant cruising against the incoming tide throughout the night. In a restricted waterway of varying depths, a mixture of darkness and strong currents could prove disastrous.

In an unsuccessful search for a mailbox, I wandered up a winding, gravel road toward the highway. My consolation came near the top of the incline where I noted a dense bed of forget-me-nots cascading down a steep, wooded slope. Seen through the trees in the fading light, the pale blue blanket of tiny blooms resembled a waterfall. I considered retrieving my camera from the boat, but the dim light was already unlikely to provide a decent exposure. Instead, I stood staring at the spectacle for several seconds, consciously locking the image into my memory.

We planned to embark at daybreak, so I chose sleep over all other personal comforts. This time, I didn't even determine whether or not the marina *had* shower facilities.

CHAPTER SIX
North of Forty-Eight

For reasons best known to oceanographers, the frigid Labrador Current creeps inland along the bottom of the St. Lawrence River and resurfaces in the vicinity of Cap à l'Aigle. The upwelling current noticeably cools the local environment and attracts a number of unexpected species of marine wildlife.

At 5:30 a.m. on June 21, *Lap Cat* motored out of Cap à l'Aigle into the salty St. Lawrence River. The air temperature dropped as the river's banks diverged and its bottom fell steadily away toward the Gulf of St. Lawrence. The VHF crackled with excited reports of sea lion and seal sightings. We, in turn, reported large numbers of beluga whales and several finbacks throughout the morning.

Aside from a slight, wind-rippled swell, the river's surface was flat until about midday. Then, a steady rain overtook us out of the south-east, and the wind began to build. For much of our eastward passage, we had relied on our diesel auxiliary when traffic, wind direction, or the confines of the river's banks made sailing impractical. Finally, with those impediments behind us, we raised the yacht's 540-square-foot sail and sped toward Rimouski on a beam reach.

Cooky served ham, fried tomatoes, scrambled eggs, and toast for brunch. The hearty meal was especially appreciated because the temperature on deck had fallen below fifty degrees Fahrenheit. In response, we zipped up *Lap Cat*'s cockpit enclosure and donned sweaters and jackets. Our environment slowly transitioned from tolerable to almost comfortable.

I was at the wheel, though in reality, it was the electric auto helm that was steering *Lap Cat* toward her next waypoint almost ten miles distant. The depth of the water was no longer a navigational concern, so my primary duties included watching for other vessels, monitoring the GPS to ensure that we were adhering to the prescribed path, and noting changes of wind direction that might cause the rig to jibe. The GPS indicated that our reported location was accurate to within thirteen feet, less than half of the hull's length. It was connected to the skipper's laptop computer, so we could follow our progress on the digital chart displayed on its screen.

There was nothing to be seen above the horizon but the dim hint of a far-off shore and, in our wake, a mosquito-like smudge that we knew to be *Kalinka I*, a thirty-five-foot Heritage. She was skippered by Noel Lien, a proud claimant of Viking ancestry. He and his first mate, Sally, had exited Cap à l'Aigle about forty-five minutes ahead of us and sailed north around Île Rouge whereas *Lap Cat* had taken the southern route and picked up a 2.8-knot lift due to a local tidal current. *Lap Cat*, moving over the bottom at nine knots according to the GPS, was now three miles ahead of *Kalinka I*. As unlikely as it appeared at the time, our relative positions would suddenly reverse before we entered our next port.

As *Lap Cat* rounded the outer marker and began her entry into Rimouski harbour, the skipper started the engine while the crew dropped her sails. Our routine approach was disrupted when, without warning, the Volvo's oil pressure alarm sounded. Adrian immediately shut down the engine.

The rest of us watched his face for an indication of understanding. He was, after all, an auto mechanic by trade. Initially we speculated—and indeed, hoped—that gravity had drawn the crankcase oil away from the pump due to the boat heeling while we were sailing. The skipper looked perplexed as he removed the engine cover, confirmed that the oil level was adequate and looked for other indications of a problem. Finding nothing, he mused about a faulty sensor and suggested I restart the engine. Within a couple of seconds, the sound of metal against metal forced me to quickly shut it down.

A twenty- to twenty-five-knot wind blew directly out of the harbour toward us. Sailing into the narrow entrance was impractical, so Adrian called *Kalinka I* on the radio and requested her assistance while I rigged a towline and secured it to *Lap Cat*'s bow cleat. When *Kalinka I* came alongside with Sally at the helm, I threw the line to Noel. Sally radioed the marina which provided line handlers on the dock and dispatched a Zodiac rescue boat to escort us into the harbour. Then, Sally broadcast a Sécurité call on channel sixteen to warn other vessels that *Kalinka I* would be towing a disabled vessel into the harbour at two knots. The towline's slack was gently taken up until the line grew taut. Noel took a perfect line at the appropriate speed, dragging us expertly within two feet of the dock before dropping the towline. We virtually handed our mooring lines to the marina staff on the floating dock.

I was still a relative novice on my arrival at Rimouski, but even years later as an experienced sailor, the mere thought of engine failure triggered a wave of anxiety.

The stress of the challenge was mitigated by Adrian's calm demeanour throughout. I'd begun to read him better as I got to know him, and I was sure he too was anxious in spite of outward appearances. Nevertheless, I noted the effect that a calm skipper can have on his crew, and I vowed to practice what I'd learned. Unfortunately, I never achieved my elusive, unspoken oath.

As soon as *Kalinka I*'s dock lines were secured, we invited her crew aboard for their reward. Relaxing over our celebratory glasses of ship's scotch, we reviewed the events of the passage from Cap à l'Aigle. We had performed well and had overcame the engine problem with the precision of a practiced team. It was great training for crisis management, and I was at least twice as confident as I had been on the day I signed on.

Ian began preparing dinner while Adrian worked on the engine. In the mean time, I sat on my berth sipping scotch and recording the day's events in my journal. There wasn't room for me to help either of them, but I expected to earn my keep the following day since I was scheduled to replace the VHF antenna at the top of *Lap Cat*'s mast.

The number of flotilla participants had been reduced by the collision at Yacht Club de Quebec and would continue to fluctuate as boats joined and left our group at various points along the way. *Pampero* was a motor-sailer, generously roomy and capable of cruising at twelve knots. I had met her skipper, Al Di Metric at Yacht Club de Quebec. With the exception of Bongo, the dog, Al had been sailing *Pampero* solo until a crew member, coincidently also named Al, joined him at Rimouski. We promptly dubbed the pair "Al squared".

We slept until half-past-seven on the twenty-second. I grabbed my things from my clothing locker and followed the dock in search of the showers. Paradoxically, mariners work hard at staying dry until they go ashore where, at their first opportunity, they find a shower so they can get wet!

Adrian advised us that the e-mail system was again up and running, after being down for several days, so those letters and cards I had recently posted were about to become old news. In the year 2000, those of us with adult children had only recently been admitted to the technology era, and email had not yet become a common tool among travellers.

"Isn't technology amazing?" I mused from the perspective of one who grew up in the era of the slide rule.

Lap Cat's VHF antenna, mounted at the top of her fifty-two foot mast, had somehow been lost en route, so I was hauled aloft to install an appropriate length of stainless rod as a temporary substitute. Because the Nonsuch is *cat-rigged*, with the mast all the way forward at the bow, it carries only one sail. As a result, *Lap Cat* was equipped with a single halyard. Since common sense dictated that the mast-monkey should be attached to a back-up halyard, Noel rafted *Kalinka I* alongside and attached her halyard to the bosun's chair as a safety line. It offered little assurance, however, since *Kalinka I*'s mast was at least twelve feet shorter and fifteen feet away. To ensure that I wouldn't swing into *Kalinka I*'s mast if the primary halyard failed, I snapped my tether to my harness and wrapped it around the freestanding mast. I also loosely embraced the aluminium spar with my legs and arms during the ascent.

Ratcheting clicks rose from the winch below me, accompanied by the grunts of Cooky and the skipper. My upward progress lurched a foot or two with each heave of the halyard. While, at the deck, the mast was a robust fourteen inches in diameter, its top—the point from which my lift line appeared—tapered to approximately four inches. Without stays or shrouds, the *stick* was entirely free standing and responded to every shift of my weight as would the stem of a daffodil. Eventually, I reached a point just below the masthead and shouted, "OK."

Working above my head, I fumbled with a pair of lineman's pliers until I managed to secure the rod in place. Then I wrapped the antenna's base with rigging tape to keep moisture out of the connection. Far below, the crews of other boats craned their necks and shaded their eyes with weathered hands as they followed my progress. When I finished, I took a moment to look around at the riverscape from my privileged vantage point before asking to be lowered to the deck. Two or three minutes later, I felt a slight trembling in the muscles of my legs as I stood on the cabin-top. I had been up a number of shorter masts previously, so I recognized the adrenaline induced symptom. With my responsibilities behind me, I walked briskly through the harbour and into the town of Rimouski to look around and burn off the effects of the experience.

In the afternoon, I accompanied Sally and Noel to the Pointe-au-Pére Musée de la Mer, four miles down river. In addition to the decommissioned Pointe-au-Père Lighthouse, the museum featured relics related to the 1914 sinking of the *Empress of Ireland*.

The Liverpool-bound passenger liner had sailed from Quebec City less than twelve hours before her demise and had just dropped her pilot at Rimouski when she entered a fog bank in the early morning hours of May 29. Her crew detected an unseen Norwegian collier, the 6,000-ton *Storstad*, by the distant, low-frequency blast of its foghorn. She cautiously reversed her engines to reduce speed while the *Storstad*, equally confused by the disembodied wail of the *Empress*'s horn, turned to port to avoid a collision. The chisel-like prow of the collier struck the 570-foot ocean liner amidships at 1:50 a.m.

As to be expected, most passengers were asleep in their cabins and had little opportunity of escape during the fourteen minutes that the ship remained afloat. Only forty-five passengers survived to mourn the 1,012 victims who perished in the frigid depths of the fog-shrouded river. The course of history would not have been irrevocably altered for hundreds of families had the *Empress* not slowed or the *Storstad* not turned.

The Empress of Ireland sank into the icy water off Pointe au Pére, bringing the desperate struggles of those still aboard to an end. Many confused passengers never found their way from their cabins to the lifeboat deck. Perhaps a handful survived for a while, trapped in pockets of air as the ship settled onto the riverbed. Of the 138 children listed on the ship's manifest, no less than 134 drowned.

Though a tragic loss of life echoing the *Titanic* disaster of 1912, the *Empress of Ireland* carried no prominent Americans to garner the prolonged attention of U.S. newspapers. A month later, their focus turned to the assassination of Archduke Franz Ferdinand and the subsequent outbreak of the First World War.

I climbed the iron spiral-stairs of the vintage Pointe-au-Père Lighthouse with Sally and Noel. We looked out over the river and took a few pictures before visiting a Rimouski restaurant for fish and chips. Later, in the evening, I joined them on *Kalinka I* to celebrate the birthday of one of her crew. In the weeks that followed, Sally and Noel often invited Cooky and I to join their explorations ashore and graciously included us in a number of social functions.

On the morning of our thirteenth day, I mounted an additional antenna on *Lap Cat*'s stern rail to augment the performance of our handheld VHF radio. While the rest of the flotilla departed for the port of Matane, a local marine mechanic tore our Volvo diesel down to remove and test the suspect oil pump. I had a couple of post cards to mail, and it was time to get my hair cut, so I again walked into Rimouski. Life aboard a small boat is confining, and once ashore, sailors tend to embrace walking as their primary means of getting around.

With my hair neatly cropped and a bottle of cabernet sauvignon in hand, I returned to the docks to determine what progress had been made on the engine. In my absence, the mechanic had removed and tested the oil pump, determined that it was performing normally and found the problem to be much simpler than anyone had anticipated. The lubrication system was pressurized, so the crankcase was designed to be airtight. A small leak had developed in the dipstick gasket, so the mechanic fabricated a new gasket, reassembled the engine, and invoiced the skipper more than six hundred dollars for his considerable labour. With the diesel operational and tested by late afternoon, we scheduled our departure to coincide with the morning tide. *Lap Cat* had, by then, fallen fifty miles behind the flotilla.

There was no time on the twenty-fourth for a shower or shave. We rose with the sun at four-thirty and left the dock at five o'clock. With insufficient wind to consistently fill our huge sail, and eager to rejoin the flotilla, we motored throughout the day. At 2:15 p.m., in flat water, I was relieved from the helm and went below to update my journal. We'd been underway in excess of nine hours and expected to arrive in Sainte-Anne-des-Monts a little after seven in the evening, having bypassed Matane where the other vessels had spent the night. The river had grown so wide that the north shore had long ago slipped beyond the horizon. The day's highlights amounted to a couple of distant seal sightings and a pair of dolphins swimming two hundred feet off our bow. By referring to my calendar, I calculated that another thirty-five days would pass before I would again see Trisha.

Cruising on a sailboat, especially as crew on someone else's yacht, provides ample time for quiet reflection. I had forgotten what it was like to have that luxury and appreciated the opportunity, but the downside was being exiled from the ones I loved. My remedy was writing to them and recording the expedition in my journal, so my wife and family could share the adventure when I returned. I penned a postcard to seven-year-old Emily, one of my grandchildren, cramming as much into the restricted space as I possibly could.

My Dear Emily,

By the time you get this card you'll be in your new house, and I'll be in Corner Brook, Newfoundland. I've seen lots of beluga whales, dolphins, finback whales, and ducks. Everyone here speaks French, and I wish you were here to interpret for me. We're sailing to Anticosti Island next. Ask Mommy to show you where it is on a map. Are you looking after Nanny while I'm away? When you read this card, I will be only four weeks from coming home again—maybe less. We've had very nice weather most of the time though it has rained from time to time, and once in a while, it gets cold for a few hours. But mostly, it's sunny and cool. Can [sic] you explain to Jack where Papa is for me? The captain thinks Papa is an "excellent navigator," so he relies on me to look after that for him. Sometimes we sail at night while you're sleeping.

P.S. I forgot to tell you that I went up to the top of the mast the other day to fix the radio antenna, and I could see for miles and miles around, but I couldn't see you.

I love you Emily and I'll see you again soon.

It was during the 2000 Flotilla that I began to really enjoy the process of writing. I had resolved to keep a journal of the six-week passage to Labrador and Newfoundland, and it quickly became a source of entertainment. I had taken a book to read, but often there were too many distractions to become comfortably immersed in its story. Writing passed the time when I wasn't on watch or asleep in my berth, and I looked forward to sharing my narrative with Trisha on my return.

On the fifteenth morning of our adventure, our little fleet departed Sainte Anne des Monts and set a course for Port Menier on Anticosti Island, a ninety-five nautical mile, downwind crossing. Throughout the day, the vessels of the flotilla gradually dispersed as wind speeds increased through twenty-five toward thirty-knots, and three-meter waves surged around us. *Lap Cat*'s full and beamy hull rolled in the heavy seaway as she momentarily surfed down the faces of successive waves. The grey sky darkened with every passing wave crest. Eventually, beyond the glare of our backlit instruments, the rain-soaked black of night rendered us sightless.

I was on the helm late in the evening when an unidentified vessel overtook *Lap Cat*. Invisible, aside from its red, masthead, port light, it appeared to be on an intersecting course, thereby posing a serious threat to the safety of both vessels. Cooky and I anxiously studied the disembodied light as it edged toward us. *Lap Cat* was running with the wind on a starboard tack, so turning out of the vessel's path to port meant enduring a violent jibe in severe winds, a manoeuvre likely to cause damage to our rigging. Dropping the Nonsuch's massive sail in the dark without coming about was equally ill-advised. Though neither of us were able to accurately estimate the distance between the two vessels, we believed our opportunity for safely turning across the other boat's bow had passed.

Every effort to contact the phantom by radio failed, and shining our brilliant spotlight in its direction went unanswered. I searched my mind for a solution, and finding none, I woke the skipper. Following a brief assessment of the situation, with no other option apparent, he began hauling in the mainsheet and ordered me to ease the wheel to port. My heart raced as I reluctantly put our stern to the wind. I braced myself in anticipation. The chaotic noise of the massive, wish-bone boom swinging fiercely to starboard was amplified by the darkness. The mainsheet tore off our loran antenna, mangled the stern rail VHF antenna, and wrapped around the inflatable dinghy on the stern.

The skipper's wife, eyes wide with fear, appeared from below in filmy white lingerie. Clearly shaken by the noise on deck and *Lap Cat*'s sudden and violent heel to starboard, she appealed to her husband for reassurance.

Lap Cat could not maintain a downwind heading with the mainsheet fouled and was in danger of broaching. Adrian took the wheel while I snapped my tether to a pad eye and scrambled over the stern rail to clear the mainsheet. With no visible reference by which to steer, the skipper was unable to hold a steady course in the high winds. *Lap Cat*, completely out of control in the confused seas, jibed twice more while I clung like an insect to the rail. With my left hand and left leg occupied with hanging on, I worked desperately to free the lines with my right hand while Adrian fought to recover our heading in the coal-black darkness. More through luck than by design, I managed to clear the lines, the mainsheet resumed its essential role, and *Lap Cat* settled into a steady rhythm once more. I wearily climbed back into the cockpit to find my pants shredded beyond further use, reducing my post-Quebec City wardrobe of two pairs to one.

In the confusion, the unidentified intruder vanished into the night. Why hadn't the phantom changed course as she approached? Perhaps her sails had obscured the helmsman's view of our stern light. Or might he have been asleep and sailing on autopilot? I came off watch at midnight and climbed into my berth to restore the physical and mental energy I'd expended, but sleep proved elusive. Rocking gently in my berth, I searched in vain for a solution that didn't include gybing. With the morning light, it came.

When the wind had blown *Lap Cat* into St. Lambert lock ten days earlier, had I not reversed the engine to slow her forward motion? Of course! It was such a simple solution, and yet it had been overlooked amid the tension of the previous night. None of us had considered starting the engine and putting it into reverse to slow *Lap Cat*'s headlong rush to intersect the other vessel's course. That simple act would have allowed the other boat to pass safely

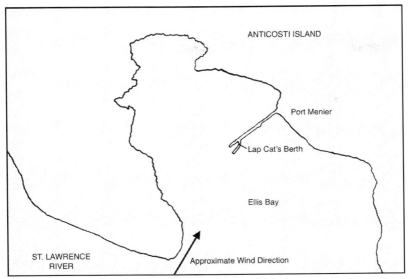

Map 9. Port Menier

beyond our bow.

On June 26, at about eight in the morning, we arrived at Port Menier. The entirely artificial harbour was located at the end of a three-quarter-mile-long man-made causeway and looked, on the chart, like a giant tuning fork with the southern tine bent slightly inward. With open arms, the wide southwest-facing entrance welcomed wind and waves into the harbour's interior throughout our short stay. Every boat in the flotilla was battered relentlessly for twenty-one hours.

Lap Cat's skipper docked along the interior wall of the southern tine, just beyond the bend. It appeared to provide the best possible protection. Even so, we rose and fell turbulently on three-foot swells. The buoyant hull was repeatedly sucked away from the rusting, steel, fluted wall and then violently slammed against it. The six-foot climb from the deck to the top of the jetty was awkward and dangerous. Descending to the rising and falling deck was no less challenging.

Our two-by-four fender board, hung outboard of three ten-inch fenders, was at risk of being chewed to splinters. We considered ourselves lucky when we found a bent, aluminium ladder among the rocks on the seaward side of the southern tine and lashed it to the starboard fender board to absorb the repeated impacts. On board, the motion and the jarring collisions with the jetty made concentration difficult. From atop the pier, the loudest sound in Port Menier foreshadowed Labrador's primary characteristic, the ever-present wind.

I walked the causeway's gravel road to a cluster of barn-like buildings on shore, mailed Emily's postcard and examined the merchandise in a couple of shops. The stores' scant inventories offered nothing of interest, so I returned to the harbour and made an unsuccessful attempt to reach Trisha on one of the dock's two weathered payphones.

We made our escape at 5 a.m. on Tuesday morning, sailing southward out of Ellis Bay into a twenty-knot wind. *Lap Cat* turned west to round the north-west tip of Anticosti Island. About 6 a.m., a voice on the VHF reported that a thirty-foot C&C, named *Windthrush*, had struck a rock just west of the buoyed channel that led out of Port Menier. *Windthrush*'s skipper, Peter Briffa, advised that she was stuck fast. *Lap Cat*, now an hour away, was not in a position to render assistance, so all we could do was listen attentively to the rescue efforts on the VHF.

None of the flotilla vessels were able to operate safely in the dangerously shallow water near *Windthrush* though *Sea Therapy*, a twenty-six foot MacGregor with a retractable keel, made a valiant attempt to drag *Windthrush* from the rock. In the end, she simply lacked the necessary power though her captain, Jeremy Hilliard, managed to rescue two of *Windthrush*'s crew including Linda Briffa, the skipper's wife. Her husband and one member of his crew remained aboard.

As the day wore on, the wind speed increased to thirty knots, putting Briffa, his crew member, and his vessel at considerable risk. I was below when Adrian leaned into the cabin from the cockpit to relate what he had just heard on the radio. Late in the afternoon, *Burin Star*'s skipper, John Dunford, used his Zodiac tender to deliver a tow-line to the grounded C&C. By early evening, the forty-six foot ketch, *Burin Star*, had successfully towed *Windthrush* free of the rock. No doubt, everyone in the fleet exhaled with relief.

Ask any cruising sailor, and he will assure you that the vast majority of his or her sailing experience has been *into* the wind. Our windward struggle to round Anticosti's western tip in the morning should have been to our benefit once our afternoon course pointed northeast, but predictably, the wind in the Strait of Jacque Cartier was blowing in the opposite direction. *Lap Cat*'s foredeck-mounted mast and single giant sail performed well off the wind, but when close hauled, she was less efficient than a sloop. We faced a long, hard slog to our destination.

Lap Cat tacked toward Harve-Saint-Pierre much of the day, but late in the afternoon, while still among the islands along the north shore, the skipper elected a daylight anchorage over a night-time arrival in a strange port. He and the other skippers in our vicinity briefly studied their charts and selected Baie Quarry on the north shore of Île à la Proie. *Kalinka I* and *Pampero* preceded us into the bay.

What a beautiful, sheltered anchorage! Aside from a line of five red mooring buoys, there were no signs of technology, nor any visible indications that humans had ever inhabited the island. There were only rocks, trees and wildflowers. We picked up one of the available mooring buoys two or three hundred feet off the beach and tied off for the night.

CHAPTER SEVEN
Beyond the End of the Road

Île à la Proie is one of about thirty islands that collectively form the Mingan Archipelago National Park. A small building on the shore of Baie Quarry, equipped with a large wood-burning cook stove, was available for public use at the time of our visit. The island's southern beach, littered with limestone formations carved over centuries by local currents and tides, formed a unique, photographers' dreamscape.

On Wednesday, the twenty-eighth of June, I motored to the island in *Lap Cat*'s ember-orange Zodiac, beached it on the gravel shore, and with my camera in my hand, I walked along the water's edge. Gently lapping waves accompanied me onto a rocky point, well away from the boats.

Seal sunning herself on a rock near shore of Île à la Proie.

There, I encountered a grey seal sunning herself on a rock. I'm not sure how I concluded that she was female, since I know absolutely nothing about seals. Perhaps it was her doe-eyed expression or her strangely passive behaviour. Though a mere thirty feet of shallow water separated us, she was completely indifferent to my presence. I stood on the shore, quietly observing her for a couple of minutes. Click, click, click, click! She didn't stir. Finally, in an effort to have her look toward my lens, I spoke to her in what I intended to be a gentle, friendly tone. Without turning, she slipped lazily—and rather rudely, I thought—into the water.

I retraced my steps to the dinghy, where a narrow boardwalk wound leisurely through the island's middle toward the southern

Hoodoo-like rock formation located on the southern beach of Île à la Proie.

shore. Photo opportunities appeared along either side of the walkway's weathered, grey planks in the form of colourful, unfamiliar flowers. I stepped from the last plank onto a sandy beach occupied by a number of grey limestone formations.

Weathered by millions of years of wind and rain and tinged with rust-coloured lichen, they towered fifteen feet above me against a backdrop of wispy, white clouds and brilliant blue sky. Click, click, click!

The boats' crews assembled in the island's only building to share a shore dinner featuring fresh cod and a bucket of wild mussels they had gathered from the bay. There, on an island normally silent aside from the sounds of wind and waves, laughter and the clanking of kitchenware filled the night. I was getting to know many of the flotilla's crews, and I enjoyed the group get-togethers immensely. Our skipper and his wife slept ashore in their tent that night, leaving Ian and I to our books and rum.

By seven o'clock the following morning, *Lap Cat* had already been underway for a couple of hours. We had replaced a batten in the mainsail, prepared and eaten breakfast, and had even begun repairing a minor rip in the sail.

The ill-fitting, makeshift antenna that I installed at Rimouski never worked properly, and, like its predecessor, it too had vanished. When *Lap Cat* rolled in heavy weather, the masthead swung violently over a greater distance than any other point on the boat. Only a commercially manufactured antenna with a tight-fitting base could hope to survive the violent whipping action.

I had acquired a better understanding of at least one aspect of cruising since leaving the comfort of Yacht Club de Quebec. Salt, a wick to moisture, was invading everything aboard, especially my canvas deck shoes. As a result, my feet felt continually damp and clammy. *Lap Cat* was developing her own scent. Mildew, rum, curry and salt air combined into a unique blend, like a fine wine—gone bad. With four of us living aboard, she probably needed a good cleaning, but that wasn't likely while we were in mid-voyage.

I too was becoming a little "salty." I had accumulated a four-day beard since leaving Sainte Anne des Monts, but I couldn't find the opportunity or the inclination to shave.

Another notable feature of cruising in northern latitudes is the frequent and dramatic fluctuation of temperatures. Cold, overcast mornings bumped up against sunny afternoons, and the latter usually alternated between pleasant and uncomfortable temperatures. I often donned a jacket when the sun vanished behind a cloud layer or stripped off a sweater when it emerged to bath us in its warm glow.

About noon, I spotted my very first puffin, its wings beating furiously as it crossed our bow a few feet above the water's surface. A short while later, a long, low island appeared on the horizon off the port bow. We thought little of it initially, but after reviewing the chart and finding nothing in that direction for more than 300 miles, we were baffled by its presence. It appeared to be surrounded by steep yellow cliffs or banks of golden sand topped with the dark green colour of thick foliage. We checked the chart again and viewed the island's shimmering reality through binoculars for some time before it began breaking up into a line of smaller islands. Gradually, the mysterious land melted into the gulf, vanishing altogether.

The uncharted island was a mirage—*a genuine mirage!* Not a wavering, indistinct image but a stable, realistic representation of land. What a privilege it was to witness one of nature's spectacular illusions, one that I had read about in my youth; a phenomenon that had, in childhood, seemed so magical. I still cherish the memory of that rare spectre of refracted light so infrequently witnessed by man.

Lap Cat was on auto helm when I took the wheel with slightly more than three weeks remaining to Quirpon Harbour. According to the chart, the remote settlement was situated at the tip of Newfoundland's Northern Peninsula. It was *there* that my passage was scheduled to end. *Lap Cat* would continue her exploration of Newfoundland's east coast without me, while I found my own way home. With the Nonsuch's sail lashed to the boom and her diesel purring contentedly, we slipped eastward over a smooth, gently rolling sea.

I remained on the helm for more than half of the day's passage, plotting and logging *Lap Cat*'s position hourly. The cruise was proving to be the ideal training exercise. We passed the day on lazy swells resembling flexible glass. Hour after hour, we gently rose—and gently fell.

Shortly after six on Thursday evening, with eleven hours of sailing behind us, we reached a tiny outport on the remote coast of Quebec named Natashquan.

When I awoke the following morning, I shaved off my five-day beard, reorganized my kit and walked into town to buy a few stamps. Did I say "town"? Natashquan had first appeared in 1859 as a small fishing settlement, and it looked, in the year 2000, as if the community's development had peaked in the early 1950s. Wind-worn and tired, the little outpost was literally the end of the road. To the east, the next coastal road of any consequence was a day's sail across the gulf in Newfoundland.

It turned out to be a lovely day, in the mid-seventies on the

Fahrenheit scale and sunny. I commented on the pleasant weather to a resident and he, standing in the middle of the dusty road while casually pawing at clouds of mosquitoes, claimed, "We get about three days like this almost every year."

Since leaving Mimico, I had been reading *Angela's Ashes* when I could find the time, enjoying both the narrative and the periodic escape it provided. A thirty-foot boat is not, however, a library. Often the skipper or one of the crew interrupted Frank McCourt's story when I was required on deck or simply asked to lend a hand for a moment. The requests were entirely understandable and in most cases justified, but the inevitable result was that I had difficulty finding an opportunity to read more than a few lines at a time.

Marine radio transmissions, from four boats that embarked a day early, reported dense fog a few miles out. In spite of the mosquitoes, I was content to be in sunny Natashquan where I might have an opportunity to read without interruption.

Like most communities along our route, the village scheduled a reception and dinner in honour of the flotilla's visit, but neither Ian nor I had known in advance of the potential expense. We simply hadn't taken enough cash to attend all of the receptions, even though the cost was in most cases quite reasonable. At Natashquan, we chose to remain on board and once more partake of Ian's tasty curried chicken.

On June 30 at Natashquan's latitude, darkness came about 10 p.m. Less than six hours later, the eastern horizon betrayed the coming of July. It was a new month, a new day and a new departure.

I was below, guiding *Lap Cat* through a cold fog with the aid of the GPS, the radar, and the electronic charts that had been downloaded to the skipper's laptop. The gulf fog obscured our vision, the frigid air numbed my fingertips, and the steady pounding of the nearby Volvo engine overwhelmed my hearing. We were bound for Coacoachou, the stepping-off point for the hundred-and-twenty-mile passage to Newfoundland's Corner Brook.

Lap Cat's radar indicated the blips of two other flotilla vessels, a mile-and-three-quarters and two miles off our starboard bow. A third and fourth followed on our starboard quarter though one of them was returning a rather weak and intermittent signal. Periodically, while I waited to confirm its relative position, the smaller boat's blip failed to appear for a few sweeps of our revolving antenna.

Lap Cat, represented on the computer's display by a two-dimensional outline of a little red boat, laid down a track in the form of a blue line. A poker-straight red line, emanating from its bow, represented our heading. In addition to scattered water depths at intervals all around the little red boat, the lap-top's chart indicated a shoreline a mile off our port beam. On deck, the skipper saw only the whites and greys of the fog, supplemented by *Lap Cat*'s true heading on the GPS mounted at the wheel. We contacted other vessels on the VHF occasionally, exchanging details of our relative positions as indicated electronically. Every crew eyed their radar screens to ensure they and their neighbours maintained a safe interval between boats.

Adrian, framed by the companionway, stood at the helm, intently scanning the impenetrable whiteness and periodically adjusting the electric auto helm. The device eased the wheel slightly to port and, a few seconds later, jerked it back to starboard, precisely maintaining the assigned course. From below deck, I guided the skipper through a deep channel separating two shoals, flashing ten fingers twice and pointing to port to avoid shouting above the engine noise. He reset the auto helm twenty degrees in that direction. I turned back to the screen and watched the red, projected course align with the middle of the channel. A second later, I gave him a thumbs up.

It occurred to me that I had for some time been blindly trusting both the skipper and our electronics with my safety. How things had changed since that first day on Lake Ontario.

I was glad to be below, in close proximity to the heater, though I still wasn't half as warm as I would have been in the garden at home. I remained semi-cosy when Ian took over on deck, allowing the skipper and his wife to retire to their berth.

By noon, the obscuring fog had cleared, exposing an expansive, bright blue dome. We motored throughout the afternoon in sunlight with a light breeze on our nose.

I was slightly intrigued by an unexpected new skill that I had developed over the past three weeks. I was, at will, able to sleep soundly in fifteen to twenty minute increments. Much of that afternoon, I awoke, checked the laptop to ensure the auto helm was adhering to the appropriate course, and immediately went back to sleep.

My personal provisions had lasted beyond my expectations. Still among them were a few packages of Kleenex and several Cadbury chocolate bars. Both were important to me. The sweet taste of chocolate had a restorative effect whenever I felt isolated from civilization and family, and on occasion, minor allergies and sinus issues made tissues essential. I found that I wasn't using my toiletries as often as I would have at home—*uggh!*—so they would undoubtedly last until I reached Quirpon. Lots of dry socks and

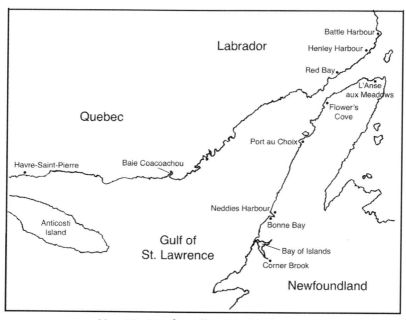

Map 10. Newfoundland and Labrador

underwear remained sealed in plastic produce bags as they had been at the outset of the passage. I had laundered clothes on two occasions and re-bagged the clean garments to prevent the intrusion of the salty dampness that permeated everything else on board. Clean, dry, warm clothes are essential at sea. Equally important in this remote region of the gulf were the half-dozen bottles of beer I had stowed safely in the cool bilge beneath the cabin sole.

At day's end, we anchored amid seven other members of the

fleet, encircled by treeless tundra in the well-protected eastern arm of Baie Coacoachou. From the deck, the terrain appeared as I had envisioned Labrador though the barren hills were actually within the province of Quebec. I saw no sign of a settlement in the vast wilderness surrounding the bay. Nature appeared to be winning the conflict with man in this part of the world.

I listened to the BBC on shortwave 6174 kHz. While a welcome connection to civilization, the announcer's formal report of the day's international events seemed only to heighten my sense of isolation. Yet, in a bittersweet way, I enjoyed the overall absence of commerce, politics and responsibility. When the skipper and his wife went ashore to explore and gather mussels, they hauled their inflatable dinghy a few feet onto a remote, gravel beach. An hour or so later, the rising tide and westerly wind conspired to re-float the Zodiac and blow it out into the bay. While the presence of other vessels mitigated the incident to an inconvenience, Adrian later acknowledged that failing to secure the dinghy was a serious error of seamanship. Had they been anchored in Quebec's coastal wilderness on their own, the couple would have faced a treacherous hike of several miles around numerous inlets to recover their dinghy on the other side of the bay. As it happened, Sally and Noel retrieved the bright orange tender as it drifted by *Kalinka I* and eventually rescued the castaways from the isolated beach.

Skippers consulted on the VHF and visited one another's vessels while the flotilla awaited a weather window to undertake the long passage to Corner Brook.

Ian prepared spaghetti for dinner, and I seized the opportunity to indulge myself with the bottle of Cabernet that I had purchased in Rimouski. The grocery and variety stores in Sorel, Rimouski, and Ste Anne des Monts offered half bottles of many varieties, and I had acquired a couple for periodic treats.

When I open my eyes each morning, the spark that ignites my consciousness is tea—steaming hot, slightly sweetened tea with a drop of milk. In the chill environs of Baie Coacoachou, the near-essential beverage took on an additional significance. I could go unwashed for a day or two, and I seldom drank water in its pure form, but having no water to make tea was unthinkable. And yet, *Lap Cat*'s twin forty-gallon water tanks were found to be empty only five days after being refilled at Port Menier. While the skipper suspected a faulty seal on one of the tanks' inspection plates, Cooky believed consumption was the culprit. He had on several occasions expressed his concerns about water conservation to the skipper's wife, and I had silently concurred.

I brushed my teeth with salt water directly out of the bay and waited anxiously until noon for that first cup of tea, courtesy of *Kalinka I*.

Cooky and I finished our brunch of scrambled eggs, peameal bacon, and fried tomatoes with toast—and the aforementioned tea. Still, the fog clung tenaciously to the bay though, admittedly, the familiar grey shroud had grown a shade lighter. I felt irritable and trapped. It seemed everyone was constantly talking and, too frequently, asking me to move out of the way so they could get at something they needed. Of course it wasn't them at all—it was *me*. I was simply suffering from cabin fever, and the others likely experienced similar feelings at times.

I motored ashore in the dinghy to explore the tundra, take some photographs, and simply escape my crewmates for a while. Contrary to my first impression, the landscape included a few trees though the vast majority of them were crooked and so stunted that, when viewed from the boat, the hills appeared completely treeless and barren. Once among these repressed victims of the northern, maritime climate, I found them to be a near impenetrable mass of tangled scrub. Fortunately, they were confined to the hollows and ravines, so once I pushed beyond them, I could follow the rocky ridges to the highest outlooks with relative ease. In most areas, the rocks were blanketed with six to ten inches of spongy moss and lichen, generously sprinkled with the multi-coloured blossoms of wild flowers.

With my back to the bay, I stood on a ridge overlooking a distant circular lake. It was enclosed within a prominent rim and appeared to be an ancient, water filled impact crater. Not unlike a movie screen, the lake's mirror-like surface reflected the brilliant blue sky and passing cumulus clouds.

The relentless white noise produced by the wind assailed my ears, rendering them essentially deaf to all other sounds, and yet, I thought I heard someone call my name. Thinking myself isolated from all humanity in the vast wilderness, I froze. I suppose I was a little startled and somewhat mystified. Scanning the terrain for an aberration of shape or colour that might betray the source of the distant shout, I settled on a tiny silhouetted figure atop the next ridge.

There, barely discernable on the crest, beneath waving arms, was Wanita, a member of *Dreamweaver*'s crew. She and her partner, Derek, had cruised to the Azores en route to Africa, where they explored the Gambia River. I was familiar with their story because, months earlier, my wife and I had attended their slide presentation at the World Cruising Club in Toronto.

While I had set out to get away from my shipmates a few minutes earlier, I was ready to socialize with someone with a different perspective. In spite of the maze of tangled scrub inhabiting the ravine that separated us, I took the plunge, persevered, and eventually climbed the ridge to join her, somewhat out of breath. For a half hour or so, we walked together, chatted and took photos.

Perhaps due to the relentless wind, the local bug density seemed less extreme at our altitude. Nevertheless, clambering over the uneven barrens involved some effort, so our exhalations and perspiration likely helped those in our vicinity to find us. We routinely swatted and waved at the pesky critters as we explored.

I was struck by the variety of colours among the flora. White flowers similar to lilies-of-the-valley, mauve periwinkles, deep purple irises, and large, yellow buttercup-like flowers dotted the moss-covered landscape along with a strange looking burgundy plant that Wanita identified as "a pitcher plant".

"It's the official flower of Newfoundland and Labrador." she explained.

Wanita went on to describe how it catches dew and rainwater in a leafy, trumpet shaped receptacle and feeds on the minute insects that get trapped in the water.

At a precipice, we braced ourselves against the wind and looked down on the bay where the yachts slumbered on its rippled surface. What a gorgeous panorama! I thought of Trisha and wished she could have been there to share the sight. I noted that *Marguerite*, a Frers-designed yacht from Rochester, New York, faced steadily into the wind while other vessels slewed from side to side, and for the first time, I noticed the riding sail hanked to her backstay. It provided *Marguerite* with directional stability at anchor, in the same way that the feathers on an arrow point the arrowhead in the direction of its flight. The cruise was turning out to be the school of seamanship I had anticipated, with a few botanical titbits thrown in.

The wind was expected to veer from the south to the southwest by dawn on July 3, and the barometer was rising, so our best opportunity for a comfortable crossing to Corner Brook appeared to be early the following day. The flotilla's captains were planning to take advantage of the weather, but I'd seen plans change frequently on this trip, and I didn't really expect to leave on time. A skippers' meeting was scheduled for 6 p.m. when a final decision would be made.

We hadn't been able to buy a radio antenna at any of the recently visited ports, and the one generously offered over the VHF by *Windthrush* turned out to be a loran antenna. Subsequently, our only operative radio was the handheld model with a rail-mounted antenna—cut to the appropriate length from a coat hanger—to augment its range. The skipper resolved to locate a proper aerial when we reached Corner Brook.

To keep us from tumbling out of our berths onto the cabin sole in heavy weather, I rigged lee cloths on the port and starboard berths. Thereafter, Ian and I found sleeping in a seaway much more comfortable. Nevertheless, long periods of sound sleep continued to elude me because my subconscious insisted on hearing and feeling environmental changes while we were underway. A change of wind direction, a steepening of waves or an adjustment to *Lap Cat*'s point of sail had an equal and immediate impact on my state of consciousness. Nor could I shake the loneliness that I had begun to feel early in the cruise. Trisha and I had been close for thirty-five years and our separation frequently occupied my mind while I awaited sleep.

Writing letters to family and friends eased my feelings of isolation, and though I was experiencing one of the greatest adventures of my life, I kept a careful count of the days that separated me from home. According to our sail plan, twenty-five more days and twenty-four nights would pass before that moment arrived.

Uncertainty lingered in the sheltered bay on Sunday morning while, out in the gulf, the wind raged. In the early afternoon, at yet another meeting, the flotilla skippers collectively agreed to begin our crossing to Corner Brook.

The fleet seemed to take forever to reach the outer marker where we would set our course for the next twenty-four hours. When the time came, I had mixed feelings.

The crossing, amidst three to four-metre waves spurred on by thirty-five knot southerly winds, was to be uncomfortable and memorable. Even so, I had confidence that *Lap Cat* would endure the blow and noted that her skipper showed no signs of apprehension. *Lap Cat*'s enclosed cockpit protected us from the constant spray as we clawed our way out into the Gulf of St. Lawrence. It may also have rendered the weather a little less threatening from our perspective.

Cooky and I took the six-to-midnight watch, and for the most part, the evening passed routinely though, on one occasion, I crept forward to secure some gear on the foredeck and suddenly found myself weightless, *a couple of feet above the deck*. Each time we dropped off a wave, I became momentarily airborne though I maintained a firm grip on something at all times. My tether, while an impediment to my progress, provided a welcome sense of security. Aside from another substantial bruise, this time to my hip, I returned to the cockpit without further incident.

CHAPTER EIGHT
"The Rock"

As the flotilla pitched and yawed toward Newfoundland on the evening of July 3, a seemingly endless series of radio transmissions occupied the airwaves. A few were routine navigational calls, but most dealt with a crisis aboard *Patient Nancy*, the thirty-one-foot trimaran built and sailed by Jerry Coulson. The sixty-one year old skipper described himself as a boat-builder and a Dogrib Indian. Though conditions were uncomfortable for the entire fleet, Jerry's home-built tri-hull was particularly vulnerable because she was much lower and broader than the other boats. As a result, waves that steeply tilted her one moment washed over her the next.

Late in the evening, *Patient Nancy's* anxious skipper began experiencing chest pain and numbness in his left hand, symptoms that his crew, son Cory and brother Marvin, identified with a heart attack. The Coulsons called the Quebec-based Coast Guard at Riviére-au-Renaud. I later learned that their operations officer was hesitant to launch a helicopter to facilitate Jerry's rescue. Because *Patient Nancy* was bound for Corner Brook, the call was redirected to the Port aux Basques Coast Guard Station which, in turn, contacted members of the Auxiliary Coast Guard in Corner Brook. Ironically, Jerry's rescuers were in a Corner Brook theatre with their wives watching *The Perfect Storm* when their pagers went off in unison.

The rescue was potentially complicated by the fact that Jerry's crew, described as inexperienced sailors, might not be capable of safely delivering *Patient Nancy* to Corner Brook on their own. Nor were any of the flotilla vessels able to transfer crew to the trimaran or get close enough to take Jerry off.

Medical practitioners tried to assess Jerry's health over the radio, proposing a number of steps to stabilize his condition, but the crisis remained unresolved at midnight when Cooky and I were relieved of our watch.

We briefed the skipper based on what we had overheard on

the radio, and he manoeuvred *Lap Cat* closer to *Patient Nancy* to stand by in case someone came up with a means of providing assistance. Because Adrian's wife slept through her scheduled watch, I remained on deck throughout the night, snuggled into the leeward cockpit seat, half listening to scraps of radio transmissions and half clinging to a fitful sleep. At irregular intervals, the sudden crackle of the VHF stabbed at my consciousness, awakening me for a few seconds and causing my heart to race momentarily. The omnipresent howl of the wind was, by contrast, soothing.

When I awoke on July 4, in the dim grey light of early dawn, the storm had blown itself out. The wind and waves were mere remnants of what they had been a few hours earlier. Beneath his furrowed brow, the skipper's eyes were dead with fatigue. I followed his gaze beyond the bow to where the horizon should have been. In its place, a black band appeared between the sea and the sky, both of which were lighter in colour. To which did the dark band belong?

Initially I thought, "What *is* that?" but quickly identified it as a distant cloud bank. The skipper perceived it differently.

"What's the matter, Adrian?" I queried, in response to his bewildered expression.

"I'm not sure," he answered vaguely, "It looks like a large oil slick on the water."

Adrian had already altered *Lap Cat*'s course to avoid sailing into the slick-like blackness. After observing it for a few minutes, I realized the dark band was growing in size and rising into the sky as we approached. Then, through the fog of our fatigue, we understood that *both* interpretations were wrong. The mysterious black band was neither an oil slick on the water nor a cloud bank in the sky. The more or less featureless shape, unrecognizable to a pair of over-tired boaters, was in fact the cliffs of Newfoundland's western coast. A Newfoundlander would have recognized it in a second.

Adrian updated me on Jerry Coulson's situation. During the night, a nearby fishing vessel named *Reef Rat* responded and managed to attach a tow-line to *Patient Nancy*. In the mean time, the Corner Brook Auxiliary Coast Guard raced out into the gulf aboard *Summer Wind*, a thirty-eight-foot power boat. Her crew managed to get a line to the trimaran, and using an inflatable zodiac, transferred Jerry to Summer Wind where he was treated by a paramedic. The rescue vessel returned to Newfoundland and delivered Jerry to a waiting ambulance at Lark Harbour. From there, he was rushed by ambulance to the hospital in Corner Brook for diagnosis and treatment.

The flotilla staggered out of the Gulf of St. Lawrence into the Bay of Islands where sheer coffee-coloured cliffs surrounded us. I stood on *Lap Cat*'s foredeck, Minolta in hand, framing, focusing and clicking as we sailed beneath an isolated lighthouse. The stalwart white structure clung to a rock shelf well above the bay as if saluting our passage. Remnants of winter's lingering snow glared down from sunless crevices high in the stone cold mountains. We motored into the relatively calm waters of the Humber Arm in search of Corner Brook. Twenty-five miles away, at the eastern end of the arm, The Bay of Islands Yacht Club awaited our arrival.

About noon, the fleet arranged itself into a single file behind its flagship, the *Burin Star*. Thus, we made an orderly arrival at the yacht club, dressed in all our bunting and waving to the CBC news cameras, hoping to be seen fit and safe by our respective families on the evening news.

The flotilla was scheduled to remain at Corner Brook's recently renovated yacht club from Tuesday afternoon until early Friday morning. Then, we would return to the Gulf of St. Lawrence and sail northward up the west coast of "The Rock" to Bonne Bay, a well-protected fishing village in the heart of Gros Morne National Park.

Trisha's birthday was now little more than a week away. I had secretly wrapped her gift and hidden it in the basement prior to my departure, so I wrote to her, wishing her a "Happy Birthday" and disclosing the gift's location. Then I walked into town to buy a pair of pants to replace those torn in the crossing to Port Menier a few days earlier. I also planned to mail Trisha's letter and perhaps reach her from a pay phone along the way. Corner Brook's business district was much farther from the dock than I had anticipated. At the time, cell phones were relatively scarce and phone booths could be found on almost every street corner in southern Ontario. It appeared, however, that Newfoundlanders had little use for public telephones because I walked almost three miles along Griffin Drive toward the heart of the city before I finally located one.

Though I hadn't been comfortably warm since Natashquan, Newfoundland's interior was a pleasant seventy-two degrees Fahrenheit. I noted buttercups, daisies, forget-me-nots and other flowers along the side of the road. It occurred to me that I wouldn't have noticed such things back home since distances in excess of a few hundred feet invariably involved the use of a car. Aside from the health benefits of physical exercise, walking provided an opportunity to smell the roses, or in this case, the buttercups.

As previously mentioned, the communities along our route staged reception ceremonies involving a meal or refreshments of some kind, but I often learned of these events at the last minute and sometimes only after the fact. This was one such occasion. When I returned to Corner Brook's Bay of Islands Yacht Club, I found that while a reception featuring a three-piece band was still under way, the food and beer had been entirely consumed prior to my arrival. Still, I was offered a glass of wine and sipped it occasionally while chatting with members of the club and the flotilla. I first visited with Bob and Hilda Bergoffen, skipper and first mate of *Ombre Rose*. They had been cruising full-time on their Gozzard 36 for eight years, and I found them to be interesting and gracious people, eager to mentor less experienced boaters. I had no idea at the time that I, along with two other flotilla participants, would crew for Bob on *Ombre Rose* the following year.

As the evening continued, I chatted with Wanita, the *Moonshadow* crew member I had encountered at Baie Coacoachou. We talked about my dream of a trans-Atlantic crossing, and she shared her experiences in the Azores, recommending the port of Lajas on Flores as the most protected entry port for crossings originating in Canada. The 1,600-nautical-mile passage could be accomplished in fourteen days with favourable weather, though fair conditions were already proving to be elusive in 2000. My uninformed choice had been Santa Cruz, which Wanita explained offers little in the way of protection. If my plan succeeded, that titbit of information would become invaluable.

Wanita advised me that Brian Strutt, *Moonshadow*'s skipper, was absent because he had fallen down the boat's companionway to the cabin sole seven feet below, cracking several of his ribs. Brian's accident was a reminder that life under sail is unpredictable and fraught with risks that made constant vigilance essential.

Before the evening ended, I learned that the construction of the yacht club's new facility had been completed just in time for our arrival though the site's pay phone, ordered six months earlier, had not yet been installed. Ironically, it was that installation delay and my subsequent quest for a telephone that had excluded me from most of the afternoon's celebrations.

As the reception dissolved, the crews of several boats invited me to accompany them to dinner in Corner Brook. I declined and chuckled as I watched the last of them cram themselves into three overloaded taxis. I couldn't afford to dip further into my cash reserve, and having just walked several miles, I was simply too tired to party. Instead, I returned to *Lap Cat* and wrote another letter. It was well after midnight by the time I sealed the envelope and crawled sleepily into my berth. Even Cooky's snoring couldn't keep me awake.

The following day, I joined a group of flotilla crew who were scraping, sanding and painting the yacht club's flag pole. The club members had been exceptionally hospitable, so we were naturally anxious to show our appreciation in any way that we could. Midway into our little project, Al Di Metric invited a number of people, myself included, to dinner aboard *Pampero*. Ian volunteered to cook the steak, so on my arrival, I joined him and several others in the galley. I peeled a few vegetables, admired the Nauticat's interior and chatted with Al's guests. The dinner was delicious and more than ample, but most memorable was Hilda Bergoffen's tasty Ritz cracker spread, made with equal parts of Heinz chili sauce and mashed sardines, to which she added a little fresh lime juice. It was an unfamiliar combination, but the simple appetizer proved popular and quickly disappeared.

Friday morning, when the flotilla's scheduled departure arrived, Brian Strutt was still recuperating from his injuries and was forced to remain in Corner Brook. We cast off the yacht club's docks at 5:50 a.m. Minutes later, the rising sun briefly painted our vessels with brilliant gold light as they slid smoothly over the glossy, black water of the Humber Arm. Four hours later, beyond the Bay of Islands, we turned northward and ran up the coast ahead of a southerly fifteen-knot breeze. As we sailed past the island's western cliffs, a ragged hole in the thickly overcast sky spilled sunlight onto the rich green highlands of the interior.

Well into the day, I watched *Kalinka I* come alongside a small fishing boat but thought little of it at the time. Later, as we tacked into Bonne Bay, Sally called us on the radio to invite us to join them for dinner. We rounded Norris Point and rafted alongside *Kalinka I* in Neddy Harbour, amid dramatic views of Gros Morne's mountains. Noel had traded six bottles of beer for a couple of sizable, freshly caught cod. He fried the ultra-fresh fillets in butter and joined us aboard *Lap Cat* for dinner. I'm sure Cooky prepared something tasty to serve with it, but the cod was so exceptional and the company so comfortable that I can't recall what else we ate that evening.

In the morning, we relocated both vessels to the docks at Woody Point, rafting alongside a couple of commercial fishing boats. As is customary among cruisers, we set out as a group to explore the community. Though snow still lingered in the higher elevations of the surrounding mountains, the day was rainy and warm enough to induce the removal of my sweater. Our first discovery of note was a youth hostel where a hot shower could be had for two dollars.

The modern local interpretive centre featured the flora, fauna, and geology of Gros Morne National Park. The facility's displays held our attention for three-quarters of an hour, after which we returned to the docks.

In the afternoon, aboard *Lap Cat*, my shipmates and I leisurely explored a six-mile-long, picturesque fjord known as East Arm.

That evening, the settlement of Woody Point hosted a reception for the fleet at Branch 45 of the Royal Canadian Legion. The legion hostesses prepared a home-cooked dinner as tasty and complete as any I'd ever had, with mashed potatoes, gravy, and even pumpkin pie for dessert, charging each sailor the paltry sum of seven dollars. The meal proved to be the most satisfying and the least expensive dinner of all those that I attended during the cruise. With appetites satiated, we were led a short distance through the evening darkness to a large, two-story clapboard building. A simple wooden sign above the double-door on the building's front wall read, "Woody Point Heritage Theatre." We shuffled over the theatre's creaky floor and took our seats. There, in a dark and remote little-known corner of Canada, a troupe of surprisingly talented local residents treated us to a live variety show for the remainder of the evening.

I rose early on the ninth of July, and since I'd been assigned no duties aboard *Lap Cat*, I decided to climb the paved road leading southward into the tablelands. I hoped to get a closer look at some of the national park's prominent features and take some photos of the area's unique landscape. Along the way, I stopped to photograph a grazing cow moose, various views of the surrounding mountains, and an unusually dense patch of wild, breeze-blown daisies. As time passed, I noted the mountain wind was howling at twenty-five knots or more. I assumed the wind's velocity was due to my altitude or perhaps my particular location, high above the fjord known as the South Arm. When I finally turned to retrace my route, I observed white caps on the fjord two or three hundred feet below the road. Sheets of wispy white spume swept northward into the air above the waves. Within minutes, the wind's velocity increased to a sustained thirty knots or more. When the harbour came into view, I observed *Ombre Rose* and *Windthrush* pitching furiously in the wind driven surf at the settlement's southern end.

Propelled by gravity, adrenaline, and the wind at my back, I raced down the hill toward the beach where two tiny figures launched a dinghy and bounced through the wind-torn surf toward the boats. I ran in awkwardly long strides, the soles of my sneakers slapping heavily onto the asphalt as the hill dropped away beneath them. Minutes later, I stood breathless at the water's edge, bracing against the wind to watch Bob Bergoffen's struggle to prevent Ombre Rose from dragging onto the beach. Particles of wind-borne sand and salt blinded my eyes and stung my face as I squinted toward the churning surf. Fifty-five-knot gusts repeatedly laid the cutter onto her beam-ends and held her there, so that at times she appeared to be lying on the bottom in shallow water. The fierce gale made it impossible to stand on the sand without frequently stepping backward to brace oneself.

Throughout the drama, the passage of time slowed, and the struggle to save the vessels seemed to take forever. With Bob at the helm, *Ombre Rose* slowly clawed inch by inch toward deeper water, but when her skipper hauled on the ground tackle, he found it fouled in debris on the bottom. With no viable alternative, Bob released a three-hundred-foot length of chain to free *Ombre Rose* from her anchor and ran for shelter beyond Woody Point. I recorded the drama with a couple of quick photos and joined several others in a race to the sheltered end of the village. Fishing docks on the north side of Woody Point would provide *Ombre Rose* with protection from the wind, and we wanted to be there to take her lines when she arrived. Radios buzzed with urgent messages, barely audible over the tempest's fury. We ran from one weathered fishing stage to another in search of one capable of accommodating the Gozzard's four-and-a-half-foot draft. Having escaped the frothing surf, *Ombre Rose* rounded Woody Point and found a berth alongside a rickety dock at the leeward end of the village. With her keel barely clear of the rocky bottom and a third of her length extending beyond the stage, *Ombre Rose* hunkered down for the duration of the blow.

I raced back to the south end of the settlement where preparations to bring *Windthrush* into the shelter of the point were underway. She hadn't dragged her ground tackle, but she was pitching violently in the surf and trailing lines and sails over the side. I volunteered to go aboard as crew, but Peter, her skipper, pointed out that the dinghy could safely carry only two people. I was left standing on the beach again as Carl Lundgren of *Marguerite* joined him in the rescue effort. They too dropped the anchor rode, abandoning it on the harbour bottom before *Windthrush* motored around the point into quieter water near *Ombre Rose*.

As the thirty-foot C&C approached the sheltered northern side of the point under power, a trailing line, overlooked in the confusion, fouled her propeller. Peter shut down the engine and deployed the vessel's secondary anchor, but in the deep water and high wind, the anchor dragged steadily toward the harbour's exposed entrance. With nothing but open sea beyond the distant gap, Windthrush was in need of a tow if she was to avoid being swept into the gulf. A local fisherman telephoned a friend who owned an open fishing boat tied to a nearby dock. While waiting for the man's friend to arrive at the harbour, I ran back to the settlement's windward end to retrieve a heavy tow line. I gulped for air as once more, with the lengthy coil slung over my shoulder, I ran the breadth of Woody Point. Within minutes, the fishing boat's owner arrived on the scene, launched his motorized dory and towed *Windthrush* to safety alongside *Ombre Rose*. Relieved and satisfied with the outcome, we celebrated aboard Bob's boat with generously filled glasses of "Old Sam".

A couple of hours later, we heard that a search was underway for a local fisherman whose overturned dory had been spotted among the whitecaps off the coast. When the fishing vessel was finally recovered the following day, the man's body was found inside. He had tied himself to the boat to avoid being swept overboard or perhaps to ensure the eventual recovery of his body. In the sparsely populated fishing communities of Newfoundland, where frigid waters offer little hope of survival, few if any fishermen learn to swim, in spite of the fact that they spend most of their lives on the water.

At nine that evening, we gathered at a dingy, dockside bar bearing the lofty name Sea Breeze Lounge. Most of the modest, wooden structure overhung the water, supported by pylons that had been driven into the harbour bottom. Inside, a hand-written sign announced that the price of all drinks was $2.50. Norm, the community's deputy mayor, was waiting for us along with several other locals. We could see that we were in for an evening of camaraderie and impromptu Newfoundland style entertainment. I expect the event was representative of the famous "kitchen parties" of which I had heard so much. We drank, laughed, and sang along with guitars, fiddles and button accordions until midnight, by which time fatigue had drained the last of my reserves. Alone, I made my weary way back to my nearby, floating refuge.

I stumbled through a tangle of nets and fish-crate shadows on the unlit wharf and crossed the decks of two commercial fishing boats, wedged between *Lap Cat* and the dock's concrete wall. As I was about to step down into *Lap Cat*'s cockpit, a light appeared where no light should have been. My eyes were drawn to phosphorous green flashes in the water, between the vessels' hulls. Enveloped in the inky night and mesmerized, I watched the lights of ten-thousand individual sea creatures suddenly appear, subside, and reappear as the motion of the boats disturbed the fragile marine life on the bottom. Several minutes of fascination slipped by before I finally stepped aboard and groped my way to my berth in *Lap Cat*'s belly.

Someone snored softly in the darkness as I settled into my sleeping bag. Though I had played a minor role in the rescue of *Ombre Rose* and *Windthrush*, I was proud of our triumph and thoroughly exhausted—both physically and mentally.

It was 4 a.m. Tuesday when we emerged from our warm berths to begin our run up the windswept coast toward Port au Choix ahead of gale warnings and the rest of the fleet. Charcoal grey, scudding clouds pursued us relentlessly throughout the day. Between five and six o'clock in the morning, they dramatically contrasted with distant, vibrant green, sunlit coastal mountains. I occupied a few minutes with attempts to capture the colours on film.

Lap Cat continued to lead the fleet until *Pampero* overtook us a little after noon. Then, two hours short of our destination port, some of the larger sailboats also overtook us.

Port au Choix's harbour provided a sheltered and secure respite for the night. First thing Wednesday morning, I installed yet another antenna at the masthead. This one, purchased in Corner Brook, was our third since leaving Toronto. Unlike the makeshift stainless steel rod that I had installed at Rimouski, it came with a new, matched mounting base, and I was confident it would survive a full gale. Once more, we used *Kalinka I*'s main halyard as a safety line in the event that *Lap Cat*'s halyard failed. With her mast a few feet shorter than ours, the halyard hung slack while I worked, and the motion of the boats caused it to jump the sheave. With *Kalinka I*'s crew unable to raise or lower their halyard, I had to unclip the shackle and let it go before I could descend to *Lap Cat*'s deck. Once released, the main halyard fell into place on the sheave again though its end, now thirty feet above the deck, was out of reach. I was obliged to go up *Kalinka I*'s mast on her jib halyard to retrieve it, cementing my role as the fleet's mast monkey.

Afterward, we all attended Hilda Bergoffen's birthday breakfast aboard *Ombre Rose*. Sally and Noel contributed oat bran muffins, and *Marguerite*'s Carl and Patty Lundgren prepared and served waffles with ice cream and fruit toppings. Keith, of *Margaret Elizabeth*, played "Happy Birthday" on his accordion, followed by a number of traditional Newfoundland tunes. Celebrants numbered about fourteen below deck and several others crammed into the cockpit.

Kalinka I picked up an additional crew member in Port au Choix. He had driven into town and checked into the local motel the previous day. Before checking out, he offered the use of his room to those of us who wished to shower. In the tiny community, inadequately equipped to meet the needs of wandering sailors, it wasn't surprising that several of us accepted enthusiastically.

Still glowing from my glorious, hot shower, I went to the local laundromat to dry and fold the clothes that Cooky had loaded into the washers earlier. Workers, engaged in tarring a nearby roof, had used the machine just before Ian loaded it, and when I withdrew my laundry from the washer, I discovered indelible, tar-like smudges on every freshly washed garment.

In late afternoon, a bus collected the fleet's crews from the dock and delivered us to the local Lion's Club Hall where we were served a an all-you-can-eat seafood dinner for fifteen dollars. Following the more than ample, fishy feast, we returned to the harbour. There, we refuelled the boats equipped with diesel auxiliaries from a tank truck, driven onto the dock for the purpose.

The scene was bizarre and memorable. A pair of high pier lamps swayed in the wind amid the masts of our vessels. Beneath, in the glare of their light, yellow rain gear and emergency-orange floater jackets mingled with yellow plastic jerry cans. Flashlights flickered among the shadows and dark corners of the windswept wharf. I snapped another picture, but it could not quite equal the one in my head. A mere photo could not capture the cold wind's salty smell, the fleeting sulphurous odour of diesel fuel, nor the sounds of the constantly changing scene, but most importantly, no image could illustrate the camaraderie of the shadowy figures on the dock. I realized at that moment that I had been quietly initiated into a fraternity of mariners, immersed in an adventure that would permanently alter my perspective.

CHAPTER NINE
The Labrador Coast

Cooky and I reluctantly rolled out of our berths just prior to 7 a.m. on July 13, but the skipper and his wife were nowhere to be found. They had slept ashore in their tent, and we had no idea where to look for them. Concerned that we wouldn't be ready to leave with the flotilla, we began preparing *Lap Cat* to set sail. With the engine warming up and nothing left to do at the dock, Cooky scanned the shore one more time and suggested we move the boat across the harbour to take on fresh water. I concurred.

A few minutes later, with both water tanks filled to capacity, I spotted the skipper and his wife approaching along the road that skirted the harbour. I released the dock lines and stood by as they tossed their bundles on deck and climbed aboard. We eased away from the wall, motored out of the harbour on the heels of the fleet, and turned north toward Flower's Cove.

The one-day passage up Newfoundland's west coast was uneventful, but it was a special day for me nevertheless. It was Trisha's fifty-fourth birthday, and for the first time since meeting one another, we were celebrating the occasion independently. That marked the second family birthday I had missed since leaving home, but if things went according to plan, I was expecting to see my wife and family again in a little more than a week.

I awoke at the dock in Flower's Cove the following morning and retrieved my glasses from the shelf where I had placed them the night before. The temple arm, though in the normal folded position, was detached from the frame. The sailboat's cabin is a cramped, unstable and often disorganized space, especially with a crew of four living aboard, so minor accidents happen easily and frequently. I was nevertheless disappointed that no one mentioned breaking my glasses. I quietly repaired them with epoxy and committed to wearing my prescription sunglasses for the next twenty-four hours while the epoxy hardened.

The tiny settlement of Flower's Cove was a little short on tourist facilities, but the hospitality offered by its residents remains unsurpassed. Jackie Moores, the local harbour master, appeared on the dock after breakfast and invited us to her home to use her family's shower. Cooky and I were among those who eagerly accepted her generous invitation.

After our showers, Jackie drove us to a nearby bakery where Cooky and I bought a couple of pies. Sally, of *Kalinka I*, was born on July 14 in some undisclosed year in the past, and we planned to celebrate her birthday on board *Ombre Rose* later in the day. Fresh homemade pies would likely make a welcome contribution to the event.

Under a clear, blue sky, the air temperature climbed to 55 degrees Fahrenheit in the afternoon. When the locals insisted the summer was "a warm one," I was thankful that I hadn't arrived during one of their cold summers.

Everyone in Flower's Cove was extremely friendly, and as I walked the quiet streets, I was amused by the fact that motorists waved to me as they passed.

The skipper told us to be ready to leave by 6 a.m. the following morning, so Cooky and I excluded ourselves from the scheduled get-together and dance in the village, retiring to our berths before 10 p.m.

At 5:10 the following morning, I reluctantly dragged my butt out of my warm berth. In fact, I don't recall ever getting out of bed eagerly in the early summer of the year 2000. At six o'clock, I was standing by with the engine running. I'm pretty sure the skipper and his wife were warm and comfortable in their bed-and-breakfast because they didn't arrive on the dock until eight-thirty. By the time we slipped our dock lines, I had been up in excess of three and a half hours, so I was feeling a little unappreciated.

Lap Cat enjoyed a speedy east to west passage across the Strait of Belle Isle. On one occasion, while I was on the wheel, we surfed down a steep wave at an incredible 11.7 knots. The crossing was otherwise routine, and at one in the afternoon, we anchored in the harbour at Red Bay, Labrador.

Remnants of winter's white blanket clung to a handful of shaded hillsides and the deepest coastal ravines. Aside from the lingering snow, the barren landscape looked much like the north shore of the Gulf near Coacoachou, Quebec. Admittedly, there were a few trees though they were scrawny conifers, hardly deserving of the term tree. Even Red Bay appeared rather bleak; just a scattering of weathered clapboard cottages and a few modest wooden fishing boats.

Though I was still enjoying the entire experience, I had noted in recent days that my enthusiasm was beginning to wane. I coveted the heat of the familiar southern Ontario summer. I missed my family, my friends and the conveniences of my own comparatively spacious home. Cruising is, after all, not unlike camping in many respects. I wrote home, "It's really cold here—and it's July! I'm looking forward to getting home, where people sleep naked just to stay cool and sail in bathing suits instead of long underwear and bulky survival suits."

When I was advised that the community of Red Bay had scheduled yet another reception dinner in our honour, I checked my wallet's contents and thought about my trip home. As it happened, *Lap Cat*'s entire crew passed on the event, and Cooky announced that we were having pita pizza for dinner. He prepared a number of separate garnishes and set them out on the table, so each of us could dress our own small pita according to our individual tastes. Once each designer pizza had been prepared by its hungry creator, Cooky baked it in *Lap Cat*'s little oven while we enjoyed our drinks and honed our respective appetites. At fifteen minutes per pizza, an hour passed before our cook got to eat, and by then, the rest of us were ready for a second serving. Needless to say, it was a very leisurely meal supplemented with lots of Bacardi's.

Sunday morning, Noel Lien called Ian and me on the VHF to invite us to go ashore to visit the federally funded local museum. Jim, the Red Bay lighthouse keeper, provided a complimentary water taxi service, transporting interested boaters from their respective anchorages to the government dock in his wooden dory.

The museum's displays described in detail how, in 1540 and possibly much earlier, the Basques of Spain and France were attracted to Red Bay by an abundance of humpback whales. During their outward passages, clay roofing tiles served as ballast in the otherwise empty holds of their ships. On arrival, the red-coloured tiles were off-loaded and used to roof shelters which the whalers erected over their rendering facilities. Today, the structures are known as tri-works because each facility housed a trio of cauldrons.

The Europeans reportedly killed no fewer than twenty-five bowhead whales along the Labrador coast each summer. At summer's end, having rendered the whale blubber into oil, the Basques transported it back to Europe in barrels that they manufactured on site. Red Bay owes its name to the mariners' importation of clay roof tiles. Four hundred and sixty years after the whalers constructed their tri-works, the area's gravel beaches remain generously speckled with well-worn but recognizable fragments of red roofing tiles.

The history of the whalers might have been lost to time, except that one of the Basque ships sank in the harbour and was subsequently found in the late 1960s. Its discovery led to a search of Spanish archives which contained obscure sixteenth-century descriptions of the local whaling industry. The resulting research underscores the importance of archaeology's role in compiling world history. If that sunken vessel hadn't been examined by trained observers with a will to uncover its story, the Spanish accounts of whaling in Canada might never have been studied.

When we exited the museum, Jim ferried us to the island in the harbour where the Red Bay lighthouse towered above his ancestral home. Sadly, due to the island's recent designation as a national park, he and his family were no longer allowed to live there though, as light keeper, Jim was permitted to use it in the course of his duties.

We wandered leisurely around the island on a raised boardwalk, occasionally stopping to read plaques identifying key archaeological sites. Before returning to the mainland, we visited with Jim in his family home and shared a pot of steaming tea while discussing life in Labrador. Afterward, he delivered us to our respective vessels where we prepared potluck dishes to be shared at the fish plant's lunchroom by the town dock. There, along with a couple of local residents, we enjoyed an eclectic assortment of culinary surprises with the crews of about six flotilla vessels.

The fleet was scheduled to leave Red Bay on Monday morning, stopping overnight at Henley Harbour on its way to Battle Harbour. From there, one day of sailing would see us in Quirpon,

Newfoundland, from where I expected to depart for home. With a little luck, we hoped to see icebergs during the final eastward transit of the Strait of Belle Isle.

Lap Cat got underway at 7 a.m. on Monday, July 17 and entered a bitterly cold fog as she emerged from the harbour at Red Bay. Unlike southern Ontario, where the presence of fog is generally associated with an absence of wind, the Labrador coast frequently hosts wind and fog simultaneously. I stood at the wheel as we sailed northward along the unseen, barren coast. As was customary on a downwind run, the back of the cockpit enclosure was removed to prevent the mainsheet from chafing against the enclosure's canvas. I found the frigid wind barely tolerable and envied the rest of the crew, sheltered below in the cabin.

The skipper was advised that the abandoned settlement at Henley Harbour offered few docks capable of accommodating our fleet, so he chose instead to anchor in Temple Bay, four miles or so to the south. We tentatively entered the narrow mouth of the bay and anchored at the fifteen-foot contour of a steep beach to the left of the bay's entrance.

As was my habit wherever we landed, I went ashore to stretch my legs. I photographed a few dilapidated shacks and a vintage cemetery, the scant remains of a long abandoned fishing settlement. The last grey remnants of a few anonymous lives were celebrated by deep purple irises, descendants of someone's once lovingly tended flowerbed. The spongy, uneven ground was mostly covered with thick moss that ingested my feet as I walked. I plodded forward amid the squishing and splashing of bog-water.

Halfway up a saddle that joined the rocky coast to the inland hills, I stepped into a bottomless abyss. Its presence was indiscernible beneath the surrounding ground cover though its density differed little from water. When my foot descended into the unseen void, I instinctively threw my body backward, sinking above my knee before my back hit the spongy ground behind me. I wondered how deep the bog was as I rolled and slithered onto a firmer patch of moss-covered ground. I was momentarily shaken at the thought of the watery bog being over my head and swallowing my body completely.

With no witnesses to the event, my disappearance in that wilderness might have forever remained a mystery. I shuddered, rose to my feet and warily retraced my steps toward the ghost village.

On my return to the shore, I noted a peculiarly shaped mountain on the southern side of Temple Bay which, due to a nipple-shaped outcrop of brown rock, took on a striking resemblance to a well-endowed woman's breast. I had no map of the area to determine if the mountain had already been named, but feeling much like an explorer in the moment, I took a photo and unilaterally named the mountain in honour of my wife.

Jeremy Hilliard, *Sea Therapy*'s skipper, was celebrating his birthday—sufficient reason for another impromptu party. From my locker, I retrieved a recently read book describing a sailor's passage to the Faroe Islands. Every mariner enjoys reading about the sailing experiences of others, so I wrapped the book in newspaper and, with a black marker, scribbled "Happy Birthday, Jeremy" on the wrapper. I tucked the gift inside my jacket and boarded Jeremy's water-ballasted, MacGregor sailboat-come-powerboat for the four-mile trip to Henley Harbour.

Through the bay's entrance, I glimpsed my first iceberg though I was disappointed that the huge chunk of brilliant white ice was at least five miles to seaward. From that distance, the berg resembled an unimpressive bit of white origami. I hoped to see more at closer range in the days to come.

Sea Therapy slipped into a dense fog at the entrance to Henley Harbour. Though a little clichéd, I recorded in my journal that evening that "the water was like black glass and the fog, pea soup."

At dead slow, we groped our way from marker to marker. Gradually, we began picking out distant human voices and occasional laughter over the buzz of Sea *Therapy*'s outboard motor. Soon afterward, Jeremy's little MacGregor squeezed in among the other vessels at the rickety, forgotten fishing stage.

There on a dock in a decaying abandoned settlement, miles from any other human beings, the crews of a half dozen boats celebrated a birthday with delicious food, slightly more than ample drink, and uproarious laughter. The fog eventually lifted, and at 10:30 p.m., we said our farewells as the full moon began rising into the cold night sky. Back home in Hamilton, the time was 9 p.m. and the evening air was likely still warm from the summer sun—not so in Henley Harbour.

On the eighteenth of July, we relocated *Lap Cat* from Temple Bay to Henley Harbour. Strewn with the bleached skeletons of fishing dories of classic, high quality construction, the settlement exuded a genuine ghost-town character. Most of the fishing boats appeared to have been abandoned while still in reasonably good condition. Their white bones lay passively amid the tall grass, patiently though vainly awaiting the return of their owners. A few of the buildings were still in good repair and apparently used as vacation homes from time to time. Peering through the windows, I could see that they contained the basic utilities of a simple life. In this barren and remote land, where everyone knew everyone for dozens of miles around, they had little reason to lock their doors, so access to the buildings was restricted solely by our respect for private property.

On a pathway at the corner of a greying shack, I found a cluster of three spent nine-millimetre casings. I tried to imagine the events that left this macabre evidence behind. I envisioned a vintage World War II German Luger or perhaps a modern automatic pistol held firmly in a hand as the shooter hid quietly behind the corner of the building, pointing his weapon at something—*or someone*. He must have squeezed the trigger three times in quick succession, the casings ejecting onto the same spot on the path at his feet. But why? I wondered, as I walked away, if he had hit his target and what had become of it.

The morning of July 19 offered little hope of seeing the sun or even a bit of blue sky.

While casting off the Henley Harbour dock in the ever-present fog, *Stand Sure* fouled her propeller with her dinghy painter and began drifting toward a tangle of nearby black rocks. *Sea Therapy* promptly responded to her request for assistance and towed her back to the dock. Then, one of *Stand Sure*'s own crew donned scuba gear and plunged into the icy water. He spent forty minutes cutting away the line, and by the time the task had been completed, the crewman was suffering from hypothermia. Several hours passed before he fully recovered from the chilling experience.

As far as I was aware, this incident constituted the fleet's third fouled propeller. Yet again, I recognized the value of this seven-week-long practical school of seamanship. I consciously noted the potential for a similar crisis involving my own *Alice Rose* and resolved to be vigilant every time I approached or cast off a wharf, to avoid fouling her screw.

Throughout our passage to Battle Harbour, *Lap Cat* was once more immersed in featureless fog with no more than two or three hundred feet of visibility at any time. As we approached our destination, the GPS indicated that we were 1,113 nautical miles from home—where the sun undoubtedly shone warmly on my home and family.

Uncharacteristically, the skipper showed signs of apprehension as we came within a few dozen yards of a fog-shrouded island, but I was closely monitoring our position on the chart and assured him that we wanted to be exactly where we were. He likely found the opaque fog and the confused waves, the latter an indication of nearby shores, intimidating. Suddenly, a wall of ochre granite loomed over the bow and *Lap Cat* spun about, retreating along the path of our approach. Though I too was apprehensive, I reassured the skipper that the chart indicated a narrow passage through the rock just a few feet beyond the point at which he had abandoned our course.

Again, with our bow rail less than a hundred feet off the face of an apparently impenetrable rock wall, Adrian questioned our position—and I didn't blame him. Unable to see the tickle that led into Battle Harbour, we circled cautiously in the fog. Then, each of us in turn, perceived the faint thumping of a one cylinder engine. Seconds later, two men in a fishing skiff emerged from the gloom to lead *Lap Cat* into the elusive passage between Great Caribou Island and Battle Island. The narrow tickle had been right where the chart said it was. It was simply invisible, hidden by rocky outcrops until we were virtually at the base of the steep rock face.

The skipper zigzagged along behind our escort, eyeing the jagged rocks to port and starboard. He watched the depth sounder with equal concern until we emerged in the rock-lined harbour several minutes later. The village appeared suddenly from behind yet another pile of granite, and *Lap Cat* was secured once more to a dock where she and her crew could relax and regroup for the next passage.

It eventually came to our attention that the traditional approach to the harbour was from the north, and Lap Cat was the only member of the fleet to enter through the shallow, serpentine southern entrance.

Battle Harbour was essentially a government-sponsored living museum, a restored facsimile of the original mercantile fishing outport that had once thrived there. External communication was entirely dependent on radio-telephone, T-shirts cost twenty-four dollars and a six-pack of Labatt's Blue lager could be had for twelve dollars—a lofty price still not reached a decade later in Ontario.

Thursday, the day after our arrival, I joined Sally and Noel in an hour-long exploration of the tiny community. The homes and service buildings, most of which were loosely clustered around the wooden government dock, were linked by a maze of raised wooden walkways. Without them, moving between buildings would have proved a challenging clamber over uneven rocks on a steep hillside. The bulk of Battle Island consisted of barren rock, rising a hundred feet or more above the settlement on the edge of the strait between Battle and Great Caribou islands. After our walkabout, I invited Noel and his wife on board for hot chocolate, a seemingly odd beverage for a mid-July afternoon, though not when the local climatic conditions were taken into account.

Later, finding myself somewhat chilled by *Lap Cat*'s damp, cave-like interior, I walked to the post office to warm myself by the wood stove. The squeaky wooden floor and radiant heat of the unseen flames awakened memories of my 1950s childhood when, in the midst of winter, the Quebec heaters in our farmhouse became gods of warmth and security.

I was beginning to get a little bored with the routine of cruising. Or perhaps it was just the imminent end of the voyage and my longing to return home that nibbled at my enthusiasm. The conversation, food and weather were all becoming rather repetitive—especially the weather. I felt somewhat like an exile, cut off from the civilized world, and I wondered if my attitude would have been different had I been cruising aboard my own *Alice Rose*, choosing my own destinations.

CHAPTER TEN
The Iceberg

The following day, I joined a group of flotilla members aboard *Moonshadow*. We lounged in the vessel's spacious cockpit, drinking, chatting and laughing together as if time was without consequence. That's where I met George, a *Moonshadow* crewman and a genuine "Newfie" in every sense of the word. He had signed on a couple of weeks earlier at Corner Brook, and when he learned that I was planning to pick up Carl Lundgren's van in Port au Choix and drive it to North Sydney via Corner Brook and the Port au Basque ferry, he suggested we travel together from Quirpon to Corner Brook. To cement the arrangement, he explained that he had friends in the Quirpon area and assured me that he could arrange a ride to Port au Choix. In fact, he proudly boasted that everyone knew everyone on the Rock! I enthusiastically, and somewhat naively, accepted the offer which appeared on the surface to simplify the first phase of my return to Ontario. When we landed at Quirpon a few days later, George's elusive friends would be nowhere to be found.

As the afternoon sun inched imperceptibly toward the horizon, the potential for recording a spectacular sunset prompted me to hike to Battle Island's summit. With my battered Minolta slung over my shoulder, I said my goodbyes and ascended the granite slope toward a conspicuous antenna tower at its peak. After a few minutes of focused exertion, I reached the highest rock and climbed up onto it to wait. The distant sky warmed in colour, but the brisk wind grew discernably colder. My overheated body quickly cooled in the chill air, and I began to shiver. Like the proverbial watched pot, the reddening sun mocked my discomfort. One of my few notable virtues being perseverance, I eventually outwaited the sun and won the standoff. My trophy is a rare Kodak slide of a very nice sunset taken from a hilltop in Labrador. Given the remote location, the limited number of fog-free days and the effort it takes to reach the hill's summit, it just might be the only one ever taken from that inaccessible, frigid perch.

During our passage to Quirpon on the twenty-second of July, we were treated to a truly magnificent sight normally reserved for fishermen, commercial mariners and seabirds. A ripple of excitement ran through the crew as *Moonshadow*, a mile off our starboard bow, sailed by a sparkling iceberg. The giant chunk of brilliant white extended above the water's surface well over two, and possibly three, times the height of the vessel's sixty-five-foot mast. While everyone is familiar with the icebergs of documentaries and mag-

180-foot-high iceberg encountered in the Strait of Belle Isle

azines, the wonder and emotion of seeing the real thing in three dimensions is incomparable.

As *Lap Cat* approached, hints of colour appeared among the white-hot facets of the ice. We sailed to within two or three hundred feet of the monster, ogling its delicate swirls of blue, turquoise and green. Shutters clicked behind me as I stood on the foredeck, focusing and framing each image with the care usually reserved for a glowing bride on her wedding day. The light changed several times, affording a variety of moods and perspectives as we circled the huge mass. *Lap Cat*'s depth sounder reported sixty feet of water beneath her hull, though the chart indicated something in the order of 380 feet.

We were sailing over the iceberg's massive, submerged base.

A sudden, loud report preceded the collapse of a multi-ton chunk of the berg. It plunged heavily into the water, generating substantial waves. Recalling tales of these giants unexpectedly rolling over, I secretly hoped the skipper would ease away from the spectacle—now that I had my pictures.

Even if I hadn't thoroughly enjoyed my other forty-three days aboard *Lap Cat*, our encounter with the iceberg would have made the entire passage worthwhile. Then, in the late afternoon as we approached Quirpon's harbour, about five miles east of L'Anse aux Meadows, Nature opened the curtain on act two of her July twenty-second show.

A pod of Atlantic white-sided dolphins crossed ahead of us, circled and began playing in our bow-wave. I quickly reloaded my camera with film and rushed to the foredeck, snapping wildly in an effort to get a shot of these sleek creatures swimming almost within my reach. Periodically, a lone dolphin veered off to starboard and momentarily disappeared before leaping into the air a hundred yards away. I couldn't be sure, but I believe it continued its circle, re-joining its comrades in our bow wave. But even before the lone dolphin had time to complete its circuit, another of the pod veered off to starboard to mimic the ritual. We watched in fascination as they performed their antics with what appeared to be playful enthusiasm. A few minutes later, the show came to an end, and we once more turned our attention to our intended landfall.

Having secured *Lap Cat* to a foul-smelling, salt-worn shrimper, I sought out George aboard *Moonshadow* to discuss our departure.

"It's all arranged," he boasted. "He's gone into town to buy some beer, and he's going to pick us up in an hour or so."

I rushed back aboard *Lap Cat* to pack my gear and say my good-byes. Unable to carry all my things, I began giving some away. Finally, with my selected possessions stuffed into a mid-sized hockey bag on the dock, I climbed aboard *Moonshadow* for a last beer with a few fellow adventurers. When, by 6 p.m., our ride hadn't yet materialized, I began to feel a little embarrassed. I had been saying good-bye for several hours and there were no indications that we were being picked up anytime soon. I knew that I'd have to leave immediately or spend another night aboard *Lap Cat*, so filled with resolve, I informed George that I was going to hitchhike to Port-au-Choix.

I stepped ashore and picked up my bag, indifferent as to whether or not George finished his beer. He, having already consumed a snoot-full, drained his bottle and staggered along behind like a stray dog. As we lugged our gear off the dock, the ever-resourceful George appealed to a couple of shrimp truckers who were waiting for the fishing fleet to arrive. I pushed on when I learned that the drivers might not be loaded for another twelve hours. George assured me that he knew people in nearby St. Anthony who would be happy to drive us to Port au Choix, and once more, I believed him.

From a nearby pay phone, I summoned a taxi to drive us to St. Anthony and split the forty-three-dollar fare with my travelling companion. Once in St. Anthony, instead of seeking out a particular residence or business, George simply wandered about aimlessly, apparently hoping to see someone he knew. Even taking his intoxicated condition into account, George's behaviour appeared bizarre. I went into a variety store, bought a large black felt-tip marker and scrounged an empty cardboard carton. I then cut the side out of the corrugated box with my pocket knife and on it, in large capital letters, printed:

PORT
AU CHOIX
WE PAY GAS

Within ten minutes, we had been driven to the highway in a car that was barely big enough to accommodate us and our bulky bags. There at the asphalt's edge, we stood for another half-hour before getting a second ride with a local couple who were just "out for a drive." Eventually, we were dropped off at the side of the road and watched as the driver made a U-turn. By then it was cold and almost dark, and the mosquitoes were thick and hungry for our warm blood.

George and I donned our brilliantly coloured survival suits to retain our body heat and keep the mosquitoes from jabbing at our exposed skin. Then we waited, extending our thumbs each time a southbound vehicle passed. Our weird costumes likely discouraged drivers who would ordinarily have welcomed us into their vehicles. For whatever reason, a couple of hours passed before two young men stopped to pick us up. They drove south for an hour or so to a road that left the highway for the coastal settlement of St. Barbe just north of Flower's Cove. The community was a tiny ferry terminal with a population of 1,200, not the sort of place I wanted to spend the night while still a couple of thousand miles from home.

The rural highway, edged with wide shoulders of two-inch, crushed stone, consisted of one well-surfaced lane in each direction. As far as I could tell in the darkness, the roadway formed a raised causeway through an endless forested bog. Waiting by the roadside at one in the morning seemed pointless, but since we were only able to carry our heavy kits a few yards at a time, no other option came to mind. Besides, there was still a remote chance that we would get a ride to Port-au-Choix in the next passing vehicle. My gear-filled hockey bag was large enough to lie on if I bent my knees and rested my feet flat on the ground. In this position, I was able to relax my tired muscles, but sleep was persistently elusive throughout the night. I was simply too absorbed in listening for approaching vehicles. If we hoped to reach our destination before morning, we had to be ready to spring to our feet and look as harmless and needy as possible. In retrospect, I'm pretty sure I wouldn't have stopped in the middle of the night for two men in the midst of the black, Newfoundland wilderness either. At best, we must have appeared alien and frightening to those inside the vehicles that sped by at intervals of about forty-five minutes. Within a short time, we became less than optimistic about our chances of getting another ride before daylight.

On one occasion that night, as my consciousness drifted within reach of sleep, I lifted an eyelid and spotted the loom of headlights just north of our location. The sound of the vehicle's engine suggested it was approaching at high speed, so I jumped to my feet in anticipation. There, on the nearby shoulder of course limestone, lay the Newfoundlander, deep in sleep on his back. George's entire right arm and shoulder extended out onto the pavement like a speed bump. His resistance to my pleas and physical efforts to get him to his feet probably made us appear drunk to the passing motorist.

For me, the seemingly endless night passed sleeplessly.

Shortly after 5 a.m., in response to our extended thumbs, the drivers of two identical dump trucks slowed to a stop. Each of them generously accepted one of us, along with our equipment, into his vehicle. That ride got us to an intersection about twenty minutes farther south where we enjoyed a hot breakfast in a motel restaurant before returning to the highway. Then, on the shoulder of the road, we spied a man reading the morning paper in his idling car. George offered him ten dollars to drive us to Port au Choix, and the man accepted, after which he divulged that he and a friend for whom he had been waiting were going there anyway. Again, we shared the cost and bundled into the back seat, barely able to stay awake. At Port au Choix, we located Carl's van within minutes and began the four-hour, coastal drive to Corner Brook. Along the way, we passed once more through Gros Morne National Park though my fatigue limited my ability to fully enjoy it from a different perspective.

Finally, we arrived in Corner Brook where I dropped George at his door and continued wearily toward the ferry at Port aux Basque. My homing instinct overcame my common sense, and in spite of being severely impaired by fatigue, I persisted through the two-and-a half-hour drive in a zombie-like trance. The opportunity for several hours of sleep aboard the ferry provided my justification for continuing. At Port aux Basque, I passed through a row of fare kiosks and drove onto the car ferry. After parking and locking the van, I made my way to the ship's lounge where I slumped into a long deferred, deep, dreamless sleep.

I don't know how much time elapsed before all the cars, trucks and trains were loaded, or exactly when the ferry departed, but I awoke almost eleven hours later, when the vessel thumped heavily against the dock in North Sydney. Before disembarking, I made my way to the men's room that was connected to the lounge. Apparently, I had slept comfortably through an unusually rough passage because I found the bathroom floor awash with the vomit of my fellow passengers.

Now a seasoned sailor, an old salt, I was capable of sleeping through a full gale like the proverbial baby.

The first thing I noticed when I stepped out of the lounge onto the ferry's steel deck was Nova Scotia's genuinely warm summer air. The sun shone benevolently on the city and its inhabitants, barely acknowledging the Atlantic's proximity. After weeks of living in a sub-room-temperature environment, I could once more take my comfort for granted.

Having spent a night on *Lap Cat* in Battle Harbour and the next on the crushed-stone shoulder of Newfoundland's Highway 430, the plush room at the Northstar Motel was a piece of heaven. I didn't even flinch when the desk clerk answered my inquiry with "A hundred and twenty dollars, sir."

I had previously called Trisha briefly from a Corner Brook pay phone, but I placed a second call from the motel so we could enjoy a longer, more relaxed conversation. I told her about my day, and she brought me up to date on what had transpired while I was away. When our conversation ended, I hung up the phone and spent at least a half hour in the shower, washing away all but the memories.

At seven in the morning, the connecting bus to Montreal picked me and several other North Star guests up at the motel's entrance before jostling us uncomfortably toward Truro. Initially, we made frequent stops to pick up fares and drop them off at service stations and variety stores along the Cape Breton highway. At Truro, I changed to another coach and continued into New Brunswick with noticeably fewer stops. Within a couple of hours, the cheeks of my butt burned, and I couldn't resist sliding forward until I found myself slouched awkwardly low in my seat. I straightened up, felt comfortable for a bit and, a few minutes later, found myself back where I had started. Late in the evening, well beyond the traditional dinner hour, the driver turned into a parking lot shared between a motel and a restaurant. He parked and invited his passengers to get something to eat during our thirty-minute stop. After waiting my turn in line and awaiting the preparation of my food, I had about five minutes to eat before re-boarding the westbound Greyhound.

My seat companion for the Truro to Montreal portion of the ride was a pleasant French-Canadian woman. She was returning home from a visit with her husband who was employed on the construction of the thirteen-kilometre-long Confederation Bridge connecting New Brunswick to Prince Edward Island. Our conversation gradually waned, and I retreated into a state of uncomfortable and frequently disturbed semi-sleep. It occurred to me during a brief interlude of groggy consciousness that the bus's ragged, jerking progress differed immensely from the gentle motion of the sea. By the time I arrived in Montreal, I retained only vague recollections of the deserted streets of Riviére-du-Loup, garishly lit with yellow streetlights and fast food restaurant signs. I felt like a marathon runner, completely numb with fatigue and intently focused on the approaching finish line.

At a cost of more than 400 dollars, including my extravagant motel room in North Sydney, a coach to Toronto and another to Hamilton, my pilgrimage ended at the Hamilton terminal on the twenty-fifth of July. There, I dropped my bag and embraced my wife for the first time in more than six weeks. Trisha drove me home where, after forty-five days of living among unfamiliar surroundings, I slept in my own bed alongside my wife as soundly as ever I had before.

CHAPTER ELEVEN
Ombre Rose

In the spring of 2001, I was invited to join the crew of *Ombre Rose* on a passage from Nassau to Rockland, Maine. Crewing for other boat owners had already proved to be a great way to learn the intricacies of cruising, and I accepted the invitation without reservation.

The thirty-six foot Gozzard was a roomy, well-appointed vessel that I had come to know during the previous summer's cruise to Newfoundland and Labrador. Her skipper, Bob Bergoffen, was an experienced mariner and an affable host. His gracious, relaxed manner put those in his company immediately at ease, and I was looking forward to sailing with him. In addition, I was eager to cruise the warm waters of the Gulf Stream after my chilly exposure to higher latitudes a year earlier.

Though the northward journey was originally conceived as an offshore passage with a layover in Bermuda, Bob modified our sail plan in response to a prolonged northeasterly wind. The opposing forces of the north-flowing Gulf Stream and the northeast wind generated unusually steep waves, assuring an uncomfortable passage at best. An astute and cautious sailor, Bob chose the alternative and more leisurely Intracoastal Waterway (ICW) route.

On the twenty-sixth of April, I flew out of the Buffalo airport along with two other Canadians to rendezvous with Bob in Fort Lauderdale. The one-way flight was the crew's only out-of-pocket expense aside from the cost of a car rental to get home from Maine at the end of the passage.

Les and Geoff, my travelling companions, had also participated in the exploration of Newfoundland and Labrador outports a year earlier. Bob met us at the airport and drove us to Cooley's Landing Marina on the Tarpon River. There, we familiarized ourselves with his spacious cutter while preparing her for the five-week cruise.

The sheltered ICW route appeared to be a rather laidback vacation-like passage, whereas I had hoped to experience the open sea under the tutelage of a veteran skipper before attempting my own Atlantic crossing. In the end, the experiences and challenges of the passage further enhanced my cruising knowledge, and I found the alternate route more beneficial than I had initially anticipated.

Much of the ICW follows the coast behind sandbanks, many of which are heavily populated and connected to the mainland with bridges. Some though, are windswept and primarily barren or sparsely adorned with weathered cottages and random patches of beach grass. Periodic gaps between the sandbanks provide glimpses of the Atlantic in exchange for exposure to its wind and waves. In northern regions, protective sandbanks are less common, though rivers, canals and bays provide intermittent shelter from the open sea.

In a little more than a month, *Ombre Rose* passed beneath 184 lift bridges, each of which involved an exchange of VHF radio communication. On our approach to a bridge, we first identified it by referring to our chart or cruising guide. Then, we called the bridge operator on channel nine to identify our vessel and report the direction from which we were approaching. Once our call had been acknowledged, we determined whether the bridge routinely lifted at specific times or in response to the request of individual boaters. I learned very quickly the importance of radio protocol when, on one occasion, I inquired whether the bridge lifted at scheduled times or "on demand".

The bridge operator responded politely with, "The bridge lifts 'on request,' Captain. Over."

Embarrassed by my gaffe, I chose my words more carefully thereafter.

Next, we either acknowledged that we would enter at the scheduled time, or we provided our estimated time of arrival, so the operator could stop the road traffic and lift—or swing—the bridge at the appropriate moment. Of course, we always reported when our vessel was clear of the bridge and thanked the operator, who invariably wished us a "good day."

It's worth mentioning that every bridge operator with whom we communicated in the U.S. was very courteous and respectfully addressed our radio operator as "Captain."

Our progress through much of Florida was marked by urban

environments, ostentatious homes and luxury yachts though the landscape varied immensely as we snaked northward through subsequent states. So too, did the people.

While Bob handled navigation, we all took turns on deck, at the wheel, preparing meals and cleaning. Most evenings we set a table worthy of a fine restaurant, including on occasion, a white tablecloth, stemware and wine. Every meal was relaxed, delicious and more than adequate. Bob was a generous man and a gracious host.

Ombre Rose had only been underway a couple of days when our skipper, while trimming Les's hair with electric clippers, looked over his reading glasses at my windblown grey locks and jokingly offered to give me a buzz cut.

"What the hell," I thought. "Why not?"

I felt like a teenager rebelling against convention. Within a day of the haircut, I could feel the sunburn on my exposed scalp. Having taken the first step, I completed my make-over by not shaving for the rest of the voyage.

Map 11. The U.S. Atlantic Coast (South)

Just south of Florida's border with Georgia, at a small oceanside town named Fernandina Beach, we tied up at a marina for the night. As we followed the maze of floating docks to the marina office, we were treated to an odd display of what appeared to be amorous animal behaviour. A diver, engaged in a dockside repair to a boat's rudder, found himself repeatedly interrupted by the unsolicited attentions of a manatee. The large, elephant-like creature, though repeatedly pushed away, immediately returned to rub up against the diver as he tried to work. Fascinated, we watched for a few minutes before continuing via the marina office to a local restaurant for dinner.

Following our meal, Bob and I gathered our laundry and carried it to the marina's coin-operated laundromat. The dryers proved rather inefficient, so it was after midnight when I walked toward the little building to retrieve the last of my clothes. In the dimly lit parking lot between the dock and the laundromat, I

Map 12. The U.S. Atlantic Coast (North)

encountered for the first time what I consider to be one of nature's weirdest-looking creatures. With disproportionately short legs and a gait indicative of urgency, a frightened armadillo scurried through the shadows toward a clump of dwarf palmettos at the edge of the parking lot. I couldn't help smiling as I watched the strange little armoured critter waddle out of sight.

The following morning, we continued our passage into the coastal waters of Georgia, sailing inshore of the Cumberland Island National Seashore where wild horses have survived since their introduction by Spanish explorers in the sixteenth century. *Ombre Rose* wandered through lazy, southern salt marshes amid hundreds of acres of dry, yellow-brown reeds. The thin spears of vegetation rose well above her deck and sometimes completely obscured our surroundings from view. The shallow waters made approaching the shore impossible, so many coastal residents installed docks that measured hundreds of feet in length. The private wooden walkways jutted out into the waterway atop spindly pilings.

Periodically, we passed crude raft-like working platforms, each occupied by a lone local entrepreneur, shoeless and shirtless. Their home-built piledrivers, powered by what appeared to be lawnmower engines, thumped rhythmically as they drove pilings into the bottom to support new docks or extend old ones.

At one such South Carolina dock, owned by a retired naval commander and friend of the Bergoffens, we tied up for the night and visited the nearby town of Beaufort to re-provision *Ombre Rose*'s galley. Bob's friend welcomed us into his home and proudly showed off his guest-room which he had redecorated to simulate a U.S. Navy ship's interior. The door to the room was convincingly designed to resemble a steel hatchway in a bulkhead. Overall, the tiny room, equipped with bunks, portholes, and riveted seams, attained an impressive level of authenticity.

The sun-warmed Carolinas came and went, along with fishing ports, holiday resorts, busy harbours and tangles of colourfully painted crab pot floats.

The ICW entered Norfolk, Virginia by the back door, via a thirty-five mile canal system that began in North Carolina. We spilled into Norfolk's Naval Shipyard in the dark, having picked our way for an hour or more from one numbered buoy to another with the aid of a powerful flashlight. From my position at the forward end of *Ombre Rose*'s six-foot bow sprit, I called out the colour and the reflective identification number on each marker. In response, the skipper soundlessly spun the wheel in the appropriate direction. At dead-slow, the Gozzard's engine purred passively in the night.

The shipyard, part of the world's largest naval base, proved an extremely confusing complex of activity and glaring lights. The sparkling flashes of welder's torches and the clangs of metal against metal defied the hour as we picked our way through the night and on into the harbour in the early light of dawn. From the midst of massive, grey naval vessels of all sizes and descriptions, we emerged into Chesapeake Bay.

Crab-pot floats were especially thick in a number of areas in Chesapeake Bay, but we somehow avoided snagging them though the odd float bumped against *Ombre Rose*'s hull from time to time. Following a straight run of almost 200 miles, we entered the Chesapeake-Delaware canal at the top of the bay and emerged into the Atlantic through the Delaware River. After a brief stop in Cape May for lunch and a walk-about, we continued up the coast of New Jersey where I witnessed a truly memorable sight.

I rose from my berth in mid-afternoon, having been on a four-hour watch from 11:30 p.m. to 3:30 a.m. and another from 7:30 to 11:30 a.m. Emerging from the relative warmth of *Ombre Rose*'s cabin, I looked instinctively outward, beyond our tiny island of fibreglass and teak. The four-cylinder Westerbeke thrummed routinely in the distant reaches of my consciousness. Four miles or so to the west, the ragged blue coastline inched toward the equator. Atlantic City, still somewhere in my future, crouched on the horizon off the port bow. She was, in her own way, still asleep.

With more than three weeks of the northward passage over the stern and my mug of coffee still steaming, I slipped easily into the on-board routine, adjusting a jib sheet and glancing seaward for signs of other vessels.

After dinner, the iconic city slid silently past the port beam as the sun eased demurely into her bar-graph skyline. The gaudy pinks and mauves of the evening sky melted imperceptibly into the darkness beyond the glamorous glare of red neon. She awakened, brilliantly adorned in the language of electricity and, within the hour, dominated the night. I watched from my privileged vantage point, seduced by her scarlet halo. Creeping snail-like along the horizon over the next few hours, she faded into my past beneath a sprinkling of celestial pinpoint lights. By the time I was relieved of my watch at 1 a.m., her passing was marked only by a distant dome of pink haze. Few will have an opportunity to experience what I saw that evening, and I will forever cherish the gift of its memory.

Ombre Rose carried her crew comfortably around Sandy Hook, beyond Staten Island, and into New York Harbour where every feature was wrapped in a gauze-like aura of familiarity. The Statue of Liberty looked down on our passing while a school of Sunkist Staten Island Ferries swarmed around us. My battered Minolta's shutter, seeking a perfect souvenir composition, clicked again and again. Through the camera's viewfinder, the harbour appeared overpopulated with working tugs, ships, ferries and water taxis. A chorus of sounds assailed my ears and brilliant sunshine pressed heavily on my eyelids.

Hidden beyond the glassy glare of Manhattan's concrete monoliths, anonymous eyes followed our insect-like progress toward the East River. The shadows of the Brooklyn and Manhattan Bridges passed all too quickly overhead as we sped down the East River. The rigid green slice of the United Nations Building rose above us on our approach to Roosevelt Island. Unknown to me at the time, I would transit the river in the opposite direction four years later, aboard *Alice Rose*.

Eventually, with the Throgs Neck Bridge shrinking beyond our port quarter, *Ombre Rose* turned into Long Island Sound, and the city of the Twin Towers lapsed into memory.

Our east-by-northeast heading would, in two hundred miles, terminate in Buzzard's Bay at the south end of the Cape Cod Canal. On our way there, while picking a path through a minefield of crab pots, we finally snagged a float line, fowling *Ombre Rose*'s propeller shaft. The skipper tried to shed the line by reversing the engine, immediately regretting his impulsive reaction. He had simply made things worse.

Initially, the event appeared to be a minor incident since Geoff was an experienced diver, but after several free dives during which he cut away at the tangled, nylon line, he began to shiver in response to the fifty-one-degree water. A couple of dives later, Geoff had to be taken aboard to avoid sinking deeper into hypothermia.

Dried and wrapped in a blanket, Geoff drank some hot chocolate and fell into a sound sleep while Ombre Rose drifted in the middle of the sound. Almost three hours passed before he awoke and tried once more to clear the prop shaft of the choking rope. Each time he surfaced for air, we enveloped his head and shoulders in hot spray from the shower nozzle located on the swim platform. Without an air tank and weights, Geoff was unable to work more than a few seconds at a time, and his efforts proved ineffective. Once more, we brought him aboard to recover from the sound's frigid environment. In the end, the skipper called Boat US on his cell phone to request the services of a professional diver. The towing company's diver, equipped with an air tank and wetsuit, resolved the problem within a few minutes.

Our route took us through the Cape Cod Canal beyond Boston to Gloucester and, ultimately, into the coastal waters of Maine. As *Ombre Rose* neared her destination in Rockland, we steered into a shallow inlet adjacent to the village of Tenants Harbour and tied to the dock of a lobsterman named Virgil. Bob's acquaintance, our overnight host, was outgoing and brash as he ushered us around his home and his eclectic assembly of personal trophies. An unlocked glass cabinet held a half-dozen long-arms and a handgun or two. A ragged stack of boxed ammunition occupied the cabinet's summit. Virgil's double garage housed a huge, orderly selection of tools and an impeccably restored 1954 Cadillac. He and his wife owned shiny new matching grey pick-up trucks, distinguishable only by their respective light-grey and dark-grey interiors. Virgil was a collector of impressive things.

The dock to which we had tied *Ombre Rose* was stacked with what appeared to be new lobster traps. Our host explained that he hadn't put them in the water because of an ongoing dispute over local fishing rights. Some of his traps had in recent weeks been cut free of their floats in retaliation for alleged encroachment on a fishing ground claimed by another lobsterman. I failed to comprehend the significance of his explanation at the time.

We accepted Virgil's offer to drive us into the village to replenish our provisions and followed him to his crew-cab pick-up in the driveway. When I opened the rear door to get into the vehicle, I noted the barrel of a shotgun protruding from under the seat. Based on the lobsterman's storage of firearms in the house, I suspected the weapon might be loaded and motioned to Geoff to give it a wide berth as he climbed into the truck. I sat behind Virgil and watched as he removed a jacket from the front passenger seat, revealing a holstered Smith & Wesson .38 revolver. As Bob got into the cab, Virgil spun the weapon's cylinder, and confirming that it held six rounds, returned the piece to its brown, leather holster. No one said a word, and we all acted as though what had just happened was as routine as buckling a seatbelt. Still, my mind wrestled with the implications of what I had just witnessed. We obtained our groceries without incident, stowed them aboard *Ombre Rose*, and returned to Virgil's dining room where we enjoyed a tasty home-

Ombre Rose and Crew. From left, author, Geoff, and Skipper Bob (Les is taking the photograph).

cooked dinner which his gracious wife had prepared during our absence.

On our arrival in Rockland the following day, a casual conversation with the harbour master revealed that the "lobster war" among Tenants Harbour lobstermen had recently resulted in a pick-up's rear window being shot out.

Another dockside restaurant dinner, a group photo, and a visit to the local lighthouse museum signalled the end of our adventure. The following day, *Ombre Rose*'s Canadian crew rented a Nissan Sentra and drove from Rockland to Buffalo where Trisha met us and drove us home.

A few days later, I filled a photo album with images of my shipmates, river barges pushed by brightly painted tugboats, gigantic dredging machines, and the undersides of famous New York City bridges.

CHAPTER TWELVE
Farewell Penetanguishene

With my confidence bolstered by a second lengthy passage, I took the next step toward fulfilling my dream of cruising the world. Though *Alice Rose* was, from my point of view, the ideal vessel, she would require a complete refit before I attempted a trans-Atlantic crossing. That would involve hundreds of hours of work, best done in a boatyard closer to home. I began planning *Alice Rose*'s delivery from Georgian Bay to Hamilton through Lakes Huron, St. Clair, Erie, and Ontario. I researched every aspect of the passage and made endless lists of provisions, personal gear, charts, tools, safety equipment and spare parts.

There are those who enjoy solo sailing, but I never counted myself among them. I had neither the confidence nor the inclination to be alone for long periods of time, and besides, I enjoy sharing my adventures with others. While I had ample experience on the radio, navigating, and on the wheel, tending to these responsibilities simultaneously would be inconvenient, and doing so over a period of several days would be exhausting, so I needed crew for the week-long passage. The number of crew was dictated by *Alice Rose*'s cabin size and the seaway authority's requirement that private vessels, while transiting the twenty-six-mile-long Welland Canal, carry a minimum crew of three.

Alice Rose's descent from Lake Erie to Lake Ontario through the eight locks of the Welland Canal would be an important element of the trip. Unlike the Trent-Severn Waterway, through which I had skippered a rented houseboat years earlier, the busy Welland Canal catered primarily to commercial shipping. *Alice Rose* and I would be sharing the seaway's facilities with massive freighters, some up to 700 feet in length. Though my previous year's experience with the locks of the St. Lawrence Seaway would be helpful, this time I would be entirely responsible for both vessel and crew. With no one more experienced to whom I could turn, I would be solely accountable for all navigation, communications, and piloting.

Tim Armstrong, a friend and neighbour of several years, agreed to crew for me throughout the passage from Penetanguishene to Hamilton. He and I had worked on numerous home and yard projects together, and he had skippered his own boats for several years. I enjoyed his company and looked forward to having him aboard. My son, David, though not very experienced at cruising, was an industrial electrician—enthusiastic, strong and capable. Midway through the passage, David's mechanical skills proved to be a valuable asset to our endeavour.

On the fourth of June, 2001, David, Tim and I launched *Alice Rose* and stepped her mast, checking each task off my list as we progressed. We adjusted her shrouds, loaded our gear and filled her fifteen-gallon tank with diesel fuel. At 9 a.m. the following morning, *Alice Rose* sailed out of Penetanguishene Harbour into Georgian Bay as she had innumerable times in her past. We cruised through familiar waters toward Hope Island and trimmed our mainsail to get the most out of the light southwest breeze. Giant's Tomb Island slipped by our starboard rail. With Hope Island now off our port bow, we set a north-westerly course toward Cabot Head, near the tip of the Bruce Peninsula (see Map 3). Sailing comfortably on a beam reach at four and a half knots, we relaxed under a predominantly clear blue sky. By mid-afternoon, Hope Island had become little more than a smudge on the horizon, and at 3 p.m. we found ourselves abeam of Double Top Island, almost halfway to our first scheduled anchorage. All was going according to plan.

Alice Rose porpoised forward, dipping and rising and dipping again through the afternoon and evening. We sailed past Lion's Head and rounded Cabot Head in darkness. The tiny screen of my Garmin 48 GPS glowed green in the light of a crisp, full moon. We located the red range lights for Wingfield Basin about midnight and kept them aligned, one above the other, on our way into the narrow-mouthed bay. Forty minutes later, with our anchor securely embedded in the soft bottom, we crawled sleepily into our berths for a few hours of cherished slumber.

On June 6, I listened to the marine weather forecast, updated the log, and entered the day's waypoints into the GPS. By 10 a.m., we had eaten breakfast, cleared the sheltered basin and turned toward Devil Island Channel, beyond the strait between Tobermory and

Russel Island. My crew and I adopted an overlapping watch schedule based on four-hours-off and eight-hours-on. The system guaranteed all crew members a total of eight hours off duty in each twenty-four-hour period. It also ensured that two crew were on watch at all times, and that during our watch, we spent the first half

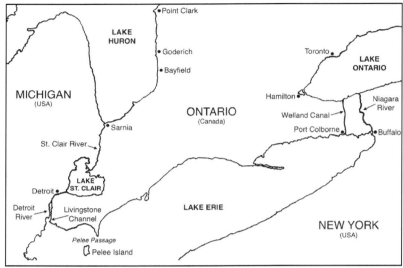

Map 13. Goderich to Hamilton

with one shipmate and the remainder of the watch with the other. The schedule's only shortcoming was that we slept in four-hour increments instead of eight.

Our second day proved as relaxing and uneventful as the first. The evening ended in Lake Huron with a spectacular sunset, and after dark, we again found ourselves bathed in brilliant moonshine. Light winds prevailed, yet *Alice Rose* managed to maintain five knots in the direction of Sarnia at the southern tip of Lake Huron.

As a scrawny farm boy, I joined the Boy Scouts of Canada. Among other things, I learned a life-altering lesson—the Boy Scout motto: "Be Prepared." Doing the preparation prior to a crisis seemed to me to be simple logic. It eliminated a lot of uncertainty, since I almost always had a plan, and if something went wrong, I often knew in advance how I was going to respond. I believe preparation enhances one's education as well because, while researching and planning contingencies, we're also learning. I've always been the guy with spare batteries in his pocket, the one who organizes the flights and accommodations—*the guy with the list.*

Our sail plan included a sequential list of the names and numbers of the charts that we would need, associated with a schedule of estimated times and locations. Navigation lights along the route and descriptions of their colour and flash sequence were listed too, along with potential anchorages and ports of refuge in case of heavy weather, a medical emergency, or mechanical failure. I was prepared for almost anything though I continued to worry about what I had overlooked.

A little after sunrise on the seventh of June, *Alice Rose* slowed, her mainsail alternately collapsing and refilling as the light morning wind became a whisper. We were becalmed just south of Point Clark, off Goderich Harbour. I started the engine and shifted into gear, but something was seriously wrong. My anxiety grew in direct proportion to the diesel's RPM as I increased the throttle. *Alice Rose* wasn't moving!

Improbable as it was, I guessed we had lost our propeller, but the problem was far worse than that. David removed the engine cover and, on close inspection, determined that the visible portion of the propeller shaft wasn't turning. It appeared that the fault was in the reduction gear, the repair of which would require the complete removal of the two-cylinder Yanmar engine. That would be a big job, best undertaken in port.

We hanked our 120% genoa onto the forestay and made the halyard fast, hoping to catch every breath of wind in our vicinity. Quietly, and at first almost imperceptibly, *Alice Rose* began to move. At 9:30 a.m., we turned her bow toward Goderich. With all eyes glued to the sail, we gently eased the sheet and waited for it to fill with air. It did, but almost immediately, it collapsed under its own weight. With minute adjustments, the process was repeated time after time as the serpentine entrance to the harbour grew closer throughout the morning. With great care and concentration, and a little advice from my crew, I steered the double-S route into the marina and came alongside the dock. I was a little surprised at our success and greatly relieved.

With blocks rigged beneath the boom and centred over the companionway, we lifted the engine from its mounts and set it gently onto the cabin sole. David quickly and efficiently disassembled the reduction gear, removing the irreparably damaged spline. Our only hope was to locate a replacement part, and I hardly knew where to begin.

The snail-paced sail into Goderich, along with the engine's removal and the subsequent diagnosis, consumed several hours. It was mid-afternoon when, together, we walked up the hill to the marina office. In response to our inquiry, the manager identified a likely source for a replacement part at Bayfield, about twenty miles south of Goderich. She offered me the use of the marina telephone to call the marine supplier, and having confirmed the part's availability, she provided us with the keys to her personal vehicle to retrieve it. While mariners are renowned around the world for their generosity and readiness to assist one another, I was overwhelmed by this lady's empathy for our situation. We drove the aging Ford southward, eager to locate the marine repair business before it closed.

The mechanic at the Bayfield marine yard offered us a used spline and upper propeller shaft coupling in good condition for $200. I readily accepted his proposal and exhaled a genuine sigh of relief. In addition to buying the desperately needed part, we filled the Ford's fuel tank and purchased a bouquet of flowers to thank the marina manager for her kindness.

With the lightly rusted treasure safely in our possession and our clothing and skin still smudged here and there with grease from our earlier work, we walked toward the dock and climbed aboard the boat. A wave of resignation swept over me when I looked below at the confused mess of parts, tools, and rigging. We were hungry and had little interest in working into the late evening, so we agreed to defer the repair until the following morning. We collected our toiletries and clean clothes, showered, dressed, and set out for the nearby Park House Tavern and Eatery.

There's nothing quite like the camaraderie of crewmates in a pub. By the time the first round of drinks were set on our table, our misfortune was forgotten, and we were occupied with our server's cheeky sense of humour. Sandra was an immediate and lasting hit with us. She kept us entertained throughout our pre-dinner drinks, our appetizers, dinner and the mariners' traditional substitute for dessert—after-dinner drinks. With our bellies full and an evening of flirting with our outgoing hostess behind us, we staggered back to the docks along a dark cliff-top trail, laughing and stumbling every inch of the way.

Thanks to my son's mechanical expertise, the replacement spline and coupling were installed without further complication, and *Alice Rose* was again seaworthy by noon on June eighth. We added thirteen gallons of diesel fuel to our tank and retraced our route out into Lake Huron.

Within twenty-four hours, we sailed beyond Sarnia via the St. Clair River and entered the shallow lake of the same name, passing numerous oncoming freighters and barges en route. Once again, in an overzealous effort to avoid impeding the progress of other vessels, I strayed slightly out of the channel as the mammoth southbound *Mesabi Miner* overtook us. *Alice Rose* dragged her keel, gently though abruptly terminating her forward motion. Indifferently, the impossibly massive red hull of the *Miner* slid by our starboard rail. The thickly silted bottom inflicted no physical damage, and with the application of a little reverse power, it grudgingly released its grip.

At 8:15 p.m., we dropped anchor in eleven feet of water, east of the entrance to Livingstone Channel, at the southern end of the Detroit River. Though enormous ships passed within two hundred feet of our sanctuary, we were unaffected because of their confinement to the channel on the other side of a narrow strip of dredging spoils. With the river's current setting southward and the breeze out of the south, our floating accommodation took up an unstable east-west attitude throughout the night. In retrospect, I should have set a second anchor or rigged a riding sail to maintain a north-south alignment, but as usual, I was anxious to flop into my berth for a few hours sleep.

At 5:45 a.m., Sunday, June 10, under a cloud-filled sky, we extinguished the anchor light and motored toward the Detroit River Light in Lake Erie. Mist, rain and ultimately thundershowers dogged our eastward progress through the shallowest of the Great Lakes. Around noon, we passed north of Pelee Island, Canada's southernmost point of land, and continued into the narrow shipping lanes of Pelee Passage. Shortly after clearing the passage in late afternoon, the wind picked up and continued to build throughout the evening. By midnight, and for the next forty hours, our environment was dominated by twenty-five to thirty knot winds and waves as high as three metres from trough to crest. My memories of the next two days are vague, and our log entries record little more than Coast Guard weather broadcasts. I confess, I've often been derelict in maintaining the ship's log, only to regret it once the passage ended. Two incidents involving other vessels were not recorded in the log, likely due to our preoccupation with navigation and weather conditions as both events occurred at night.

During our first night on the lake, an overtaking ship called us on the radio to determine if we were in distress. When I responded that we were not, the nameless voice reported that we were displaying a flashing white light, an international signal of distress. We quickly identified the source of the flashing light, explaining that the flapping of our Canadian flag was intermittently obscuring our white stern light. The lake freighter's long, low shadow rumbled by without further comment. Though the incident was mildly embarrassing, it was nice to know that the ship's crew was vigilant and concerned for our safety.

Late the following evening as we were being overtaken by a thunderstorm, I crawled into my berth and slipped contentedly toward dreamland. *Alice Rose* was faithfully sailing a pre-determined course, maintained by her electric auto helm and monitored by two capable crewmen. Only occasionally was my slumber disturbed by the nearest of the lightning strikes.

With the time for my next watch still hours away, Tim summoned me on deck. Though he and David felt inclined to alter our course, they were understandably reluctant to do so without consulting me. In shallow waters, three-metre waves, and high winds, a quick decision to deviate from a planned course at night is likely to have consequences though, in this case, my crew had good reason. A sailing vessel, identifiable at night by the configuration of its lights, normally has the right of way over a privately owned power vessel. Nevertheless, Tim reported that a rather large motor-yacht had stubbornly maintained a collision course with *Alice Rose* for the past half-hour. We speculated as to whether she too was being steered electronically, and wondered if anyone was on deck. Perhaps her crew had fallen asleep long before our navigation lights became visible. On the other hand, they might be keeping a radar watch from below, in which case the rain and waves could be obscuring our reflected signal. At a range of 400 yards, I disengaged the auto helm, eased the wheel to starboard, where if anything the water was likely to be deeper, and watched the lights pass on our port side. Then, having resumed our original heading, I returned to my warm berth. The incident, though trivial, demonstrated the need for constant vigilance and adherence to marine regulations.

Toward evening's end on the eleventh of June, the storm began to subside. By morning, the air was still, warm, and unusually humid. I came on watch just before sunrise.

Our world had changed dramatically. Everything glowed with an eerie red-mauve light, diffused by the moisture-laden atmosphere. The lake and sky were barely distinguishable from one another. The former's mirror surface rose and fell like the breathing breast of a giant beast. A ghostly, red-mauve freighter appeared to be stalking *Alice Rose*, a mile off our stern.

David and Tim brought me up to speed, explaining that the ship was stationary and likely awaiting clearance to enter the man-made route to Lake Ontario. The Welland Canal, as indicated by chart number 2100, was just beyond our visibility somewhere in the rosy gloom beyond the bow. I noted our position on the GPS and, waving a swarm of insects away from my face, worked out the bearing to the canal entrance.

In an instant, *Alice Rose* was overwhelmed by millions of tiny flying insects known variously as fish flies, shadflies, dayflies, and dunes. There are 1,500 species worldwide, and, at 300 million years old, they are believed to be the oldest insects in existence. I later confirmed that the shadflies had recently taken to the air, having been lurking in the lake-water as nymphs for up to a year. For months they had awaited the precise water temperature required to trigger their metamorphosis into winged insects. Desperate to find a dry place to alight, they blanketed our clothes, our skin and even the lenses of my glasses. Brushing them off left a green though otherwise blood-like smear. David closed the companionway to bar them from the cabin, and we got underway toward the canal. I hoped to escape the swarm by fleeing the area, but my efforts were in vain. Within minutes my khaki pants were permanently stained green in the midst of a red-mauve world. The encounter was beyond bizarre.

On arrival at Port Colborne's Sugar Loaf Marina, we hosed down *Alice Rose*'s deck and rigging to rid her of the millions of clinging shadflies and enjoyed the rest of the day ashore, exploring and taking care of business. We returned to the boat in the evening and spent what we anticipated would be our last night together, tied to one of the marina's floating docks. The next day, we expected to reach the far end of the canal by late afternoon, David's week of vacation would end, and he would return to work—or so I thought!

On our ninth day out of Penetanguishene, we rose early and left the marina just prior to sunrise with the hope of completing our eight-lock canal transit in a few hours.

Just inside the canal entrance, we secured *Alice Rose* to a dock designated for small craft clearance. There, I picked up the receiver of a telephone provided for contacting the seaway authority. A series of questions and answers established *Alice Rose*'s identity and size along with particulars of her crew. The Welland Canal is a busy waterway, and I wasn't expecting VIP treatment, so I stood by the phone for some time after being directed to await a call-back. Eventually, I returned to the comfort of the cockpit a few yards away and had a coffee, still within earshot of the phone. There had been no indication of when the call might come, and I had foolishly assumed that it would be only a matter of minutes.

We waited impatiently for hours. When at last the phone rang, I leapt onto the dock and ran to pick up the receiver.

"Hello?" I answered breathlessly.

An anonymous male voice curtly directed me to proceed toward Lock Eight. We were officially cleared to proceed—*finally!*

I obediently set our marine radio to the assigned frequency and reviewed my reference documents to ensure that I understood the light signals and instructions that we would encounter as we motored northward through the canal. The sun was already overhead and the transit was expected to take up to eight hours. In the end, it was a longer and more complex process than any of us had anticipated.

Port Colborne, the town through which the canal moves vessels between Lakes Erie and Ontario, had an agreement with the seaway authority which ensured that only one of the town's pair of lift bridges would be closed to road traffic at any one time. Consequently, when one bridge jammed in the up position, the agreement prohibited lifting the second one. We, along with a half dozen commercial freighters, waited impatiently while repairs to the bridge mechanism were completed.

The gates on the up-bound end of Lock Eight eventually opened, allowing the ship within it to proceed into Lake Erie. The signal lights changed from amber to green, and *Alice Rose* entered the first enormous lock along with two other small vessels. David and Tim stood by fore and aft to take lines from the seaway workers while I handed the $160 canal fee to an official who waited at the lock's rim. A few minutes later, we motored out of the giant concrete reservoir to continue our downward journey.

Well into our 326-foot descent toward Lake Ontario, everything stopped once more when a faceless voice on the radio directed *Alice Rose* to "stand by." With no further explanation, we again waited for several hours between locks. At the time, we were unaware that divers were inspecting one of the locks for damage after an empty down-bound laker, carrying excessive ballast, had grounded on its sill. Long after the last of the sun's rays had been obscured by the glare of floodlights along the canal's edges, we received clearance to continue.

Alice Rose finally reached the north end of the Welland Canal at 1:30 a.m. on June 14. After nineteen hours of compliance with the seaway authority's direction, our transit of the canal's eight locks was complete. Drained of every ounce of energy, we tied to the small vessel dock, signed "No Overnight Stays," and slept until morning.

David returned to work, leaving Tim and I to complete the Lake Ontario leg of the passage on our own. The sixty-mile run to Hamilton was *not* uneventful.

Oddly, strangely, weirdly—for the *second* time in three days—my little sloop endured a plague of insects. The second attack, involving millions of slightly undersized common houseflies, took place a mile off the southwestern shore of Lake Ontario, twenty-five miles east of Hamilton. The flies, eager as their Lake Erie cousins to find a safe refuge, invaded every nook and cranny on deck. Tim and I took shelter in the cabin, reluctantly poking our heads out of the forward hatch periodically to briefly check the water ahead for other vessels.

By the supper hour, *Alice Rose* had passed under the Burlington Canal lift-bridge and sprinted the final four miles through Hamilton harbour to a berth at Harbour West Marina. There, another thorough hosing-down of the deck restored her dignity.

Finally, moored just a thirty-minute drive from home, *Alice Rose* was about to begin the detailed refit that was so vital to her next adventure.

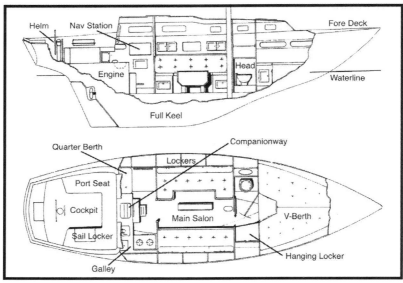

Alberg 29 Profile and Plan

CHAPTER THIRTEEN
Alice Rose's Rebirth

Alice Rose had not changed much since I had taken possession of her in 1996. Aside from reupholstered quarter berth and V-berth cushions, the only significant improvement was the conversion of her temperamental hydraulic steering to a pull-pull cable system in June 1999. Now that she was readily accessible, she would undergo a comprehensive refit in preparation for her trans-Atlantic crossing.

At the same time, having just sailed north from Florida to Maine and then south from Penetanguishene to Hamilton, I had simply had enough of boating for a while. Besides, I had neglected other aspects of my life long enough. Social commitments had accumulated during my absence, a lengthy list of home repairs and upgrades demanded my attention, and service issues with both of our vehicles awaited resolution. Though my dream was never far from conscious thought, *Alice Rose* would just have to be patient.

Bob Sebrosky, a close friend for more than forty years with an aptitude for mechanical and electrical systems, was to be my crew and fellow adventurer. I had always found experiences more satisfying when shared, and in any case, I wasn't prepared to undertake a solo crossing of the Atlantic. My trust in Bob's ability to cope with whatever unknowns we encountered made him an indispensible partner in the venture. We planned to sail to Sydney, Nova Scotia and on to the Azores before turning northward to Southampton, England—*all in one season.*

With *Alice Rose* safely berthed in England, we would fly home for the winter. Trisha, unwilling to endure the crossing, would join us the following summer for a leisurely circumnavigation of the United Kingdom.

Bob and I towed his float trailer to Penetanguishene to retrieve *Alice Rose*'s steel cradle. Later that summer, we delivered it to Fifty Point Marina, situated in a quiet rural setting on Lake Ontario's southern shore. The recently established marina was about fifteen miles from my home and offered competitive docking rates and modern facilities including a restaurant. When October arrived, I sailed my neglected Alberg to her new home at Fifty Point and had her hauled for winter storage in the marina's boatyard. With her mast removed and a blue polyethylene tarpaulin stretched over a wooden two-by-two frame on deck, I was able to begin *Alice Rose*'s refit while somewhat protected from Ontario's winter wind and snow.

When time allowed, I pored over a book of North Atlantic pilot charts that I had purchased the previous winter. Pilot charts are divided into five-degree blocks and identify within each block the average wind speeds, wind directions, current strengths and current directions for each of the months of the year. Seven such blocks span the route from Nova Scotia to the mid-Atlantic islands known as the Azores (or, in Portuguese, the *Açores*). Ice limits and average wave heights are also indicated on the pilot charts. By giving careful consideration to each of these factors, I was able to plot a somewhat efficient course from Sydney, Nova Scotia to the tiny island of Flores in the Azores.

Whenever I tired of double checking dates, calculations, and entries on the dozens of plotting sheets that I had prepared for the crossing, I studied the infinite details of the charts for the Azores archipelago and the English Channel, working out the specifics of those legs of the passage.

With invaluable help from Bob, Trisha and David Jr., the rebirth of *Alice Rose* began in earnest. I prepared lengthy lists of tasks and essential equipment in anticipation of the January boat show, where vender competition generated special offers and lower overall prices. Sailors look forward to boat shows the way children long for Christmas, and I was no exception.

At the 2002 Toronto Boat Show, in addition to numerous bits of marine hardware, I bought an anchor windlass, 200 feet of G4 chain, a high-capacity bilge pump, and a cabin hatch to exhaust condensation from the galley and improve airflow in warm weather. My major find, however, was a Voyager wind-vane steering system, by far the most efficient and reliable aid to cruising that I ever encountered. Despite its cost of $3,350, it was not, however, my most expensive purchase. That honour eventually went to a life raft that I acquired a couple of months prior to our departure.

Some of the planned tasks involved adhesives, bedding compounds, and epoxies that required extended periods of warmth to set up, so they were scheduled for the spring. Many other jobs that could have been done that winter were not undertaken because of freezing temperatures and frequent snowfalls. Crawling beneath the tarpaulin into the frigid cockpit from the top of a ladder was awkward and not very inviting. More often than not, I lacked the motivation to don long-johns, parka, and boots, drive to the boatyard, and labour under the glare of a work-light in the freezing cabin. It was more appealing to get out the charts, spread them out on the floor of my den, and, under the guise of planning, dream of sailing among the Azores.

During my winter boatyard visits, a small electric heater struggled against the sub-zero temperatures. After a couple of hours, the boat's interior warmed to a less than comfortable fifty degrees Fahrenheit. Nevertheless, I took countless measurements, applying them in the warmth of my den to detailed drawings of proposed installations, and spent hours in my workshop fabricating and assembling components.

In late February, I optimistically bought an inflatable life jacket for Trisha. Even before the snow drifts of 2002 melted, I began the complex process of re-wiring *Alice Rose*, and centralizing her electrical components at the navigation station. Hundreds of feet of variously coloured wire snaked throughout the vessel over the next two years. The complicated assembly of circuits that evolved were fed by the starting battery and two house batteries through a pair of isolator switches. New installations included an inverter and banks of switches with indicator lights to ensure the efficient management of our precious electrical resources at sea.

In June, I installed the Voyager wind vane steering system. The remainder of the sailing season was consumed with the re-wiring project, a myriad of minor repairs, plumbing, and refinements to deck hardware. I also painted the interiors of thirty-six lockers and storage areas with grey epoxy.

With renewed determination, I arrived at the 2003 January boat show with a list much longer than the previous year. I checked off three replacement halyards, nineteen folding mast steps, a tri-colour masthead light, and a second GPS to be permanently mounted at the nav-station. I also bought a number of engine spares and a Yanmar diesel repair manual, bringing the total bill to more than $1,400. The frenetic refit continued into the spring and summer.

On a crisp, sunny day in mid-March, Bob and I lifted *Alice Rose*'s forty-two-foot mast down from the mast rack and set it onto sawhorses. We then drilled and tapped seventy-six holes to attach the mast steps purchased in January. An instrument platform of my own design was fitted to the masthead. It was comprised of navigation lights, a radar reflector, a VHF antenna, and a wind direction indicator. The next few days revolved around *Alice Rose*'s launch and the stepping of her mast. At my first opportunity, I climbed the mast, stood on the uppermost mast-steps, and proudly looked down on an array of vessels and docks beneath me.

Bob and I spent several warm April days converting the now empty boat cradle into a trailer, so I could tow it from one boatyard to another without having to rent or borrow a trailer. June's projects included the complex installation of a twenty-three-gallon fresh-water tank beneath the port main salon berth. I also installed a small folding table in the cockpit, as well as jack-lines on the deck to which our tethers could be clipped in heavy weather.

For the most part, *Alice Rose* rocked gently in her slip that summer, rarely entering the lake except to test the functionality of recently installed equipment. Trisha seldom visited *Alice Rose*, and Bob and I contented ourselves with lounging on deck or in the cockpit during breaks between tasks. The whines and moans of power tools regularly emanated from *Alice Rose*'s cabin, and intervening periods of silence were sometimes punctuated with muffled outbursts of profanity.

In July of 2003, the main salon berths were reupholstered to match the V-berth and quarter berth that had been re-covered six years earlier. Custom-made lee cloths of matching material were fitted to secure us in our berths during heavy weather.

It seemed incredible that I had owned my little yacht for almost seven years, and yet a lengthy list of essential upgrades remained.

Finally, under the heat of the early August sun, I installed the ten-inch hatch that I had acquired at the 2002 boat show eighteen months earlier. Centred over the aft end of the main salon, it allowed galley smoke, steam, and hot air to escape while at the same time drawing in cool breezes from the ports along the cabin's sides.

Over the summer, I partitioned the chain locker to accommodate two independent anchor chains, and incorporated separate storage compartments for two additional propane tanks. Then I drenched the locker's interior with two coats of rock-hard epoxy to resist the inevitable battering that it would receive at sea. I felt that *Alice Rose* was approaching completion in spite of the list I revised almost every evening before climbing into bed.

Bob and I spent as much of our time as we could manage at the marina. As the days passed, we noted the sun was setting earlier and the evenings were getting cooler. The refit list grew, shrank, then grew again as new and overlooked items were added. The fall firmly established itself in summer's wake, and I began to worry that my dream was slipping through my fingers like dry sand. Mariners often speak of dreamers who never leave the harbour though year after year they swear they'll be gone in spring. The inference is that they lack the courage to set out, though I prefer to believe that most are victims of underestimating—of failing to recognize the enormity of the task of preparing a vessel for sea. I had clearly miscalculated both the cost and the effort required.

Nevertheless, I persevered. By reviewing my list repeatedly, breaking big projects into manageable tasks, and working diligently, I scratched them, one after the other, from the list.

I assured everyone that I was leaving in the spring and bought the charts that I would need to navigate the St. Lawrence River. The act was one of finality, as though there could be no turning back once the charts were on board. In October 2003, I bought yet another blue poly tarp and, once more, tied it tightly over a wooden frame on deck to protect my dream from the coming winter.

Each night, as I lay beside Trisha awaiting sleep, I imagined myself halfway to Flores and searched my mind for things overlooked. Occasionally, I got out of bed and crept quietly into my den to scrawl one more thing at the bottom of the list. To help finance the refit, I worked a couple of days a week at my son-in-law's factory automation firm. Many of the company's process solutions involved the fabrication of stainless steel and plastic components for use in food packaging. It had been a great opportunity to learn fabrication techniques applicable to *Alice Rose*'s refit.

The 2004 boat show, the last that I ever attended, left an enormous hole in my savings account. I began with the purchase of 400 feet of twisted nylon line with which to secure *Alice Rose* to a sea anchor in the event that we encountered a head-on gale. The line's length and construction would act like a spring, providing what I hoped would be a comfortable head-to-wind ride with as little loss of ground as possible. Its bulk, even when neatly rolled into a tight bundle, constituted a significant storage challenge.

Our sea anchor was a yellow, ninety-nine-dollar army surplus cargo parachute with a diameter of fifteen feet. I hoped we'd never have to deploy it, and I worried about the physical effort required to recover, dry and stow it after use.

In addition to a manual bilge pump, accessible from the cockpit, *Alice Rose* was equipped with a twelve-volt electric pump fitted with a float switch. I had invested in a third pump, which I fastened to the underside of a hatch cover. It had languished, unseen, in a locker since its procurement at the 2002 boat show. In an emergency, the high-capacity pump, fitted with lengthy intake and outlet hoses, could be put into service in seconds anywhere in the cabin or on deck.

As a last defence against losing my Alberg at sea, I commissioned a triangular canvas "collision blanket." With lines attached to the grommets at each of the three corners, it could be dragged under the hull to cover any significant damage. The pressure of the sea would press it tightly into a breach in the hull and slow the intake of seawater—at least in theory. The three-sided canvas would also serve as a rain-catchment device to replenish our fresh-water tank at sea, and a riding sail to keep our head to wind and minimize the erratic yawing and heeling that boats often endure at anchor.

Other boat-show purchases included spare injectors for the diesel engine, parachute flares, radar and a handheld VHF radio. Not only would the latter come in handy if we found ourselves in the life raft, but it would be our back-up if our primary radio failed. In any case, it would eliminate the necessity of going below to utilize the primary radio at the nav-station. We had experienced that inconvenience throughout our transit of the Welland Canal.

Of course, the major expense, the one I had deferred year after year as we prepared for the crossing, was the life raft. At $3,800, it was the most costly piece of equipment on board and probably the most essential—yet I ardently hoped we would never have occasion to use it.

The second most important purchase, the EPIRB (emergency position indicating radio beacon), was never made. Its purpose, should we find ourselves helplessly adrift in a featureless sea, was to transmit our exact location to searchers via satellite. Though some versions were only a quarter of the cost of the life raft, I was running out of money, and I estimated the chances of us taking to our raft were minimal. In hindsight, the decision was uncharacteristically risky, and I would caution others that an EPIRB could mean the difference between survival and a lonely death at sea.

As successive sunrises crept northward in the spring of 2004, the days grew longer, yet their passing seemed to quicken. We redoubled our efforts, installing a Force 10 LPG cabin heater, a $1,500 JRC radar system, and a custom-built mahogany bowsprit of my own design. I had fabricated it in my workshop over the winter, along with a double bow roller system to augment the chain and the anchor windlass purchased the previous year.

June 1, our scheduled departure date, slipped into the past while *Alice Rose* remained high and dry in the marina's boatyard. The days ran together as I attacked the remaining tasks with a sense of desperation. Bob and I invested countless hours in the preparation of her hull. By the end of the third day of scraping and sanding, my shoulders ached and my arms—*and brain*—were numb with fatigue. I tried to focus on one day at a time, denying the enormity of the unfinished work. With hours to her scheduled launch, we applied multiple coats of 2000E epoxy and CSC antifouling.

Finally, the marina's travel-lift lumbered toward the water with *Alice Rose* swinging gently in its foot-wide slings. Within an hour or so, we were adjusting her mooring lines at our assigned slip and preparing to get on with the remaining refit tasks.

When sailing before a gentle wind in the light of day, it's a simple matter to raise and lower sails singlehanded, but more often, the need occurs at night or in rough weather while one's shipmate is sleeping. At sea, we were likely to be alone on deck much of the time, so one of our final installations was that of lazy jacks, a spider-web of light lines designed to contain the mainsail when blustery weather appears bent on blowing it overboard.

Then, we bolted the double bow rollers, which I had fabricated during the winter, through the forward deck. With two anchors, each attached to a separate rode, we could readily adapt to a variety of weather and bottom conditions. *Alice Rose* could safely swing on 200 feet of G4 chain in forty feet of water if needed. In deeper water or heavy winds, we would simply add our five-eighths-inch twisted nylon.

To test the new bowsprit, anchor rollers and windlass, Bob and I sailed out among two metre breaking waves and anchored a couple of hundred yards offshore. The system withstood an hour of continuous battering in the unprotected waters of Lake Ontario, and though retrieving the anchor was a drenching and physically exhausting workout, the equipment functioned as intended.

One of the final installations, the project of which I was the most proud, was the complex folding salon table that stowed inconspicuously against the bulkhead when not in use, yet comfortably accommodated four diners at meal-times. Its mahogany finish was flawless and its strength was superior to comparable original-equipment tables.

I built in redundancy wherever funding permitted. I purchased a robust storm jib, and to secure the companionway against heavy weather and the occasional monster wave, I fabricated a sturdy, transparent washboard from half-inch-thick polycarbonate. A second, vented version, would serve our security needs while the boat was in port. I commissioned custom canvas weather-boards to protect the cockpit from drenching spray and wind, and to provide additional cockpit locker space, I mounted four readily accessible fender baskets on the stern rail.

Months earlier, Bob and I had taken an offshore first-aid course designed specifically for those without access to professional medical services. We learned to give injections, suture wounds and diagnose selected illnesses. Though not convinced that I could find the courage to use them, I added a scalpel and surgical clamps to our first aid kit.

The days sped by indifferently. Even as we neared our departure, new ideas materialized and competed with those stubbornly clinging to the original list. On several occasions, we rescheduled our departure a day or so until finally, with proverbial butterflies in my stomach, I knew it was time to leave. I was apprehensive, though I felt I had done everything possible to prepare myself, my crew and my vessel. Bob, Trisha and I were trained in navigation, VHF communication and most other aspects of seamanship. And although a handful of minor refit tasks remained to be undertaken while underway, the essential preparations were complete. *Alice Rose* bristled with equipment. *Union Jack*, our upturned dinghy, occupied the foredeck, secured with obsessive care and redundancy. Green and yellow plastic jerry cans containing exigency water and diesel fuel were lashed to the rails, giving a festive look to our heavily laden blue-and-white sloop.

We and our little vessel were as ready to face the sea as we would ever be.

CHAPTER FOURTEEN
East by Northeast

My crew and I made a few last minute adjustments, completed a couple of minor tasks, and visited with our children, our grandchildren, and a handful of close friends. The weather was warm and sunny, and the children enjoyed playing together in the park-like setting. Finally, after years of learning the intricacies of sailing and months of readying my vessel, it was time to go.

We posed for photos, said our goodbyes, and eased *Alice Rose* out of her slip. Well-wishers waved as we motored toward the marina entrance. Within a few minutes, we were quietly sailing eastward into Lake Ontario while the sun settled predictably toward our wake. My renewed and eager *Alice Rose* sailed out of Fifty Point Marina almost four hours behind schedule—*twenty-one days and four hours to be precise!*

My memories of those early hours are muddied by the multitude of thoughts that assailed my mind that afternoon. It was the eve of the most challenging summer of my life, and there were lots of things to think about.

The first leg of *Alice Rose*'s 2004 journey zigged and zagged from the western end of Lake Ontario to the eastern tip of Nova Scotia, a route I would find somewhat familiar due to my previous voyage to Labrador and Newfoundland. Most of the ports that the 2000 Flotilla had utilized along the St. Lawrence River would be revisited during our passage. Once safe in Sydney harbour, Trisha would return to our home in Hamilton while Bob and I undertook the fourteen day crossing south of the Newfoundland coast to Flores in the Azores.

Everything I had learned about North Atlantic summers suggested they were both short and elusive. To avoid a blustery autumn approach to the dangerous English coast, Bob and I had planned to limit our time in the mid-Atlantic Azores archipelago to a mere three weeks.

That decision, however, had been based on a June 1 departure.

Our delayed sailing hung over me like an approaching storm cloud. Even the tingle of excitement that coursed through my veins as we sailed over Lake Ontario was tempered by the realization that exactly three weeks had elapsed since our originally scheduled departure date. My entire plan was hanging by a thread, and the next few weeks would surely be dominated by a sense of urgency.

Sailing through the night, we addressed numerous adjustments, discovered oversights, and coped with minor equipment failures. Three years of refitting had left little time for sailing, and it became clear that our cruising skills had deteriorated. In the rush to get underway, I had neither read the manual for our recently installed radar, properly stowed my personal gear, nor entered way points into the GPS beyond the first two days. I had a lot of catching up to do.

Giant, ghostly hulls slipped quietly by in the darkness.

Bob and I observed a five-hour-on and four-hour-off watch system, incorporating a thirty-minute overlap at each change of watch and a minimum of eight hours off in any twenty-four hour period. Our shifts gradually rotated our duties so that we shared daylight, moonlight, sunrises and sunsets equally. Trisha, whose line-handling and housekeeping duties were most valuable through the day and into the evening, enjoyed a normal night's sleep.

During my 2:30 a.m. to 7:30 a.m. watch on June 24, I turned the helm over to the Voyager wind-vane steering system, designed and built by Peter Tietz. Peter's invention was to me absolute magic! There it was, accurately holding the assigned course with little or no monitoring, leaving me free to go below and brew coffee in preparation for Bob's upcoming watch. Thank you, Voyager!

"Otto," our Navico WP 4000 electric auto helm, would drain our batteries if we used it while under sail though it had always been a reliable helmsman while motoring. When we put it into service on our second day, it stubbornly nudged the wheel first one way and then the other in ever-increasing arcs until, eventually, it steered *Alice Rose* in a complete circle. I reviewed the manufacturer's manual and reset it, but the device repeated its mysterious behaviour. In the end, baffled by the auto helm's erratic performance, I stowed it in a locker for the remainder of the passage. Clearly, after years of unappreciated service, Otto had gone mad!

Wind is everything to a small yacht. Its direction and strength rule over every inch of the vessel's progress and every aspect of the crew's comfort. In mid-afternoon, when the sails began flapping lazily against the sheet-ends, I lowered them and started the engine. Less than two hours later, *Alice Rose* was under sail again and making 6.6 knots on a close reach. We had been underway for forty-eight hours, and most of Lake Ontario's one-meter waves were well beyond our stern rail.

My crew and I were rather tired when, at seven-thirty in the evening, we entered Confederation Basin, Kingston's municipal marina. We tied up, registered, showered, and settled comfortably down to dinner at Tir Nan Og, an Irish pub in the old Prince George Hotel on the waterfront. The pub's name refers to an Irish mythological "other world," tales of which date back almost 2,000 years. I found the establishment's atmosphere and my hot meal relaxing after more than two days of continuous sailing.

Our time on Lake Ontario had been an endless series of minor equipment failures. In fact, our maintenance log already listed a dozen items in need of our attention. I resolved to remain in port the following day to explore Kingston's core, rest and prepare *Alice Rose* to enter the St. Lawrence River.

On the twenty-sixth, I awoke at 4 a.m., dressed, topped up our water tank, and prepared to sail. *Alice Rose* passed under the La Salle Causeway Bascule Bridge at 7 a.m. and entered the inner harbour. There, we refuelled at Kingston Marina, pumped out our waste tank and hurried back to the bridge to take advantage of its scheduled eight o'clock lift.

We cruised in fine weather among the celebrated Thousand Islands throughout the afternoon (see Map 7). In the vicinity of Alexandria Bay, beyond Gananoque, the southern sky darkened and the wind picked up. With one eye on an approaching line of slate-grey cloud, I hurriedly donned my rain gear. When heavy raindrops began crashing onto the fibreglass deck, Trisha and Bob withdrew into the cabin, securing the companionway with our transparent half-inch polycarbonate washboard. Over the next few minutes, we faced the fiercest winds I had experienced on the water to date.

The initial gusts heeled *Alice Rose* dramatically to port in spite of her bare pole. I clipped my safety tether to a folding D-ring that we had installed for this very situation. The inverted dinghy on the forward deck and the fixed radar reflector at the top of our mast turned, in an instant, from conveniences to liabilities as the wind pressure forced them leeward. I feared the dinghy would be torn from its lashings as gusts of wind screamed through the shrouds. The deafening clatter of hail assailed my ears, and the blue canvas dodger and the deck became littered with ragged spheres of ice. The hail turned the river's surface white with foam, and the raging wind tore spray from the choppy peaks. With my left foot braced against the port cockpit seat back, I turned up-wind to ease the load on the dinghy. Immediately, the lenses of my rain-spattered glasses reduced my vision to blurred shadows of grey and muted blue-green.

Behind me, an ash-coloured freighter emerged from the curtain of rain. It crossed our stern and melted into the translucence. Trisha and Bob held the chart against the dry side of our transparent washboard. Our safe progress through the islands was entirely dependant on that chart and the power of our two-cylinder diesel. I wiped the beads of rain from my glasses and leaned toward the washboard, then looked about for a channel marker amid the colourless confusion. Unable to determine our position and fearing a rocky encounter with the southern edge of the channel, I spun the wheel to starboard a second time and retreated downwind. *Alice Rose* dipped her starboard rail as she turned. My perception of time crumbled in the chaos. I had no idea how long I had been on the southward heading or where I was in relation to the channel.

Then, as quickly as it began, the wind and rain eased, and the freighter reappeared a safe distance away. The channel markers bobbed excitedly among the confused waves, and *Alice Rose* resumed her northeasterly heading.

With my adrenaline still pumping, I had to admit that I had momentarily feared the loss of my boat and crew. We had no anemometer on board to measure wind speed, but I had previously sailed in thirty-five-knot winds on the Gulf of St. Lawrence for several hours. With that experience as a reference, I estimated the squall's winds had for a short period exceeded forty knots with gusts of forty-five.

Late in the afternoon, we encountered Iroquois Lock, the first of the St. Lawrence Seaway's seven locks. In response to our approach, the barrier gate lifted and the lights flashed green. The lock attendant accepted our twenty-dollar bill on the fly and advised us that we would be dropping two and a half inches—eight dollars an inch. I concluded that the surprisingly small drop was due to the spring's extremely low Great Lakes water levels. We cruised through the atypical lock without tying up and slipped between the opening gates at the lower end. Immediately east of the lock, *Alice Rose* found refuge from her long day in an abandoned seaway canal on the river's north shore. It was the Iroquois Marina, the same overnight stop utilized by the 2000 Flotilla during my eastward passage aboard *Lap Cat*. The staff had gone for the day, but we located a suitable piece of vacant wall and tied up—among a million mosquitoes.

Bonus! Whether an oversight or deliberately, the marina's shower doors had been left unlocked.

We motored out of Iroquois Marina at 9 a.m. on June 27. An hour and a half later, *Alice Rose* was making 7.7 knots over the bottom, thanks in part to our carefully trimmed 120% jenny. Of course, the mighty river's current was helping a little.

Just prior to noon, we approached Eisenhower Lock, the first of two U.S. locks in the system. A sign directed us to an unseen small craft dock, hidden behind the port approach wall. A strong following wind whipped up significant waves as it drove us into the narrow, buoyed entrance. On entering the basin, we observed a second sign indicating a depth of six feet. That meant *Alice Rose*'s four foot, six inch keel was certain to find the bottom as she bobbed up and down on two-foot waves. As is common aboard a sailing vessel, our circumstances were suddenly elevated through challenging to desperate.

From inside the entrance, we could see that the dock was barely large enough to hold the three vessels already tied up, and we had no room to turn around. My only remaining option was to reverse out of the narrow opening, against the wind and waves. Due to prop-walk, *Alice Rose* didn't back well at the best of times, and the manoeuvre appeared to be impossible. Nevertheless, gradually, with the engine revving dangerously near its maximum rpm, she began to splash her way out of the confined basin. Curiously, on this occasion alone, she answered the wheel well, and though we struck bottom several times, we ultimately escaped into the deeper approach channel. Perhaps with the reversing prop at our windward end, the rest of the vessel acted as do the feathers on an arrow, keeping us aligned into the wind. Contrary to the seaway authority's direction, we waited in the approach channel for the lock to turn.

Having cleared Eisenhower and Snell locks, a combined drop of eighty feet, we sailed without further incident into Lake St. Francis en route to our planned anchorage. A few miles short of our scheduled destination, we searched the chart for a dock with access to provisions. We selected the western end of the abandoned Soulange Canal, which had originally opened in 1899. The buoyed approach to the canal was long and narrow, and due to years of accumulated silt, rather shallow. In exchange for a fee of ten dollars, we secured our lines to bollards at the top of an eight-foot wall within the canal and slept.

With a little help, Trisha managed to climb from the deck to the top of the lock wall the following morning. We locked the companionway entrance and walked into the village for groceries. Naturally, we chose the wrong road first and the right road last, returning to the boat late in the morning with several bags of provisions, somewhat fatigued from walking the indirect route.

We slipped our dock lines at one in the afternoon, re-entering Lake Francis through which we reached the Upper and Lower Beauharnois Locks. Our little vessel was lowered another eighty feet or so toward sea level and made her way to the opposite end of the same Soulange Canal for the night. No signs of development or human activity were apparent, and the east end of the abandoned waterway appeared isolated and forgotten. The canal's wall, bristling with the rusted remnants of bolts that once held planking in place, rose at least ten feet above the water. When Bob tried to scale the wall to reach a corroded bollard in the deep grass above his head, he inadvertently dislodged a section of crumbling wall. It fell into the water, scattering a mixture of large chunks and loose gravel over the port deck with an alarming crash. We cleared the debris from the deck, inspected it for damage, and carefully examined the canal wall over a distance of a couple of hundred feet. Eventually, we located a safe section where we tied up for the night.

Alice Rose left the canal at 7:10 a.m. on the twenty-ninth, continuing downriver toward Sorel via the Ste. Catherine and St. Lambert locks. We had experienced no delays during our transit of the first five locks, but the final two took much longer than we had anticipated.

Alice Rose's engine controls, gauges, and ignition were mounted on the starboard cockpit bulkhead, a rather vulnerable position since about half of the time her crew entered and exited the vessel there. I had, on at least one previous occasion, accidentally struck the ignition key with my foot as I stepped into the cockpit. Having released our lines from the small vessel dock where we had been waiting for the St. Lambert Lock to turn, I boarded to get underway and stepped heavily on the protruding ignition key. The switch exploded into several pieces, and only Bob's extensive auto repair experience saved us from drifting uncontrollably toward the lock. Though the bits and pieces and the wires attached to them made no sense at all to me, Bob managed to temporarily reassemble the switch, enabling us to start the engine and enter the lock in the usual manner.

Alice Rose docked in Sorel too late in the day to explore the town and replenish our provisions. Still, we found time for showers, entering waypoints into the GPS for the following day's run, and most importantly, undertaking a permanent repair of the ignition switch.

It may be appropriate to point out that, in a relaxed state, I can be an easygoing and perhaps even pleasant fellow, but there is another me, the me that emerges at times of crisis. Invariably, when an urgent situation—such as the broken ignition switch—arises, my patience wanes in direct proportion to the stress I experience. Never have I been subjected to stress more frequently than as the skipper of *Alice Rose*.

Sailboats are susceptible to quickly changing circumstances, and when things go wrong, only an immediate response can prevent them from spiralling out of control. One failure often leads to another, overwhelming the crew with a complex series of potential dangers. The burden of responsibility for vessel and crew tends to amplify a skipper's perception of a crisis, and in the case of Captain Bligh and myself, it does little to enhance our human relations skills.

By 7:40 a.m. the following morning, we had refuelled, pumped out our waste tank, replenished our fresh water supply, and re-entered the river. Finally, while crossing Lac St. Pierre on June 30th, I found the time to read the radar manual and switch the radar on for the first time. With so much new equipment and the electric auto helm's erratic performance, we had spent too much time on the wheel and too little setting up and learning to use our hand-held VHF, digital camera, lap top computer and Garmin 102 GPS, the software of which differed considerably from my familiar Garmin 48.

Most sailors, embarking on long-planned adventures, struggle to meet their scheduled departure date. Even years of preparation seem insufficient in the days leading up to the celebrated start of a major passage. Often, the overwhelming workload and stress of planning for every possible contingency continues well beyond a safe start date, adding additional risks to the venture. For many, enthusiasm wanes, the dream dies, and the vessel *never* gets underway. I had always been conscious of that possibility and secretly feared putting off our departure any longer. Already three weeks late, I had knowingly and deliberately set sail with a rather limited understanding of some vital equipment.

When we arrived in Trois Riviére, Trisha went ashore to do laundry while Bob and I walked into town to get a few groceries. The laundromat's dryers weren't very effective, and the walk to town was substantial, so once again, we ate dinner late in the evening. Close quarters, inclement weather, equipment failures, stressful locking procedures, and long hours made us irritable at times. Nevertheless, our longstanding relationships, coupled with a little perseverance, kept us working toward our goal as a team.

As often happened, Bob and Trisha went to sleep while I stayed up to enter the waypoints for the next leg of the river. July 1 had officially arrived by the time I turned the GPS off and retired to my berth.

We slept late and didn't leave Trois Riviére until 8:15 a.m. on Canada Day. For us, the celebrated holiday was routine until we reached the Richelieu Rapids at 1:15 p.m. There, we noted our speed over the bottom was 10.8 knots. That was more than double our normal cruising speed and had to be due in part to a combination of river current and ebbing tide.

A thunderstorm pursued us eastward throughout the afternoon, finally overtaking *Alice Rose* just as the incoming tide reduced our forward progress to one and a half knots. Our plotted position put us six miles short of the Quebec Bridge when the deluge began. I noted in the log that it had rained every day since our departure. The downpour continued throughout the four hours it took to reach the iconic bridge, though thankfully we weren't subjected to any significant wind.

Ninety-seven years earlier, the world's largest cantilever bridge was being assembled immediately southwest of Quebec City. After warning signs were ignored, an engineering error caused the bridge to suddenly collapse into the St. Lawrence River. The iron structure plunged 150 feet toward the swirling water, killing seventy-five workers. Construction was resumed six years later, and the bridge was eventually completed in 1917, though not before a second collapse in September 1916. As a crowd of more than 100,000 gathered to watch the central span being lifted into place, a structural fault caused it to twist and crash into the river, killing thirteen additional workers. Eighty-eight years later, we looked up in awe as we passed under the centre span of the enormous structure.

An hour after sailing beneath the bridge's web of girders, we entered Yacht Club de Quebec, situated on the north shore of the river in a Quebec suburb known as Sillery. The yacht club greeted and serviced virtually every up-bound and down-bound privately owned yacht on the St. Lawrence River. Bruno, a member of the club's executive, directed us to a convenient berth and advised us how to locate the hospital, as Trisha had developed a serious infection in her foot.

Bob and I bundled Trisha into a taxi and turned to securing and cleaning up the boat which was littered with wet clothes, rain gear, and other remnants of the day's cruise. We each had a shower and a beer before Trisha called to advise she was about to leave the hospital. It was half-past midnight on July 2.

On Trisha's return to the yacht club, we learned that her foot was so severely infected that the doctor wanted to admit her to the hospital so he could administer antibiotics intravenously. Instead, Trisha opted for two prescriptions.

In the morning, the yacht club staff proved incredibly supportive and accommodating when we inquired about a pharmacy within walking distance. Eve called a nearby francophone pharmacy, ordered Trisha's prescription, and arranged to have it delivered. When the package arrived, she came to our slip to retrieve my credit card for payment and returned minutes later with the antibiotics. The experience was akin to receiving exceptional room service in a prestige hotel.

Fed up with our old, unreliable SR Mariner depth sounder, I invested in a digital Raymarine replacement. As the transducer could only be properly installed from the wet side of the hull, it had to live in a "well" in one of our forward lockers until the next time *Alice Rose* was hauled out of the water. I fitted a six-inch piece of three-inch plastic pipe to the inside of the hull, sealing the bottom edge with Sikaflex bedding compound prior to filling the pipe with water. Over the next few days, we would discover whether or not the new depth sounder was more reliable than its defective predecessor.

Trisha wasn't up to a lot of walking due to her foot infection, so she lounged aboard while Bob and I set out to explore on our own. We hiked up the nearby escarpment to the Plains of Abraham where Wolfe and Montcalm fought it out in 1759. Then, continuing to Avenue Cartier, we came upon the Turf Pub where we sat down at a sidewalk table, ordered a pint, and called Trisha to suggest she summon a taxi and meet us at the pub. Together, the three of us wandered about, had dinner, and watched the local Canada Day fireworks display which had been postponed due to the weather.

By the time we walked down the escarpment to the yacht club, we were all spent and eager for sleep. I decided to stay in Quebec the next day to finish installing the depth sounder, adjust our leaky rudder post stuffing box and sort out an electrical short associated with our number two house battery. The short turned out to be in the battery itself, so I made yet another trip to the nearby chandlery to purchase a replacement; more unplanned expense!

Our Garmin 48 had been indicating a "low memory battery" for several days, and the manual made no reference to that battery's replacement, so I inquired at the chandlery and was advised that it would have to be shipped to Garmin for installation of a replacement. A suggested alternative was to install fresh AA operating batteries to see if the lithium battery would recharge itself. I did so and figuratively crossed my fingers.

In the mean time, Bob examined our ailing electric bilge pump and discovered that the wires had been inadvertently reversed when the pump was last serviced, so it had actually been running in reverse. We were lucky that the thru-hull was above the water line, or it would have flooded the cabin by pumping water into the bilge.

I looked at my watch as we got underway for Cap à l'Aigle on July 4 and entered 8:15 a.m. in the log-book. Though it was already high water, the tide would continue to flow up-river for an hour, so we had to fight the current for the first four nautical miles downstream.

Just as the tidal current eased, we smelled burning gear oil. Bob investigated and immediately noted that the visible portion of the propeller shaft was turning more slowly than indicated by the engine rpm. We immediately shut down the Yanmar, suspecting that the reduction gear coupling had failed for the third time since I had purchased *Alice Rose* in 1996.

Though I loved my little yacht, my trust in her diesel auxiliary had always been tentative. My apprehension began during our first sailing season with a tiny leak in a fuel line. Bob saved the day by clamping his thumb over the pin-hole while I motored the mile or so back to our slip in Penetanguishene. Occasionally, particularly on cool mornings in early spring and late fall, the hard starting engine threatened to drain our battery, and I worried that it would fail me one day in an anchorage far from port. In response, Bob and I isolated the battery dedicated to starting the engine and added two "house" batteries to supply our lighting and equipment needs. The final straw came when we had to tow *Alice Rose* to her berth with our dinghy after the spline teeth on the propeller shaft coupling stripped. Though a complete absence of wind at the time rendered our sails useless, it at least gave us time to devise a solution.

Even the second failure of the coupling off Goderich, though stressful, hadn't exposed us to any immediate danger. Being swept down the St. Lawrence River on a receding tide was an altogether different matter. Without an engine or a substantial wind, we would have no steerage, and unless we stumbled on a suitable anchorage in the steep banked river, we would wreck on a rocky shore or islet. Even if we found a safe anchorage somewhere downriver, it would be difficult to obtain a replacement for the defective coupling along the lightly populated eastward shore. We would likely be forced to endure an expensive tow back to Quebec City or await a combination of an incoming tide and a favourable wind.

Overwhelmed with the complexities of the crisis, I tried desperately to suppress the panic growing within me. I felt a need to convince my wife and friend that we were in a serious predicament, and I demanded their unquestioned compliance. I began barking orders and declarations of our precarious situation. In retrospect, I suppose I behaved rather badly.

CHAPTER FIFTEEN
Retreat, Regroup and Resume

As *Alice Rose* slipped helplessly downriver, we hurriedly raised and set her sails. With our only remaining resource, a light breeze out of the southwest, we began our westward retreat. By tacking endlessly back and forth across the St. Lawrence, we fought our way upriver against the ebbing tide. Occasionally, when the wind dropped off, or we took a few seconds too long to come about at the end of a tack, we lost ground. Throughout the day, with two steps forward and one step back, Alice Rose waltzed her way toward the very dock to which she had been tied for the past three days. Without the wind and our obsessive attention to her course, she would have been swept eastward away from Quebec City and out of reach of technical support.

When, finally, we had clawed our way to within a mile of Yacht Club de Quebec, I made a VHF call to advise that we would be entering the marina under sail, and I requested someone stand by on the dock to take our lines. I was very concerned about squeezing through the narrow marina entrance amid the river's swirling currents, so when the club's radio operator asked if we needed any additional assistance, I added one more appeal. Since many boaters use Zodiacs for dinghies, I expressed a willingness to take a tow from a Zodiac once inside the entrance if someone was available. To my surprise, the yacht club's agent answered that a towboat would be dispatched to meet us. I confess that I worried a little about the cost, having heard third-hand accounts over the years of some very expensive rescues. Marine towing services often charge hundreds of dollars—even thousands for offshore tows.

Gilles and Jerome were incredibly professional. With a calmness and efficiency that I envied, they came alongside and secured to our fore and aft T-cleats. We dropped our sails and watched as they expertly delivered *Alice Rose* to "Y" dock, precisely where we had been moored earlier that day. Then, to my great relief, I learned that the club's towing fee was little more than the cost of a cross-town cab fare.

It is impossible to describe the relief that came with being tied to the dock.

Throughout the six-hour ordeal, while I continually fretted about a change in the wind, *Alice Rose* advanced a mere three and a half miles. Had the wind fallen off or changed direction, we would have had no means of reaching the familiar yacht club and its welcoming staff. Finally, with the crisis behind us, I had time to reflect. Under stress, I tended to focus exclusively on results with little concern for the feelings of my crew. I had treated them harshly, and I resolved to face the next challenge with a little more tact and self-control. Then, with *Alice Rose* secured and her crew safe, I poured generous portions of rum into three glasses.

In spite of the sense of security that came with being safely in port, I began to realize that our late start from Hamilton and our current need for repairs would likely jeopardize our planned crossing of the Atlantic. While it was still technically possible, there would be little time to explore the Azores, and our late-summer run for England's south coast would be uncomfortable, if not risky. I'd have to give serious consideration to delaying the passage yet *another* year.

I could feel my dream slipping away, and I tried in vain to stop thinking about it. Much of that night I lay awake, searching my mind for a solution that never came.

The following day, with heavy rain drenching our clothes and chilling our bodies, Bob and I rigged the mainsheet mid way on the boom above the companionway. When the downpour let up for a few minutes, we opened the hatch and lifted the engine off its mounts, setting it gently onto a towel on the teak and holly cabin sole. Once disconnected from the propeller shaft, we could see that the teeth of the spline had stripped, as they had three years earlier in Lake Huron off Goderich Harbour. We removed the reduction gear (transmission) and delivered it along with the damaged coupling to Pierre Belanger at Usinage MCP in St. Malo. Pierre had been independently recommended by several members of the yacht club. He explained that the spline damage was due to a slight misalignment between the shaft and the engine, and agreed to install a replacement coupling and realign the propeller shaft.

While a replacement part *was* available through a U.S. warehouse, the local supplier estimated delivery and customs services might take ten days or more. Subsequently, I accepted Pierre's offer to machine a replacement part instead.

The previous day's stress, the disruption to our schedule, the added expense, and the incessant rain were getting me down.

By early afternoon on Tuesday, July 6, we hadn't yet heard from Pierre. To assuage our boredom, Bob and I signed out the last two complimentary bicycles of the yacht club's inventory, and pedalled toward the centuries-old city of Quebec. For her part, Trisha called for a taxi and met us at the Chateau Frontenac Hotel. The hotel's palatial lobby and turreted exterior extolled Victorian prosperity. A promenade on the south side provided easy access to panoramic views of the river far below. Having filled our heads and cameras with images, we left the hotel property and wandered casually through the old city's narrow streets, soaking up the European-like atmosphere and enjoying the performances of a number of street buskers. Though our mechanical setback was always on my mind, I enjoyed the day and to some extent deferred my anxiety.

Like most of the world's major cities, Quebec is best experienced on foot, so being fit is a prerequisite to properly enjoying its steeply inclined streets. I was pleased to note that the streets were as clean as they were beautiful. Toward the end of our visit to the old city, the three of us relaxed in D'Orsy's Pub, ordered pints of beer, and enjoyed them at a table by a large open window. Warm breezes and snippets of passing conversations washed over us as tourists wandered by within arm's length.

We returned to the yacht club, ate cheeseburgers on the restaurant's waterfront patio, and immersed ourselves in inactivity for the remainder of the warm, summer evening. Never far from conscious thought, the delay hung over me like a cloud, occasionally isolating me from conversations concerning other matters.

Then, abruptly and with a degree of resolve I hadn't anticipated, I made a decision. It was as though I had suddenly surrendered to the obvious. It was clearly too late in the season to cross the Atlantic, explore the Azores, and complete the passage to England before the weather deteriorated. It was still possible, but at what cost? We would see little of the Azores and unnecessarily expose *Alice Rose* and ourselves to a risk-ridden passage. It was the responsible thing to do, and while disappointed, I was relieved that a verdict had finally been rendered.

Now, we could slow down a little and enjoy the communities between Quebec City and Sydney. Claude Provost of *Syjoli III*, a thirty-six-foot Bayfield, was about to embark on a circumnavigation via the Panama Canal and was very helpful with local knowledge between Quebec City and Nova Scotia. At his suggestion, I entertained the idea of a visit to the Îles de la Madeleine. His gracious gift of two relevant charts was greatly appreciated.

Today, electronic charts have all but replaced their paper counterparts, which in 2004 were costly but essential. Passing them on, both as a means of recycling and as an expression of fellowship, was a longstanding tradition within the cruising community.

Though we spent July 7 anticipating a call from Pierre, it didn't come. In the meantime, we cut a rectangular opening in the cockpit bulkhead and completed the installation of our new Raymarine depth sounder. The original instrument remained in place on the bulkhead pending an opportunity to "glass" over the circular hole. I felt a degree of sadistic pleasure as I cut away its wiring. It had been letting us down for years, even after I had personally delivered it to the U.S. for service. When I picked it up a week later, I was assured that it was working well, only to have its indicator periodically plunge to five feet for no apparent reason. In obviously deep water it was a minor annoyance, but in a tricky channel or a harbour where shallow areas were more likely, its behaviour triggered an unpleasant and instantaneous surge of adrenaline. Assuming the malfunctions were due to electrical interference, I expected more reliable performance after we re-wired the boat, but isolation from all electrical wiring seemed to have no effect. With all the difficulties we had recently faced, I was almost surprised that the new $300 instrument *actually worked*. I was really looking forward to knowing with certainty the depth of water under our keel when we continued our passage.

On July 8, Pierre Belanger had the reduction gear, fitted with a new stainless coupling, delivered to us for installation. Bob reassembled the engine while I rigged the mainsheet in preparation for lifting the two-cylinder Yanmar back onto its mounts. Again, it rained during the hoisting and installation of the 300-pound engine. Trisha supported us with towels, hot drinks and food throughout the procedure. Later in the afternoon, as we were clearing up the mess, Pierre came by to properly realign the propeller shaft. Immediately, he discovered that the aft coupling needed re-facing and returned with it to his machine shop, assuring us that he would finish the job the following morning.

Though rain continued to drench the area throughout the afternoon and evening, we were at least able to stay dry by remaining below deck. All three of us were suffering a little cabin fever, and no doubt Trisha and Bob were as anxious as I was to get underway.

Our saviour returned on July 9, re-installed the coupling, aligned the propeller shaft and drove us to the nearest Bank of Nova Scotia, where I willingly fulfilled our obligation. Although the cost of our beloved machinist's services exceeded $700, I was both relieved and satisfied that we had chosen the right person to do the work.

We reassembled the last few wires and fuel lines, primed and started the engine. It ran normally for a couple of seconds and stalled, almost certainly due to air in a fuel line. We carefully re-tightened each of the lines, primed and started it again—and again—and again! I lost count of how many times, but every time I thought the nightmare was finally over—*it wasn't*.

The clock was ticking, and my blood pressure was undoubtedly soaring. We had now been in Sillery for eight days.

When I fell asleep that night, I believed we had resolved the last air leak in our pressurized fuel system, but when I started the engine to warm it up in the morning—it quit! It appeared we still had air in the fuel line, and if we missed the tide, it would be twelve hours before we could again depart for Cap à l'Aigle.

When would I ever be able to trust the little Yanmar again?

Bob went over the fuel lines one more time while I looked on with a feeling of inadequacy. Eventually, he determined that the leak was due to a minor oversight, one that could be resolved with a simple fix. A washer had been re-installed on the wrong side of a fitting, and that had been the sole cause of the air leak from the beginning. Finally, we motored to the fuel dock, pumped out our waste tank and filled our fuel tank, then returned to "Y" dock until half past midnight.

We had a great time at the Yacht Club de Quebec, we had a terrible time at the Yacht Club de Quebec. *(Author's apologies to Mr Dickens!)* The people and the facilities were fantastic, though our mechanical issues and the associated costs destroyed any hope of sailing beyond Nova Scotia before the end of the season.

I will always appreciate the friendly and helpful staff of Yacht Club de Quebec for all of their kindness and assistance during our stay—Bruno, who in shorts and a T-shirt walked out onto the breakwall in a cold wind to guide us to our slip; Louis Alexander, who delivered a clubhouse access card to us immediately after our late arrival; Eve, who cheerfully arranged the procurement and delivery of Trisha's medication right to the boat; Gilles, the harbour master, who towed us in after our engine failure; Jerome, who, though only seventeen, helped us in so many ways and came to *Alice Rose* the night of our departure to wish us bon voyage; Francois, who with very limited English and a friendly smile made numerous trips to the dock to accommodate our needs. They were magnificent hosts and memorable individuals.

Of course, I owe a special thank you to Pierre Belanger of Usinage MCP, who worked long and hard to get us back on the water and charged us less than he deserved for his skill and special attention. Finally, it's worth noting that Trisha's endurance and support throughout our stay at Yacht Club de Quebec, along with Bob's technical skills and persistence, enabled me to get through the most trying episodes of our eastward passage.

The moon was well into its last quarter when, at the appointed hour, we re-entered the St. Lawrence. *Alice Rose* fought the incoming tide for almost three hours, before it turned and sped downriver toward Cap à l'Aigle (see Map 8). Crisp, brilliant stars glittered in the black dome overhead. There was a chill in the night air when, at 4 a.m., I sent Bob below for a couple of hours sleep.

In the faint light of early morning, I watched a blanket of fog creep across the water toward us. By 6 a.m. the grey mass had completely enveloped our little sloop. Shortly afterward, I summoned Bob to take the wheel when a following ship's foghorn sounded a long blast for the second time. The freighter appeared clearly in the form of a smudge on our radar screen, and I knew that *Alice*

Rose appeared similarly on hers. I estimated that we were already perilously close to the north edge of the channel, but because our electric auto helm was out of service, I couldn't leave the wheel unattended to fix our position on the chart. I looked over my shoulder nervously while I awaited Bob's arrival on deck. My head was strangely fuzzy, and I realized I hadn't slept for twenty-three hours.

For most of us, an inexplicable if not irrational fear is associated with the loss of sight, whether due to blindness, darkness, or, as in this instance, dense fog. Knowing that an enormous, unstoppable, and, most significantly, *unseen* ship is overtaking one's vessel rattles the nerves. A third blast increased my anxiety, and reluctantly I eased the wheel a little more to port. I continued to peer over the starboard quarter until suddenly, there it was! A towering pale-grey ghost loomed out of the monochrome fog at what I immediately knew was a safe distance. I exhaled and turned to look ahead. In the early morning light, the north shore appeared as a barely discernable shadow in the fog. A few yards off the bow, a red tower buoy waddled on the edge of the channel. *Alice Rose* was moving northeastward, precisely along the channel's northern boundary when Bob emerged from the cabin.

Several times throughout the day I tried to sleep, but I could only lie on my berth listening; waiting for the diesel to sputter and die as it had at Yacht Club de Quebec. Trust comes slowly—imperceptibly, over time.

Once more in a state of near-exhaustion, I tied our lines to the dock in Cap à l'Aigle a little after 3:30 p.m. Established in a remote section of the river by the Canadian Government as a port of refuge, Cap à l'Aigle offered basic services, and sleep was the only reason I could find to linger. We registered, showered and ate French fries at the grubby little restaurant. By 6:30 p.m., my crew and I were re-boarding *Alice Rose* to get some precious sleep. I set the alarm for 1 a.m. and closed my eyes in search of oblivion.

Consciousness returned at midnight, a full hour before the next favourable tide and our scheduled departure. Knowing I wouldn't be able to sleep that last hour, I turned the alarm switch to off and lay there waiting for one o'clock. Finally, I rose, donned my survival suit to keep warm, and prepared for our departure while my crew slept. The air was cold and still when I started the engine and slipped the dock lines. Forty-five minutes later, with fenders and dock-lines stowed, *Alice Rose* doggedly pursued her predetermined course at six and a half knots. I entered our position and speed in the ship's log and huddled against the cold in the cockpit. The engine's throb drowned out the snoring below, and I was alone with the crescent moon until 5:30 a.m. when Trisha appeared, hair askew.

July twelfth's passage to Rimouski was uneventful, aside from a few brief and distant sightings of whales. We enjoyed some exceptional speeds over the bottom, topping out at 10.4 knots as we passed to the south of Île Rouge at the mouth of the Saguenay River.

Thanks to our early morning departure on an outgoing tide, we reached Rimouski, a town of about 50,000 dating to the late seventeenth century, at about 3:30 p.m. Its unusual name was derived from a Mi'kmaq word purported by some to mean "land of moose."

Our itinerary for the next day called for a day of shore leave, so with our departure so far away, our mood was somewhat relaxed. We tidied the boat, refuelled, and walked into town to re-provision our perishables at the local IGA.

A little after lunch on the thirteenth, we rode marina bicycles to the Pointe-au-Pere Musée de la Mer where, in 2000, I had discovered the tragic story of the *Empress of Ireland*. Many of the details of the *Empress*'s demise had, since my previous visit, been blurred by time. I enjoyed the opportunity to revisit the exhibit while introducing my crew to the little-known story.

Bob and I climbed the steps of the lighthouse which was decommissioned in 1950 after only forty-one years of service. Its French-made lens, like most of that era, floated in a circular trough of mercury and was rotated by a mechanical clockwork. The machinery was driven by the action of gravity on a heavy counterweight that steadily descended at the end of a stout chain in the centre of the lighthouse. The clockwork required twenty minutes of cranking every six hours in order to raise the weight to its highest point again. No doubt the lighthouse keeper was physically fit.

Trisha was too weary to climb the lighthouse's 128 steps for a brief presentation and a bird's-eye view of the river. Instead, she hired a taxi to drive her into Rimouski where she spent the rest of the afternoon exploring the shops. In the evening, we celebrated her fifty-ninth birthday with dinner in the Marina Restaurant overlooking the harbour.

CHAPTER SIXTEEN
The Void

By 8 a.m. on July 14, we had set our course for the port of Matane on the river's southern shore. Though the morning was cold, wet, and windy, the waves were no more than a foot in height. A twenty-knot fresh breeze sped *Alice Rose* along at five-and-a-half knots on the working jib alone. The mainsail remained lashed to the boom. It was a comfortable and low-maintenance approach to sailing. The wind diminished throughout the morning until even the mainsail, combined with the 120% genoa, offered little in the way of progress. Shortly after noon, we surrendered and started the engine.

We motored on through a cold mist until we reached the commercial fishing harbour at Matane. There, we tied to the first floating dock we encountered. While there were no other vessels on the dock, I was concerned that we were occupying a berth already allotted to a fishing vessel, so I sought out the harbour master who advised that pleasure craft were not permitted in the harbour. He suggested we move *Alice Rose* to the Matane Yacht Club on the Matane River, a thirty-minute sail to the east. He pointed out its location on a chart that hung on his office wall.

The chart indicated the club's entrance channel was a mere 0.6 metres deep—*about two feet*. Laden with equipment and provisions for an ocean passage, *Alice Rose*'s actual draft slightly exceeded her specified four-and-a-half feet. Cruising was supposed to be relaxing, but it seemed that I was being challenged every step of the way.

Waiting by the yacht club entrance for high tide entailed almost as much effort as continuing downriver to Ste Anne des Monts though, if we chose to go on, we'd first have to review the charts beyond Matane and enter additional waypoints into the GPS. I had no idea how long we'd have to wait for high tide as our tide tables were aboard *Alice Rose*, a few hundred feet from the Harbour Master's office.

The local Kia dealership owner, who happened to be present

in the office, indicated the channel had recently been dredged. He offered to drive me to the yacht club to determine if the canal was now deeper than indicated by the chart. Since he appeared optimistic about our ability to access the yacht club basin, I accepted his offer.

The Matane Yacht Club attendant assured me that the river channel was much deeper than indicated on the chart, but he urged me to "keep to the middle."

Finally, at 7:30 p.m. we entered the narrow canal between two high breakwalls, eased over a silt bottom just inches below our keel, and tied up in a cold drizzle. After dinner, Bob called home. That call changed his life forever.

A few minutes later, in a voice laden with worry, Bob announced that he would be leaving *Alice Rose* in response to an urgent family matter. Thus began his daughter's lengthy struggle with cancer, a courageous fight she ultimately lost. Her death left a void in the hearts of all who knew her.

Bob was understandably shaken and absorbed in thought, while Trisha and I were torn between expressing our concern through conversation and respecting his privacy. I asked a couple of superficial questions, concluded that he wasn't comfortable talking about the situation, and decided to give him time to deal with the shock. The three of us passed the evening with minimal conversation.

Bob left in a taxi at 10:30 a.m. to catch a bus to Montreal. Suddenly, everything had changed, and I had no idea what I was going to do. I tried to think it through, but there were too many variables to even sort out the alternatives. Bob had been my key to a successful Atlantic crossing. His mechanical aptitude, physical strength and confidence were major assets at sea. He was intimately familiar with *Alice Rose*'s equipment and characteristics. We understood each other and we were comfortable with one another's idiosyncrasies.

Clearly, my best course of action was to continue to Sydney where *Alice Rose* could hunker down beneath a tarpaulin until the following spring. Her winter layover, though initially an unplanned expense, had already become inevitable while we languished in Quebec City. I would have the entire winter to determine what her future would hold.

My enthusiasm for adventure evaporated and my sense of purpose vanished. Trapped in the cabin by maritime drizzle and indecision, I felt only depression. I wasn't ready to abandon my dream of a trans-Atlantic passage, but neither could I imagine how I would pull it off.

It was still raining when Bob left. I thought about the isolation he would feel as he endured the tedious bus ride back to Hamilton. He would have twenty-four hours to contemplate the terrible news he had received. I imagined him staring with unseeing eyes at the river as it whizzed past the coach windows hour after hour.

Hot showers become somewhat of an obsession after a few days of cruising on a small boat, and the quality of the facilities at various ports is a common subject of discussion among crews. Matane's facilities were new, clean and spacious—not superior to Sorel or Sillery, but equal to or better than most along the St. Lawrence.

On the table in the clubroom stood a vase of fragrant, mauve lilac, an indication of the local climate. I was surprised to see a plant that flowered in southern Ontario in April or May in full bloom at Matane on July 15!

Rather than spend the dreary day on the boat, Trisha and I, fending off the rain with umbrellas, walked to a nearby gift shop. We stood before the shop window pondering a display of penguins crafted from painted clamshells. We couldn't comprehend the connection between Matane and penguins, unless of course it had something to do with the air temperature.

"Oh wait," I said, "Of course! They're not penguins. They're just poor depictions of puffins."

A distant shopping mall offered us an escape from the chilling rain, but we found the merchandise limited both in quality and variety. So, at a time when Internet access options were limited, we walked to the town centre to locate the local library. For those seeking Internet access in a francophone environment—especially those who skipped French class in high school!—the French word *librairie* means "bookstore" while the equivalent of "library" is *bibliothèque*. Through trial and error, we eventually located the latter and updated family and friends on our progress. The librarian allotted us thirty minutes on the computer, and while it was sufficient time to read and reply to some of our e-mail, the remainder had to be deferred to another time. The delay would amount to several days as we were about to enter a less populated area of the coast with even fewer services.

Clearly, the three-week window I had scheduled for the 2,200-mile passage to Sydney was inadequate. In addition to our late start and unforeseen equipment failures along our route, there were always things to repair, replace or reorganize, charts and weather to review, and waypoints to enter into our GPS. We seemed always to be trying to catch up. Re-provisioning, showers, laundry, and the ever-present desire to sleep consumed every minute not otherwise allocated, so we found little time for exploration of the communities we visited.

Trisha and I left the *bibliothèque* and came upon a restaurant advertising "seafood, Canadian, Italian and Chinese" food. We chose Chinese. After dinner we hired a taxi to return us to the yacht club in a driving rain.

I wasn't surprised when I awoke on the sixteenth and heard rain on the coach roof. *Alice Rose*'s interior dripped with condensation, and once again we experienced the symptoms of cabin fever. As we slowly organized our environment and ourselves for the day, I noted that the weather forecast for Ste Anne des Monts was slightly better than that for Matane. With as much enthusiasm as I could muster, I embraced the idea of moving on, and at 10 a.m., we retraced our route through the shallow river channel and turned toward the Gulf of St. Lawrence.

Now, without Bob for mechanical support, I listened and wondered if the diesel's *thrumm, thrumm, thrumm* superimposed over the more distinct *clackity clack, clackity clack* was normal. I didn't remember it sounding like that before, and there seemed to be a little more vibration recently. At sea, the auxiliary is of little importance, but in a restricted and heavily used waterway, or while entering or leaving port, our little Alberg yacht relied heavily on her Yanmar. I was relieved when the wind picked up and the engine fell silent.

In three- to four-foot seas and the ever-present rain, we raced before the wind toward Ste Anne des Monts. By midday the weather cleared though in our wake, the sky over Matane remained unchanged. We had, at least temporarily, escaped the constant downpour.

It was after nine o'clock and completely dark when we arrived at Ste Anne des Monts. Every small boat slip in the protected end of the harbour was occupied, so we were forced to tie up to a floating steel dock directly across from the entrance. The incoming swells tossed the dock about, causing the steel to protest loudly with bangs and groans. I staggered over the rocking, grated surface to the shore and made my way to the marina office at the other end of the harbour. There, I went through the ritual of registering before retracing my steps to *Alice Rose* amid the inhospitable darkness. At the time, all I wanted was to climb into my berth, get to sleep, and rise early, so we could depart at first light. Instead, I tossed and turned on the thin edge of sleep. The grumbling steel wailed and clattered mercilessly above the howling wind throughout the night.

July 17 brought another late start.

I was not familiar with the ports beyond Ste Anne des Monts because, at that point, the 2000 Flotilla to Labrador and Newfoundland had turned north to Port Menier on Anticosti Island. I felt my confidence slipping away. It was the exploration aspect of cruising that had initially appealed to me, yet I was beginning to feel apprehensive about the unknown. Trisha and I agreed to put in at Cloridorme to avoid another after-dark arrival. The harbour had been described to us by Helen of *Fly By Night* a couple of days earlier as having a new floating dock for small craft, and based on the chart, the port appeared to offer good protection from the prevailing southwest wind.

By midday when the wind eased to a whisper, we lowered the sails and started the engine. Ten minutes later, the wind returned; up went the sails. The wind often played with us like that. It was frustrating, but in the end, we were happy to have escaped the annoying, monotonous throbbing of our diesel engine.

Just prior to Cap de la Madeleine, Trisha went below to prepare dinner while I reclined lazily on the port cockpit seat. Seconds later, a great rush of air on the port side startled me awake. I turned in time to see a blow-hole and a shiny black surface sliding into the water a mere ten feet from the cockpit. Completely unprepared, I uttered a loud and inappropriate exclamation and summoned Trisha on deck with a shout. In retrospect, perhaps I should have whispered because we never saw the whale resurface, and I'm afraid I might have inadvertently discouraged its return. A Yacht Club de Quebec member had told us that whales sometimes swim alongside small boats, but I hadn't really expected to witness that behaviour and certainly not *that* close. Though the entire experience lasted only three or four seconds, the image of the black giant's smooth back is indelibly burned into my memory.

We sailed into Cloridorme at 9:30 p.m.—in the dark! Again, we registered with the harbour manager, paid sixteen dollars for our little piece of dock, and fell exhausted into our berths after another long day on the water. Like many others, this village would go unexplored. It appeared we would never have time left at the end of the day if we didn't get an early morning start.

Determined to make July 18 a short day on the water, we rose early and sailed out of Cloridorme at 7:30 a.m. As I backed away from the dock, the bow swung toward a piling. *Alice Rose* lurched as the primary bow roller slammed hard against the piling, bending the anchor's three-eighth-inch, stainless steel retaining pin.

With the wind directly over the stern, the foresail tended to back or collapse. Our normally reliable wind-vane steering required frequent minor adjustments to maintain a downwind heading. As a result, Trisha took the helm for much of the morning and to our delight we arrived at Riviére-au-Renard just after noon under a clear sky. It was a welcome change from the previous few days and went a long way toward lifting the dark cloud we had been under since Matane.

As we approached a vacant slip to tie up, a middle-aged woman in a miniskirt and high heels hurried onto the dock to take our bow line. Her cascading hair and generous use of make-up appeared strangely out of place on a fishing-port dock. This time, after registering, we found ample time to shower and roam casually through the village. The little community appeared to be lost in the 1940s aside from a few dozen modern cars and a totally unexpected chip wagon. The smell of French fries made our mouths water, so we placed our order, sprinkled the sizzling chips with malt vinegar and salt, and sat at a picnic table savouring every mouth-burning bite.

Riviére-au-Renard's mid-afternoon temperature peaked at seventeen degrees Celsius. With some surprise, we noted the community's tiny, black-sand beach was littered with sunbathers. I could only imagine the endless, dreary winters that induced a population to lay out their beach towels on such a cool afternoon.

Though the dock was comfortable and the harbour secure, there wasn't much to see aside from the cluster of rafted fishing boats that clogged the harbour. We tucked in for the night amid thrumming diesel engines and glaring work lights. No human activity had been apparent on the dock throughout the afternoon and evening, so we concluded the diesels were supporting on-board refrigeration for the catch. The brilliant lights appeared entirely pointless.

We went to sleep with the expectation that the next day would be another short run to L'Anse-à-Beaufils. There, we would gorge ourselves on relaxation and refreshing sleep before the day-and-a-half passage to the Îles de la Madeleine.

In the middle of the night, I awakened to a shrill, irritating siren, presumably an indication that one of the fishing vessels was taking on water. No one responded, and the siren continued to wail, making sleep impossible. I rose, dressed, and prepared for our departure. By 5:30 a.m., the harbour and the persistent siren were receding along with *Alice Rose*'s wake. Still stiff with morning aches, we motored out into the windless Gulf of St. Lawrence.

Within minutes, a dense fog swallowed our little sloop. For the remainder of the day, we groped blindly along an imaginary line connecting the waypoints that I had entered into our GPS the previous evening. Our radar displayed the positions of anonymous vessels and coastal features on its circular screen, the centre of which represented our location. Every two seconds, the fading image refreshed in a sweeping circular motion. The digital depth sounder continually displayed the depth of the water under our keel.

Years earlier, I learned that the first rule of flying IFR (instrument flight rules) is "Trust your instruments." The same adage applies to a vessel in zero visibility, though in both situations it's easier said than done. My tangible world consisted of a circular patch of rippled swells within a translucent white dome. With no reference of scale, I could be sure of nothing, not even the size of the circle. It could have been anything from a couple of hundred feet to two hundred yards.

Cap des Rosier Lighthouse and Percé Rock slid by the starboard rail unseen. Even on radar, their iconic identities were obscured by the ragged coastal clutter of reflected microwaves. The entire day was featureless, tedious and nerve-wracking.

As *Alice Rose* entered the two-mile gap between Percé Rock and Île Bonaventure, an anonymous blip appeared in the bottom-right of the radar screen. The target, most likely a commercial fishing vessel, maintained a converging heading, moving gradually toward us over the next hour or so. I assumed her radar was operative, but as a precaution, I altered our course to port and slowed to an idle to allow the unseen vessel to pass safely ahead of us.

We reached our final waypoint just outside of the port of L'Anse-a-Beaufils about 2 p.m. on July 19. I put the engine in neutral and peered shoreward into the grey. Neither Trisha nor I were able to see the outer marker depicted on the chart, so I plotted and entered an additional waypoint nearer to the harbour entrance. After a couple of stressful minutes of edging gingerly toward it with one eye on the depth sounder's display, the radar presented the sought-after buoy as a black speck. We crept toward it until, with the marker visible off our bow, we could just distinguish another, and beyond it, the shadowy silhouette of the breakwater.

Having cautiously made our way into the harbour, we came alongside the extreme outer end of a metal-sheathed, concrete pier, five to six feet higher than our deck. I climbed a rusty ladder to secure our lines.

Trisha and I went ashore to explore the village, but after probing a short distance into two or three foggy roadways we abandoned the idea. We did, however, stumble on a convenience store or "deppaneaur" as they are known in Quebec. We purchased bread and milk and stopped in at a bar and bistro on the pier before returning to the boat. I ordered the typically French Canadian salmon-and-potato pie. It proved suitable fare on a cold and foggy afternoon on the Gaspé Peninsula, though I've never been inclined to order it again.

Sailors, particularly skippers, are afflicted with a sixth sense that appears at times to be supernatural, though I'm sure there's a logical explanation for the phenomena. On many occasions, both before and after my visit to L'Anse-à-Beaufils, I sensed environmental changes that a superstitious person might consider magic. During the blackest hours of the early morning of July 20, I awoke and *felt* that something was not right in the universe. I lay awake for a couple of minutes before the feeling compelled me to take action. I climbed out of the cabin into the cockpit, unsure what I was expecting to find in the dark. The deck, a full five or six feet below the pier a few hours earlier, was now level with the pier. With five extra feet of fore and aft lines in the water, the vessel was free to drift away from the pier into the path of passing vessels. I cursed the god of tides, rigged crossed fore and aft spring lines to allow for the rise and fall of water levels, and crawled clumsily back into my sleeping bag.

We spent the following day in L'Anse-à-Beaufils doing our laundry, resting and preparing for the crossing to the Îles de la Madeleine.

Most ports included unlimited hot showers in their docking fees, but in L'Anse-à-Beaufils a little black box gobbled up our dollars at the rate of one every two minutes, including the few precious seconds it took to adjust the water's temperature. The arrangement was more than slightly inconvenient for a dirty old sailor with a ten-dollar bill. The only other coin-operated showers we had encountered were in Rimouski where a single dollar assured us eight minutes of body-drenching bliss.

Yet another oddity of this port's facilities was that the women's toilets were accessible only by walking through the men's washroom and showers—some sort of architectural afterthought, I suppose. Imagine me standing at the urinal, completely oblivious to local custom, when a woman unexpectedly walked in through the open doorway and passed by as if the porcelain and I were invisible. My mind whirred with possible explanations, but it didn't occur to me at the time that she had no alternative if she wanted to access the ladies' toilet or showers. Later, I wondered how long it had taken her to find the necessary courage the first time she had to pee.

Who the hell came up with that idea? Perhaps I'm not particularly worldly, but it seemed a bizarre arrangement nonetheless.

When the fog dissipated, I could see that most pleasure craft in the harbour were rafted to one another or to one of the numerous fishing boats tied to the pier. We were lucky to have secured an unoccupied space at the extreme seaward end of the pier. Across the harbour, a construction crew worked on the new marina which was scheduled to open the following summer.

With insufficient wind to warrant raising her sails, *Alice Rose* motored out of L'Anse-à-Beaufils at 3:30 a.m. to facilitate our arrival at the Îles de la Madeleine in daylight. Thirty minutes into our passage, we encountered yet another bank of impenetrable fog. Two and a half hours later, a light west-by-southwest wind began to strengthen, the fog lifted, and I raised our sails.

Trisha abandoned her warm berth, joining me on deck just as *Alice Rose* settled into a five-and-a-half-knot beam reach. Together, we shared the creation of yet another memory as our tiny yacht surged toward Harve Aubert on the early morning westerly. For most of the day, we enjoyed a great sail with the breeze backing slightly and gradually to the southwest.

Because our wind vane steering system had been lovingly designed and built by Peter Tietz, we affectionately referred to the apparatus as "Mrs Tietz." Of all the equipment on board, she had proven to be the most valuable and most reliable. As long as the wind direction remained constant, Mrs Tietz ensured absolutely accurate automatic steering, thereby freeing our minds to focus on other tasks such as navigation, maintenance, and meal preparation. Though my concern for my wife and my boat prevented me from sleeping during the passage, my confidence in our wind vane steering at least allowed me to lie down on the cockpit seat and close my eyes while Trisha took her turn at the helm.

The sky remained clear into the evening, but eventually the wind dropped away to nothing, forcing us to stow our sails, disconnect Mrs Tietz, and start the engine. With the electric auto helm out of service, I was compelled to steer throughout the night. Fatigue invaded my consciousness and dragged me toward sleep on several occasions, but by then, Trisha was once more tucked snugly into her berth, and I couldn't bring myself to wake her. Periodically, she appeared in the darkened companionway to inquire if I needed anything. On one occasion, I gratefully accepted a cup of hot chocolate, answering in the affirmative when asked if I was all right.

My eyes moved routinely from the radar screen to the depth sounder, then to the GPS and finally to the ship's compass. The process was repetitive and hypnotizing. At some point in the long night, about twenty-two hours after our departure, my eyes locked on the compass needle and I stared in disbelief. Inexplicably, our heading, which had a few seconds earlier read one-three-four degrees, now indicated three-zero-eight degrees. In my world of featureless black, I stood squinting into the glaring display, unable to comprehend the discrepancy. At first, though I knew something was wrong, I simply couldn't figure out what had happened. I struggled to interpret the implications of the disparate numbers. Then, through the fog of my fatigue, I understood—*I had fallen asleep, standing at the wheel with my eyes wide open.* How long had I been in that strange state of unconsciousness?

Whatever period of time had passed, it must have been substantial. During those lost minutes, *Alice Rose* had turned 174 degrees, ultimately sailing into her own wake. I spun the wheel southward and watched the numbers decline through 270, 240, 210, 180 and 150. I eased onto the one-three-four degree course we had charted, then shook my head in disbelief.

Twenty-four hours had not yet passed when I began observing white flashes on the horizon. At irregular intervals, lights appeared briefly in my peripheral vision and vanished as I turned toward them. Each time, I focused on the light's approximate location to await its reappearance, earnestly believing it was that of a vessel or a distant lighthouse. Time after time, the passing minutes failed to produce additional sightings in the area. Eventually, I discounted the white apparitions as mere hallucinations, manifestations of sleep deprivation.

The low, wind-swept Îles de la Madeleine first appeared as faint shadows in the distant haze. Again and again, their profiles emerged and dissolved, then reappeared only to fade into the shifting, distant mists. Not until we were three or four miles from their coasts did they take on aspects of a third dimension.

Trisha and I were somewhat alarmed when what looked like a small open boat with a single occupant appeared over the bow. The featureless shape was moving southward across our heading at a substantial speed, and in the water behind the boat, there appeared to be three or four people. Curiously, the bobbing heads were keeping up with the boat as if being swept along by an unseen current. As we closed the distance, relief and amazement replaced our apprehension when we realized the heads were in fact seal heads. What had at first looked like an open boat with a single occupant was in fact an additional member of the pod of seals. It had climbed onto the floating wall of a small, clapboard building to lounge in the sun. By the time Trisha retrieved her camera, the seal had noted our approach and cautiously slipped into the security of the sea's fast moving current.

I found the channel leading to the lagoon at Harve Aubert rather shallow though well marked, and by 1:30 p.m. on the twenty-second, we were safely anchored in sixteen feet of water. A balmy twenty-knot wind played abstract tunes in our rigging. The air was noticeably warmer than anything we had experienced since leaving Yacht Club de Quebec.

To the north, a thin collection of brightly painted frame buildings formed the remote settlement of Harve Aubert. The bay was completely surrounded by low, grassy sand banks and small dunes, rendering the water's surface calm though rippled by the brisk wind. *Alice Rose*'s mast and hull responded to the southerly wind with a gentle, sleep-inducing rocking motion. Exhausted by the passage, we lay together in the V-berth and spiralled quickly into a coma-like sleep.

CHAPTER SEVENTEEN
Sprint to the Finish

Still dazed and exhausted, Trisha and I awoke briefly, ate something forgettable, and without even checking the time, crawled back into the security of our warm berth. The better part of the twenty-third of July had elapsed when we finally crawled out of the V-berth to resume our lives. A full twenty-four hours had passed since dropping our twenty-two pound CQR onto the sandy harbour bottom.

The remainder of the day was dedicated to rest and recuperation, including a most welcome cockpit bath. Sitting on the cockpit sole, I rubbed a bar of soap into my skin while my wife poured the Gulf of St. Lawrence over my head, one bucket at a time.

Trisha and I, anxious to complete our odyssey, abandoned our plan to go ashore to explore the islands. While in Quebec City, we had looked forward to experiencing the island culture, but now we seemed inexplicably drawn to the finish line. A month of hurrying toward Sydney had tarnished my dream of leisurely cruising the world. Still, I suspected that I would one day regret the decision.

With an Atlantic crossing off the table, I just wanted to go home. Perhaps Ontario's warm summer breezes would soothe my bruised enthusiasm. I untied one of the yellow jerry cans we had stowed on deck and, steadying myself on the narrow deck beside the cabin, carefully poured diesel fuel through the deck fitting into our tank. Then, I went below to plot the final leg of our journey to the Dobson Yacht Club in Sydney Harbour, Nova Scotia.

Making sense of the maritime weather report was hopeless. First, I was familiar with the geography of the Great Lakes and easily recognized the areas to which weather broadcasts referred. In the Maritimes, however, I had no idea which of the referenced geographic areas applied to our route.

Second, I had become accustomed to Ontario's MAFOR system (*Marine Fore*cast). It presented weather forecasts for a twenty-four hour period using numeric codes. Each number in a series of six digits identified a specific period of time, a wind direction, a wind speed, and so on. It was a simple matter to work out the meaning of each number after we had written down the six digits for the area in which we were sailing. This maritime forecast was, however, presented in plain English, spoken rather quickly, and immediately followed by a French language version. I had difficulty keeping up with and interpreting the report because it dealt with numerous aspects of the weather over various periods of the day and night for

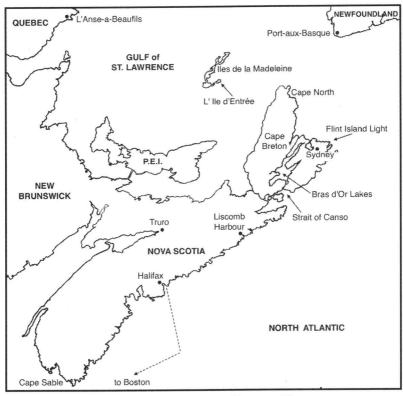

Map 14. L'Anse-à-Beaufils to Halifax

areas I couldn't readily identify.

In the end, I called Sydney Coast Guard Radio to request clarification and found the radio operator both willing and helpful. Rested, and armed with a reliable forecast, we resumed our eastward passage. *Alice Rose* would round Île d'Entrée to the northeast and then turn east-southeast toward Cape North on the north-eastern tip of Nova Scotia. Once off the cape, she would be steered southward along Cape Breton's east coast to Sydney.

The anchor chain rattled noisily into the chain locker at 6:45 a.m. on July 24. I secured the CQR with a stout anchor pin, and within minutes, *Alice Rose* was threading her way through the narrow channel toward the gulf. We hauled the main and jenny taut to take full advantage of a brisk southwest wind over our stern and followed the northwestern shore of a low sand spit for two or three miles. Our course soon put us in the lee of the only high island in the archipelago. Île d'Entrée's lumpy bulk forced moisture-laden winds skyward where they condensed into clouds that periodically shrouded her 570-foot peak. As we emerged from the shelter of the weathered, green island, short, steep waves and twenty-five knot gusts unexpectedly hammered us from the south. *Alice Rose* heeled over until her port deck was awash. With Trisha urgently assigned to the helm, I struggled to douse the jenny and reef the main. Within the hour, the wind eased enough to allow us to shake out the reef and sail under a full main and jib once more.

Threatening, gloomy clouds and haze filled in astern as we pursued the brilliant blue sky over the bow. To my surprise, Cape Breton appeared above the horizon from more than forty miles out. I watched with a degree of impatience while its silhouette grew in height over the next eight hours. As we neared the coast, the wind eased further and eventually died altogether. For the last time in 2004, we lowered *Alice Rose*'s sails and fired up the auxiliary.

The Yanmar propelled us steadily toward Cape North ahead of an ominous black squall line, but its efforts were no match for the swiftly moving weather system. Within a few minutes, a cold blast of north wind hit us. I was feeling lazy after yet another long day on deck, and the sun was low, so I didn't bother to raise the sails. It would be dark soon and the potential for strong winds was high.

We rounded Cape North at sunset and motored southward, along the coast of Cape Breton, toward the loom of Sydney's lights, still several hours distant. The long night was memorable only for its tediousness and the bitterly cold wind.

The early morning hours of July 25 provided me with ample time to awaken from my dream. Reality had firmly established itself by the time I secured our dock lines at Dobson Yacht Club. At 9:15 a.m. Atlantic Time, I made the season's final entry in *Alice Rose*'s logbook. Since leaving the dock at Fifty Point, our Alberg had journeyed 1,178 nautical miles, and still, the nearest of the Azores lay unseen beyond the horizon—a further 1,330 miles. Though we were a mere seventy-six nautical miles short of the halfway mark, Flores, our first foreign port of entry, remained elusive.

Both Trisha and I had been accumulating stress and fatigue for weeks. We hadn't seen our children nor our grandchildren since leaving Hamilton, and we were more than ready to go home.

Somewhere between Matane and Sydney, I compiled a list of options from which I would have to choose before returning to Nova Scotia the following summer. I could undertake the Atlantic crossing as originally planned with the assistance of an as yet unidentified crew member; I could return *Alice Rose* to Lake Ontario via New York City's Hudson River and the Erie Canal; I could cruise the reportedly beautiful Bras d'Or Lakes of Nova Scotia for a season while I pondered my options; I could arrange to ship *Alice Rose* home by truck; or I could sail southward via the eastern seaboard's Intracoastal Waterway. In any event, I would be compelled to make a decision by the end of the winter of 2004–2005.

As summer tilted toward autumn, Trisha and I researched alternatives for our trip home. One-way vehicle rentals, reasonably priced and readily available in the U.S., were impossible in Canada, thanks to $1,000 drop fees. Train and plane fares from Sydney were more expensive than a week at an all-inclusive resort in the Caribbean. In disbelief, I hired a taxi to drive us to North Sydney where I purchased two one-way coach tickets to Toronto for less than $200 each.

Predictably, the ride home was long and uncomfortable, but unlike my experience of four years earlier, I was not alone. Trisha and I chatted, dozed and occasionally snored throughout the thirty-hour-plus jostle homeward.

A couple of days after arriving home, I hitched *Alice Rose*'s steel cradle—modified and licensed as a trailer—to my van and drove to Cape Breton where I arranged to have the boat hauled out for storage in the boatyard. Winterized and wrapped snugly in blue poly tarps, *Alice Rose* braced herself for winter's maritime winds and relentless salt spray. It was difficult to leave her there to face the icy North Atlantic's fury by herself, but I was running out of time and money, and could imagine no practical alternative.

There would be no Atlantic crossing in 2004, and possibly none at all for *Alice Rose* and her skipper. A late start, a number of costly equipment failures, and the loss of a crucial crew member had conspired to defeat me. My enthusiasm, diminished by physical and emotional fatigue, had been battered by the worst weather in a dozen summers.

I looked over the windswept North Atlantic and realized that dreams, like dreamers, get old. I wondered if mine could somehow survive. I had hoped to sail among warm tropical islands some day, but found myself unable to escape the chill Atlantic coast of Canada.

CHAPTER EIGHTEEN
The Resurrection

It was June 1, 2005 and time to bring *Alice Rose* home to her port of registry. She had been resting passively beneath her blue tarpaulin in Sydney's Dobson Yacht Club since her arduous early-summer passage of the previous year.

I had agonized over my options throughout the winter, clinging desperately to my dream even as it slipped from my grasp. I wanted to sail to the Azores, then Britain and eventually southward to the tropics—but not without Bob. I had groomed him from the beginning, imparting everything I had learned about sailing, navigation and seamanship. We had been friends for forty-five years and got along well. He knew *Alice Rose*'s mechanical and electrical systems intimately, having worked on them as well as sailing on her for several years.

I had been unsuccessful in my search for a suitable replacement for Bob, but there were other considerations, too. One was the ongoing cost of keeping the dream alive. For several years, I had been redirecting a significant portion of my retirement income toward reaching my goal. Thousands of dollars had gone into modifications and equipment, and every year marina fees and winter storage added to the cost. Sailing wasn't Trisha's first choice of vacation options, though she had been more than patient while I pursued distant horizons year after year.

I was, for a time, tempted to spend the summer cruising Nova Scotia's Bra d'Or Lakes or sailing to Florida via the Intracoastal Waterway. Either alternative could be accomplished without Bob's involvement, but would amount to little more than deferring the decision.

No, I had to be pragmatic. I had to bring *Alice Rose* home, sell her to someone else with a dream of their own, and recover as much of my investment as I could. And so *Alice Rose* and I began our final journey together, one that was not without its share of unanticipated events.

A word to the wise: Whether it's your first voyage or your last, when you take into account all the variables associated with sailing, arriving *anywhere* at a specific time is a challenge. Sometimes it's simply impossible. Often schedules are disrupted even before departure. My plan called for Bob and I to sail out of Dobson Yacht Club at 4 p.m. on June 6. That assumption proved incredibly naive.

We left Hamilton at 3 a.m. to avoid Toronto's morning rush hour and drove eastward beneath a crescent moon. Among the tools, provisions, and equipment in the van were a dozen new class B flares and a replacement Raymarine autopilot, both essential to our homeward passage.

Alice Rose's return voyage would take us around Northern Head and Flint Island Light to Louisburg before skirting the southern coast of Nova Scotia to Cape Sable. Following a stopover and a crew change at Halifax, she would make a four-day crossing of the Gulf of Maine to Boston. There, my son, David, would join us for a coastal sail through Cape Cod Canal, Buzzards Bay, and Long Island Sound. New York City's East River would lead us to the southern tip of Manhattan where we would enter the Hudson River and follow it inland to Albany, New York. From there, the Erie Canal would guide us to Oswego on Lake Ontario. At that point, still 165 miles downwind of Hamilton, I planned to sail across the lake to the Canadian shore before turning for home in familiar waters.

Bob and I drove over the St. John River on the "World's Longest Covered Bridge" at Hartland, New Brunswick, enjoyed a late dinner at Mexicali Rosa's in Fredericton, and registered at Moncton's Beacon Light Motel a few minutes before midnight. After twenty hours on the road, sleep came easily.

In the morning, we showered with the knowledge that the yacht club showers, though adequate, did not offer the luxuries afforded by the average motel. Somewhat fatigued from our previous day's drive, yet eager to put the journey behind us, we continued eastward. I drove into the boat yard at 4 p.m. on June the second and immediately began removing the web of lines that had for ten months secured *Alice Rose*'s now shredded tarpaulin.

It was just a coincidence that our departure was scheduled for D-Day. We had precisely four days to prepare before embarking on our homeward journey, ample time if all went according to plan. It didn't!

I entered the sloop's cool, damp interior to find that insufficient ventilation and the resulting condensation had created a perfect environment for black mould. Much of the paint on the V-berth deck-head had peeled off, and the teak and holly cabin sole in the head was sopping wet and delaminating. We devoted the remainder of the late afternoon and most of the evening to cleaning and drying the cabin's interior. Ultimately, hunger and dusk drove us into nearby North Sydney in search of a hot meal.

When Bob and I arrived at the North Star Inn late in the evening, we found the dining room had already closed. As we set out in pursuit of an alternative restaurant, we stumbled on Rollie's Wharf a short distance away. From a member of the staff, we learned that local fiddlers gathered at Rollie's every Thursday night to play traditional Cape Breton music. What great luck! Twelve fiddles, a piano, a banjo, and a guitar entertained us while we enjoyed a plate of fried scallops for an incredibly low price. We washed the local fare down with cold beer and soaked up the down-home hospitality for a couple of hours before reluctantly returning to the shadows of the boatyard.

Over the next few days, we slept aboard Alice Rose, showered at the yacht club, and drove to Sydney River each morning to pick up our Tim Horton's coffee. Together, we assembled, repaired, installed, and frequently cursed a variety of equipment, ever aware that our departure date was quickly approaching. Each evening, we drove to Sydney or North Sydney for dinner.

At the end of our second day, devoted almost exclusively to ridding the boat's interior of mould and dampness, we quit work in time to enjoy the view of North Sydney's waterfront from the hilltop dining room of the North Star Inn. The tables, adorned with freshly pressed blue cotton tablecloths, were set with sparkling glasses, crisp, white napkins, and carefully polished silverware. The room was cool, quiet and relaxing—a welcome contrast to the dishevelled boatyard where, a few minutes earlier, we had been working in the glare of an unseasonably hot sun.

I spent most of June 4 cleaning the boat's interior while Bob readied *Alice Rose*'s engine and pumps for going to sea. In a demonstration of Nature's power, the pleasant twenty-five-degree Celsius environment in which we had been working was suddenly swept away by a northeast breeze. We traded our T-shirts for sweatshirts and jackets, and endured a chilly eight degrees for the rest of the afternoon. As the unseen sun approached the horizon behind impenetrable cloud-cover, we gathered up our tools, locked the companionway, and drove into Sydney for dinner.

At Joe's Warehouse, Kelly, our waitress, entertained us with her Cape Breton accent and hospitality. Evening dinners quickly became coveted escapes from the drudgery of the boatyard. They provided us with an opportunity to re-assess technical issues, talk about home, and share a laugh or two.

Thirty hours or so before our intended departure, I drove to Sydney River to have two of our four propane tanks re-filled. Then, I stopped at a grocery store for our last minute perishable provisions and returned to the boatyard carrying subs and coffee.

After lunch, we paid the $120 launch fee and waited for the travel-lift and its operator, Robert Etheridge, to arrive. When Robert hoisted *Alice Rose* out of her cradle, he began the travel-lift's turn prematurely, dragging *Alice Rose*'s hull along the aft port cradle post. The waterproof skin of epoxy and gel-coat below the waterline suffered a lengthy and deep scratch. I was not impressed.

Then, as my cherished sailboat hung high above the launch slip, one of the lifting cables jumped the sheave and jammed. Unable to raise or lower the slings, the yard crew argued the merits of various solutions amid the suggestions of opinionated bystanders. In the meantime, the travel-lift's filthy hydraulic oil dripped from a leaky hose connection onto *Alice Rose*'s white deck. My confidence in Etheridge and his equipment waned as he silently surveyed the situation.

Eventually, Robert, a professional truck driver, climbed into his pick-up to retrieve a pair of "come-alongs" from his eighteen-wheeler a couple of miles away.

Alice Rose's enormous weight strained against the come-alongs, as her seven-ton bulk lifted ever-so-slowly off of the forward sling. As the bow rose, much of the vessel's weight was transferred to the other sling, and I expected at any moment to see a chain link part. I imagined the hull crashing heavily onto the slip's sill, several feet below. Finally, in heroic though foolhardy fashion, Etheridge risked a crushed hand by lifting the heavy cable onto the sheave. Minutes later Bob and I stepped aboard, relieved and anxious to move *Alice Rose* to the nearby crane slip. There, we scrubbed the splatters of hydraulic oil from her deck and began preparing her forty-two-foot mast for stepping. Desperate to meet our departure goal, we continued working under the boatyard lights into the late evening.

Early in the morning of June 6, Bob and I stepped the mast with the hand operated mast crane. We carefully adjusted the tension of the stays and shrouds, taped the shroud boots in place, and worked relentlessly to meet our four o'clock deadline. With clevis and cotter pins installed, our vessel began to look her old self again. Nevertheless, countless tasks remained unfinished, and while I was reluctant to admit it to Bob at the time, I didn't really expect to get underway within the next twenty-four hours.

Dan McCarthy, a director of the yacht club at the time, proposed that we sail through the Bras d'Or Lakes instead of rounding Cape Breton and following the coast to the southern end of the Strait of Canso. He assured me that the inland route would be shorter, and as a local, he garnered my trust. A preliminary calculation indicated the Bras d'Or Lake option was in fact about twenty percent shorter though I wondered whether it would provide favourable winds. I made a quick trip to Sydney Ship Supply in Whitney Pier to purchase charts for the alternative route at a cost of almost $100. All of North Sydney's restaurants were closed by the time we finished working, so Bob and I settled for Kentucky Fried Chicken.

It was raining when I drove to Sydney River on June 7 to fill three jerry cans with diesel fuel. They would be secured on deck to increase our cruising range from two to five days. I also stopped at a local bank to withdraw some cash. As I thanked the teller, I slipped my travelling wallet, containing my passport and more than a thousand dollars in Canadian and U.S. currency, into the jacket pocket of my rain gear.

I returned to the boat, and a few minutes later, as I bent over to fasten the flag halyard shackle to a stanchion base, I heard a loud "SLAP!" Absorbed by the task at hand, I snapped the shackle in place before looking around to determine the cause of the sound.

My eye was drawn to a tan-coloured rectangle floating on the water's surface—*MY WALLET!*

Comprehension turned to panic, as I threw myself heavily onto the deck and reached blindly into the narrow gap between the hull and the seawall. I snatched the wallet deftly off the surface, rolled onto my back and, imagining the impact its loss would have had on our plans, took a deep, deep breath. Had I not looked for the source of the noise, or had the wallet landed on its edge, I would never have known where it had gone. Clearly, it was a very lucky escape from a careless mistake!

Our new embarkation target, now twenty-four hours beyond the original, came and went. Bob and I reviewed the list of remaining chores, a small number of which were deferred or simply deemed non-essential. With my preparation plan and my credibility in tatters, I told Bob to aim for midnight and suggested we then sleep until 3 a.m. before getting underway. Both of us were exhausted from the constant effort of preparing for the month-long passage. Bob fell into his berth at 11 p.m. while I finished a couple of last minute tasks, and at 1:50 a.m., I too collapsed onto my berth. A mere fifty minutes later, the clock's alarm rattled us awake, and we prepared to get underway.

At 3 a.m., we started the engine, slipped our dock lines in a light rain, and eased away from the sea wall. Once free of the crane slip, I engaged the auto helm, and we stumbled about the deck, stowing fenders and dock lines in the dark. Our Yanmar purred passively as we moved over the inky water of the harbour. Though our passage was just beginning, *Alice Rose*'s crew was already impaired by fatigue.

We raised the jenny and shut down the engine. *Alice Rose* zigzagged downwind, gliding from waypoint to waypoint at a respectable four knots. We made our way out of the twisting south arm of Sydney Harbour—thirty-five long hours behind my carefully calculated schedule.

When the wind eased, we raised the main, and every sailor knows what happened next. While gale force winds raged on the Bras d'Or Lakes just six hours away, the wind in Sydney Harbour ceased to blow. Down came the sails.

At 4:45 a.m. the wind returned, enabling us to sail continuously for almost five hours. During the first couple of hours, I deleted the original route from our global positioning systems, hurriedly replacing it with waypoints to and through Cape Breton's salt-water lakes. It goes without saying that navigation should, whenever possible, be completed well in advance of a passage to ensure appropriate time for a careful review of all the data. The calculation of each position and its entry into a GPS demands great care as absolute accuracy is essential to the safety of the vessel and its crew. During the early morning hours of June 8, though every waypoint was accurately located in terms of latitude and longitude, I inadvertently made three keying errors while hurriedly entering the data. These mistakes became apparent and somewhat distressing later in the day as the GPS directed us toward positions on shore and just beyond shoals that—thank the sea gods!—were clearly indicated on our charts.

Because a minute of latitude is equal to a nautical mile, my entry of "44.54 minutes" instead of "45.44 minutes" mislocated one of our waypoints about a mile south of our intended position. I cringed when I thought about the disaster to which those errors might have led on a moonless night or in fog.

My obsession with maintaining the schedule also resulted in a careless disregard for the tides at the entrance to the Bras d'Or Lakes. Not only had I overlooked how narrow the opening was, I failed to appreciate the strength of the tide's current. Yet another stroke of good luck put us into a tidal rip that propelled us *into* the lakes at 8.8 knots. Had we arrived as the tide was ebbing, our speed over the bottom would have been reduced to a fraction of a knot. Unknown to me at the time, that precise scenario would occur in New York City twelve days later.

Periodically, clusters of painted floats slid silently by the hull, betraying the presence of submerged lobster pots. With a subtle zigzag motion, *Alice Rose* danced safely through them beneath a grey, maritime overcast.

Though the late spring temperatures remained rather cool by Ontario standards, the sun emerged in mid afternoon and warmed our faces. As time passed, the lakes' shores gradually converged, providing a little shelter from the chill wind. In response to the narrowing, winding route, we secured the sails and enjoyed noticeably milder conditions while motoring toward our destination. I took the helm and Bob went below, where he opened a can of tomato soup and heated it for dinner. We lounged lazily in the cockpit, consuming our steaming bowls of soup as *Alice Rose* crept toward St. Peter's Canal.

Just prior to 8 p.m., the canal and tidal lock connecting the Bras d'Or Lakes to the Strait of Canso came into view. I radioed the swing bridge guarding the canal entrance several times but received no reply. Later, we learned from the skipper of another boat that, prior to mid-June, the bridge is unattended after 4:30 p.m. Disappointed, we tied to the canal's approach wall for the night. Though we were destined to lose the time we had just gained by taking the inland route, I was grateful for the opportunity to sleep for a few hours.

Bob and I reorganized, relaxed, and charted a course to a waypoint in the Atlantic at the eastern outlet of the Strait of Canso. Then we slept soundly until 6 a.m.

Before the dense morning mist had cleared, a Cape Breton sailor, whose boat had been berthed at the wall on our arrival, returned from the local Tim Horton's with a coffee for each of us. It was a simple gesture, but one that I appreciated greatly. The hot liquid soothed my soul as it trickled down my throat. A pattern seemed to be emerging; every time an obstacle threatened my enthusiasm, a serendipitous event restored my morale.

By 8:30 a.m., *Alice Rose* had motored beyond the swing bridge into the lock and was about to enter the southern portion of the Strait of Canso. We exchanged small talk with the lock crew as they closed the gates behind us and opened those ahead. Visibility was good as we motored southward into a light morning breeze. A long, gentle ground swell betrayed the mighty Atlantic ahead. When finally, we reached our offshore waypoint well beyond Cape Canso, I set the wind vane to steer us southwest toward Halifax. The day passed without incident and we slept in turns.

At 10:15 p.m., Bob awakened me to advise that a westbound ship was overtaking us. The freighter was within a half-mile, and though the ship's officer was undoubtedly competent and aware of our presence, I altered course to starboard until the vessel had passed and suggested Bob go below to get some sleep. An hour later, a second ship approached on our port bow, passing within three-quarters of a nautical mile. It appeared we were on the edge of a well-used shipping route, so we would need to remain alert.

I peered into the green displays of the GPS, depth sounder, and radar in turn, while similarly coloured phosphorescent plankton slid sternward along the hull. Cold and uncomfortable, I longed for a nap and occasionally closed my eyes—just for a moment. The night passed slowly until Bob relieved me just before three in the morning.

Forty-five minutes prior to the end of Bob's first four-hour watch on June 10, the GPS called for a dramatic change of course toward the coast. With no formal training in marine navigation and complete trust in my navigation and plotting skills, he complied. No crew member wants to awaken the skipper unnecessarily.

For the next three-quarters of an hour, we sailed landward toward a waypoint that had been part of our abandoned offshore route—*before we opted for the Bras d'Or Lake route.* Its purpose had been to guide us into Liscombe Harbour for our first anchorage after leaving Sydney Harbour. We had, however, slept well the previous night during our unplanned layover at the canal wall, and I had simply overlooked removing the waypoint from our route.

When I came on watch and became aware of the diversion, I simply steered a reciprocal course for forty-five minutes before resuming our passage to Halifax, now within sixteen hours or so. That loss of about ninety minutes resulted in a later arrival off Halifax, complicating *Alice Rose*'s entry into the city's harbour in complete darkness.

Throughout the morning, the wind picked up out of the southwest, forcing us to sail close-hauled. *Alice Rose* fought to maintain our heading, constantly pinching the wind to avoid the shallow coastal waters southeast of the distant harbour entrance.

As another day passed routinely, the sky darkened and the wind shifted to the west. Just prior to ten in the evening, we found that we could no longer maintain our heading which was now almost directly into the wind. Compelled to tack southward—*away from Halifax*—in an effort to make the harbour's outer marker, we changed course. Anxious to reach the security of the port, I succumbed to my own impatience, abandoning the tack too soon.

Subsequently, we missed our waypoint and found ourselves crossing a twenty-two-foot shoal guarding the deep-water channel. While the water's depth was more than ample with respect to our keel, the shoal's effect on the surface was unmistakable as we were tossed about roughly in steep chop.

Once in the channel, our environment changed dramatically. No longer alone in the night, *Alice Rose* shared the busy waterway with numerous vessels of all types. Their lights, and those lining the shore, combined into a dazzling confusion of flickering colour. The air grew noticeably warmer in the harbour's Northwest Arm. Minutes later, we came alongside a dock where a guitarist and the clinking of beer bottles accompanied the vocals of an enthusiastic group of young couples. When we called out to them, asking the location of the Armdale Yacht Club, a young lady in a bathing suit ran to the end of the dock to direct us. It was midnight when we located the club's gas dock and secured our lines.

There were no lights in the clubhouse, and the entire facility appeared abandoned. I climbed a hill to the showers and found the door unlocked, so we cleaned up before crawling into our sea-damp berths. I thoroughly enjoyed sleeping in my shorts, instead of the bulky survival suit I had worn on the Atlantic.

I awoke refreshed on June 11, and relieved that the coldest sailing was now behind us, I looked forward to a day's rest ashore. We had just crammed $102 worth of diesel fuel into our tank and jerry cans when Mark Graham, a high school chum and resident of the Halifax area, drove into the boatyard. He arranged for *Alice Rose*'s slip and helped Bob and I spread her damp contents on the deck to dry in the late spring sun. Then he drove us to a nearby chandlery to pick up a few replacement parts before continuing on to the bus depot. There, I purchased Bob's one-way ticket to North Sydney as he had agreed to retrieve my van and tow the boat's cradle back to Ontario. By the time Mark and I had sailed half way to Boston, Bob would have the van and the cradle safely back in Hamilton.

The Halifax to Boston passage was to be my most challenging sailing experience to date. To begin with, Mark and I would be isolated from the world for four days—longer than on any previous occasion—and I confess I was slightly anxious about facing the challenge. We would be entirely dependent on our own resources with little hope of immediate rescue in the event of an emergency. The passage would provide me with a taste of what it might have been like to cross the Atlantic.

Though we didn't expect to need them, our parachute flares and life raft were reminders of the risks mariners routinely face on offshore passages. Before leaving Hamilton the previous spring, I had decided we could manage without buying an $800 emergency position indicating radio beacon. Now, I wondered if I had made the right decision. In spite of the risks, real and imagined, we enjoyed the sense of adventure as we prepared for our departure.

My Halifax holiday ended at 8:15 a.m. on June 12; *Alice Rose* and I were back on schedule.

As Mark's wife, Mary, waved goodbye from the Armdale Yacht Club dock, I thought of Trisha and wished she too could have been there to see us off. I took comfort in the fact that I would see her in Boston in four days.

CHAPTER NINETEEN
The Circle of Light

Most view the sea as two-dimensional, perceiving it in varying shades of blue, green, and grey, but the reality is far more complex. The unseen world beneath its textured surface is home to hundreds of thousands of species. Mark and I were reminded of that shortly after 1 p.m., at 44° 20.9' north latitude and 63° 32.1' west longitude where we briefly glimpsed a breeching northbound whale. I wondered what other unsuspected wonders lurked beneath *Alice Rose*'s hull.

Soon after sighting the whale, we entered an impenetrable fog bank.

On the darkest of nights, though navigation lights reveal the presence of other vessels, their speed and distance can be difficult to judge, so passing ships demand one's full attention. Fog is another matter entirely. It renders navigation lights useless at all hours of the night or day. For all intents and purposes, *Alice Rose* and her crew became fog-blind on June 12, entirely dependent on sound and her electronic instruments.

A couple of hours into the eerie meringue that enveloped our little yacht, we faced our first close encounter. Fifteen degrees off our starboard bow, an unseen ship steamed toward us, ominously sounding her throaty horn every two minutes. We complied with marine law by responding with our shrill, handheld air horn. On a clear day, our passing would have been routine and forgettable, but interpreting the encounter through sound and a blip on our five-inch circular display tested my nerves. I knew the fast-moving phantom would be aware of our precise location, speed, and course, so I deliberately maintained our heading while carefully monitoring our relative positions on the radar. The ship's crew were professionals; they knew what they were doing. I thought of the fog-bound encounter between the *Storstad* and the *Empress of Ireland*. It was essential that I avoid sudden or indecisive course changes that put us in her path or introduced confusion about our intentions. I felt a little like William Tell's son, waiting for the arrow to pierce the apple on his head; I mustn't flinch.

Our radar antenna swept the unseen seascape. Each ponderous sweep of the instrument's needle etched a new image onto the screen. I tried to determine the vessel's heading by projecting the series of intermittent blips on our radar screen. As the ship approached with no obvious progress to starboard, I gradually came to the conclusion that she intended to pass starboard-to-starboard at very close range. Subsequently, I made the decision to adjust the auto helm's course one degree to port. That would put a little more distance between us, and the minor adjustment was as close as I could come to maintaining my heading.

I waited for our relative positions to confirm my assessment.

With each low moan of the ship's horn, the electronic target edged toward the centre of the radar screen. My heart pounded in my chest, and my resolve weakened. I eased another degree to port.

Suddenly, a loud blast off our port bow contradicted all my assumptions. *The ship had crossed our bow; I had been turning into her path!*

Instinctively, I spun the wheel, turning ninety degrees to starboard. Then, through the fog, I heard the rhythmic thrum of her powerful engine beyond our stern. With the incident behind us, my tunnel vision dissolved, and for the first time, I noted a second, smaller target on the radar screen. *Alice Rose* had been one of two small vessels converging on the ship's northeasterly course, squeezing her into a narrow gap between potential collisions. While the opportunity to calculate the distance between the ship and the other boat had passed, *Alice Rose* had sailed within two hundred yards of the behemoth's path as she crossed our bow, ample clearance... on a sunny afternoon!

For much of the four-day crossing, fog banks and wave heights well above the level of our deck hid other vessels from sight. Only fading, black smudges on the radar screen betrayed their presence.

With the evening came absolute darkness. Were we still fogbound or simply sailing beneath cloud cover? Regardless, we remained obsessed with the radar display.

Mark and I began informally swapping short watches, though I found sleeping somewhat difficult for several reasons. First, my longtime friend wasn't yet intimately familiar with *Alice Rose* and her equipment. Second, the cold sea was sucking the warmth out of the cabin, so the damp interior was hardly conducive to sleep. Finally, we were only one day into my longest passage on the open sea, and a vague feeling of apprehension kept me alert.

Our second day of constant motion dawned cold and damp. Clammy and uncomfortable much of the time, we motored in and out of thick fog banks throughout the morning. Fatigue, my ever-present companion, slowed my responses and degraded my motor skills. I steadied one of our jerry cans against my knee while I poured five gallons of diesel fuel into *Alice Rose*'s tank. Then I meticulously re-secured the remaining two cans on deck, and I tightened the lines that lashed our upturned dinghy to the foredeck before going below to make an entry in the ship's log. Our progress had been steady though slow and almost entirely dependent on our noisy auxiliary. The tedium was irritating, and I wished aloud for wind.

At midnight I assumed the watch while Mark tucked into the starboard berth, secure behind a lee cloth of my own design. Within a half-hour, intermittent flashes of lightning foreshadowed the coming weather system. I was pleased when a northeast breeze began to build through the night. Snug in my survival suit, I clipped my tether to a pad eye on deck and wedged myself against the bridge deck on the cockpit sole, out of reach of the night breeze. Five hours later, the growing swells off our stern glowed with the first light of dawn. The wind began gusting to twenty knots out of the east-southeast. Mark came on deck, and together, we raised the sails, engaged Mrs Tietz, and shut the engine down. *Alice Rose*'s auxiliary was relegated to cargo for the next forty-four hours.

At 9:20 a.m. on June 14, we were surfing down the face of a wave in the direction of New England when I looked up at the water's surface. A dark fin raced toward me at incredible speed. For a fraction of a second I thought it was a shark, but it was, in fact, a dolphin. It was one of a small pod that escorted *Alice Rose* for several minutes before retreating into the giant swells. By midday the sky darkened dramatically, and we withdrew to the relative comfort of the cabin. Wind-driven rain beat against the transparent, polycarbonate washboard.

Cooking became ill-advised, and while the well-spaced, twelve-foot seas weren't in themselves a concern, the motion and heeling of the vessel made moving around the cabin difficult. It would have been easy in a moment of carelessness to sustain a serious injury. Nevertheless, with the wind off the port quarter, we were making good progress toward Boston, and the seas were not threatening—as long as Mrs Tietz kept our stern more or less into the wind.

Thousands of waves slid westward beneath us throughout the day. Each one rose ominously above our stern as it approached, then benignly lifted *Alice Rose* toward its crest. By noon the massive, green giants towered over us and scattered foam into the air as the wind tore at their crests.

Throughout the afternoon and evening, the tempest grew in strength, gusting occasionally to thirty-five knots or more and piling waves up to the height of my house back home on Lisa Court. With no supporting evidence whatsoever, I kept expecting the storm to abate. By late evening the howling low had reached a ferocity I had never before experienced. Finally, at about 10:15 p.m. on June 14, I rose from my berth and stood braced in the cabin below, listening to the maelstrom outside. It was still getting worse and my uneasiness had turned to anxiety.

On any other point of sail, I would have reefed the main and put up the storm jib long ago. It was now patently obvious that I had waited too long. The wind's velocity had increased so gradually and *Alice Rose* had been running before it so gracefully that I had delayed reefing, every minute expecting the wind to ease. How often had I read about crews who failed to reef in time to avoid disaster? I was risking a knockdown, and I knew better. Reducing sail in these conditions would be difficult and potentially dangerous.

Alice Rose pitched and rolled violently as I woke Mark and switched on the deck lights. One by one, we clipped our tethers to the pad-eye on the bulkhead next to the companionway and crept on deck in the driving rain.

The awful roar of the wind, overlaid with siren-like shrieks and wails from the wires, was overwhelming and disorienting. I had never heard anything like it before. We transferred our tethers to the jack lines that ran along the deck and struggled to hang on as the vessel heeled, yawed and dropped away beneath our feet. A complex pattern of shadows darted erratically about the deck, distorting our reality. The lights above our heads glared off sheets of horizontal rain inside a thirty-foot circle. For a few minutes, our world ended where the black began, and everything beyond the circle of light became irrelevant.

The mainsail grinned through a gaping thirty-inch tear just forward of the leech near the boom.

"We have to get the main down quickly before it rips further!" I shouted into Mark's ear. He clambered monkey-like onto the coach roof and braced himself against the mast.

When I called "Are you ready?" I knew by his lack of a response that the wind had snatched my words away.

Against the enormous pressure of the wind, I hauled in the mainsheet, nodded at Mark and released the halyard. Together, we somehow managed to stuff the flapping layers of sail into the lazy jacks and lash them to the boom. When, after several minutes of focused effort, the sail was secure, I crawled toward the cockpit, battered and bruised, my hands stiff with cold. With only the jib to steady her, *Alice Rose*'s motion worsened and her speed dropped off considerably. We couldn't repair the mainsail in that wind, and in any event, we would have no use for it until the wind let up.

Mark and I went below to ride out the storm and get some rest.

By 2 a.m., sustained winds of forty-knots hammered our little yacht as she lurched toward the distant coast. On two occasions, breaking waves thundered onto the deck over the port rail. Each time, *Alice Rose* shuddered violently, and the weight of the wave forced seawater through the neoprene seals of the bronze portholes, thoroughly dousing my port-side berth.

Trisha and David junior waited in Boston, unaware that our eventual arrival would be sixteen to twenty-four hours behind schedule. I worried that they would report us missing when we failed to contact them. At 11:30 a.m., with that in mind, I made several attempts to reach the U.S. Coast Guard on the VHF.

"United States Coast Guard Radio, United States Coast Guard Radio, United States Coast Guard Radio. This is *Alice Rose, Alice Rose, Alice Rose,* Charlie-Foxtrot-Foxtrot-Nine-One-Three-Seven. Over." I listened and heard only silence.

The inference was that we were beyond the range of coastal stations, and there were no Coast Guard patrols in our area. I waited thirty minutes and tried again with similar results. For the first time in my life, I felt truly alone, and for the present, entirely dependent on my own resources.

After numerous calls over the next few hours, we finally made contact at 5 p.m. The radio operator was very patient throughout our weak and broken radio exchanges. The identification of our vessel and our position took some time, as I carefully articulated numeric details and phonetic spellings over and over. The wind had already dropped somewhat, and our position had become a matter of record. I no longer felt alone.

In response to my request, the U.S. Coast Guard confirmed that they had reached my son through his cell phone to advise of our late arrival. Things were returning to normal.

The wind had almost completely abated by 3 a.m. on June 16, when we began the long, serpentine entry into Boston Harbour amid countless red and green lights. On several occasions, we found ourselves hopelessly confused by the sea of markers though for only a few seconds each time. We always identified the next light just in time to take up the appropriate heading, and by so doing, edged ever closer to the inner harbour. At 4:45 a.m., after several failed attempts to locate it among the confusing maze of docks and mooring buoys, we bumped gently against the floating dock of the Boston Waterboat Marina.

Drunk with fatigue, I stumbled ashore, found a pay phone, and called the U.S. Customs Office. No one answered.

After several attempts, an anonymous male answered and instructed me to call back at 9:30 a.m. because the marine officer would not be available until then. Here we were, foreigners on a foreign vessel, in the midst of a major American port, unchallenged for four hours.

Members of the marina staff arrived for work, so we registered and walked to a nearby car rental agency. I was disappointed when I called my son and discovered that Trisha had begun the drive home the previous evening because Angela, my son's wife, had to return to work. I drove to the Sheraton Hotel to rendezvous with David junior and hopefully enjoy a hot shower.

It was ten o'clock when I again called customs. The marine officer invited us to attend his office to apply for entry to the U.S. and obtain *Alice Rose*'s cruising license. We did so, and the process appeared to be all but complete when the presiding officer directed us to return to the dock to await a vessel inspection in thirty to forty-five minutes. Though the entire procedure appeared to be pointless bureaucracy, I drove back to the marina and parked in the lot at the marina's entrance.

We found laundry facilities in a small floating shed. In fact, the marina consisted entirely of floating docks and buildings, occupying no land whatsoever. I spent the rest of the morning and part of the afternoon washing, drying, and re-packing my clothes in plastic bags to protect them from the ever-present dampness of our salt-water environment.

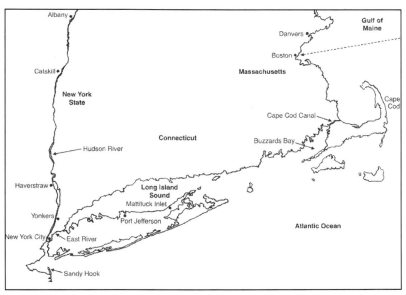

Map 15. Boston to Albany

Three times, I called the customs office to determine why their inspectors had not arrived. Finally, about four in the afternoon, two officers arrived, explained that they had been dispatched to the wrong marina, and apologized for keeping us waiting by the dock all day. In the interim, our rented car had been towed from the parking lot which was apparently not associated with the marina. To avoid inconveniencing us further, the Coast Guard officers declined to search *Alice Rose*. Instead they provided us with a name and a telephone number which we were to "call if we encountered any additional issues with the U.S. Coast Guard or customs staff" during our visit. Finally, they presented us with a handful of gaudy trinkets bearing USCG insignia and welcomed us with handshakes.

In the meantime, my son located our rental car at a towing compound in a seedy part of town, retrieved it at a cost of $110, and delivered the mainsail to Downs Sails in Danvers, Massachusetts. He arrived there just prior to closing time and related the day's events. The sail maker, in turn, complained about problems with his computer as he began repairing the sail. Within minutes, David had fixed the computer and the mainsail was on its way back to the dock with no money having changed hands.

With a single night of uninterrupted sleep, I recovered quickly and awoke about 8 a.m. It was June 17, my eldest daughter's thirty-ninth birthday, and like so many of Jacqui's birthdays I was away—but I didn't forget.

With showers and shaves out of the way, we prepared *Alice Rose* to sail and embarked at ten o'clock. We crossed the bay to refuel at Boston Harbour Shipyard Marina and set out to follow the coast southeast to Cape Cod.

Above the eastern horizon, a distant, grey blimp flew southward, perhaps seeking or returning from a sporting event. We anticipated a pleasant, uneventful sail in fine weather, sunny though still a little too cold for mermaids.

The sun touched the tops of the grassy coastal dunes as we approached the northern end of Cape Cod Canal. Even in the fading light, the entrance was easily located. I felt relaxed and secure in the shelter of the canal, where navigation was visual and simple. Mark went below to prepare dinner, popping out of the companionway like a prairie dog from time to time to scan the dimly lit shores. David sat in the cockpit with me, quietly taking in the cruising experience.

The canal's southern end was undeveloped and wound through what appeared in the dark to be marshland. David took the helm. Only occasionally marked with well-spaced buoys and subject to swirling tidal currents, our route required a little extra attention to navigation. We cruised through Buzzards Bay and Rhode Island

Sound during the night, en route to Long Island Sound. At dawn, we raised our sails for the first time since entering the canal. By mid-morning of June 18, the temperature had risen significantly. The wind died a little after lunch, and the sun began to warm our skin. We abandoned the lazily flapping sails, started the engine and engaged the electric auto helm. David lounged at the helm listening to music on his iPod, while Mark, shirtless, read a novel. A tiny fleet of military patrol vessels practised manoeuvres a few miles off our port beam.

As the day approached its end, I watched the sun descend toward the sparkling chrome surface of Long Island Sound. Within minutes, the dazzling silver turned to gold, and I acquired a few digital souvenirs with my Canon.

Late in the evening, we probed a recommended anchorage at Mattituck Inlet, but due to low tide, found it uncomfortably shallow. We continued through the night to Port Jefferson, arriving shortly after sunrise. There, we tied to the main dock, secured the companionway and went ashore for the day.

Together, we explored the affluent resort-town, wandering the streets, visiting the shops, and eating lunch at Papa Joe's. It was the kind of day that justifies the work of maintaining a boat.

We returned to *Alice Rose*, reorganized, and replenished our fuel supply. Before departing just after 6 p.m., I paid the day's docking fee which was ten times that of an overnight berth in most Newfoundland ports and by far the highest rate I ever encountered. I returned my ravaged wallet to my hip pocket and re-entered the sound in search of New York City.

CHAPTER TWENTY
New York and the Hudson

In the soft loom of pre-dawn, Alice Rose emerged from Long Island Sound, winding her way between markers toward a high, light-trimmed bridge. I referred to the chart and over the diesel's din announced to the crew, "That's the Throgs-Neck Bridge."

Minutes later, we passed beneath the arched girders of the first of seven East River bridges and entered the gloomy urban water-

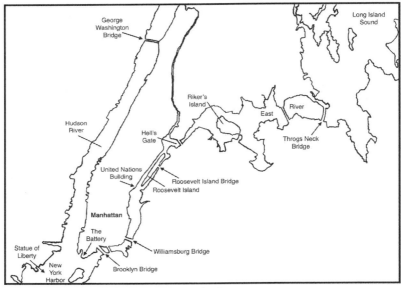

Map 16. New York City Waterways

way. Brightly coloured tugs growled with effort as they barged by, and lifeless, dilapidated freight terminals edged toward our stern in subdued light. Everyone aboard stood statue-like, staring outward in silence, absorbing the grey reality of the legendary place. In the distance, beyond Riker's Island, Manhattan hummed to life and glittered as the first rays of sunlight embraced the upper floors of its glassy skyscrapers.

There are lots of things to think about when sailing in coastal waters, including the ebb and flow of tides. They can, of course, limit a vessel's access to inlets and bays, but tidal currents can also impede a boat's progress in restricted waterways and forcibly drag it from its intended course. Because tides vary by geographic location and time, tide tables are published for all coastal areas. Consulting local tide tables is an essential aspect of navigation though I confess, I've never fully grasped their complexities. That became abundantly clear in New York City.

Mariners normally begin by identifying the nearest designated tide station, but that in itself is a challenge when sailing in coastal waters with unfamiliar place-names. Even with a station in one's vicinity identified, the data furnished isn't always the most relevant. Sometimes, where coastlines are ragged and complex, the times and heights listed for a more distant station are more applicable. I deliberately scheduled our approach to the East River to coincide with the "incoming" tide, based on the Battery Tide Station at the southern tip of Manhattan Island. It appeared to me to be the most appropriate point of reference. Based on our anticipated arrival time, I believed the tide would flush *Alice Rose* through the infamous Hell's Gate narrows into the upper East River. What I failed to understand was that the "incoming" tide doesn't approach the Battery through the East River. Instead, it roars into the mouth of the mightier Hudson River and floods into the East River in the opposite direction—*toward Long Island Sound*. I could not have been more wrong!

Within a few minutes, we arrived at the river's narrowest point at the absolute worst possible time. There, *Alice Rose* endured a head-on collision with an incoming tide in excess of five knots. She clawed her way through Hell's Gate at full throttle, more than once slipping backward momentarily. Photos taken at 6:29 a.m. and 6:59 a.m. depict the same building at distances that appear to differ no more than a hundred yards. For more than two hours, I worried about our aging Yanmar failing as it had on several previous occasions. In retrospect, I should have retreated downriver where the current was less severe to await slack water. Instead, in the hope of reaching Haverstraw Marina on the Hudson River before sunset, I stubbornly pressed on, expecting at any moment to overcome the current and surge beneath the Brooklyn Bridge into the Hudson. Of course, that isn't what happened.

To further complicate an already difficult situation, I arbitrarily chose the eastern route around Roosevelt Island. That branch of the river proved impassable as the Roosevelt Island Bridge, a vertical lift bridge, was inoperative due to renovations. Frustrated, I was forced to withdraw to the island's northern tip and enter the river's western branch. I looked at my watch when *Alice Rose* came abreast of the monolithic United Nations Building at the southern end of Roosevelt Island. The time was 10:30 a.m., and Haverstraw was still eight hours away. We had progressed a mere thirteen miles in five hours, much of it at full throttle.

Alice Rose edged southward, past the end of the urban canyon called 42nd Street. The spires of the Chrysler and Empire State buildings slipped in and out of view among countless monoliths of brick, concrete and glass. Once clear of the Roosevelt Island narrows, with high tide only minutes away, the current began to ease.

We were soon looking up at the bottom of the Williamsburg Bridge, then the pale-blue-painted Manhattan, and finally the iconic Brooklyn Bridge. Helicopters buzzed above our masthead on their way into and out of pier-based landing pads. From its distant vantage point on Liberty Island, the Statue of Liberty welcomed us to New York Harbour. We rounded Battery Park and powered into the Hudson River, boiling with the wakes of tugs, water taxis and ferries. I was physically and mentally fatigued. We were *all* tired, and we were hungry as well.

Alice Rose pressed on into the Hudson in search of Haverstraw just as the tide began receding toward the Atlantic. I had chosen the worst possible time to enter the East River and realized I was entering the mighty Hudson at the worst time too.

Someone, I think it was Mark, quickly prepared a hot lunch. There was something comforting about the warmth of the bowl as I cradled it in my hands. I wolfed down spoonfuls of wieners and baked beans on our approach to the George Washington Bridge, then went below for a nap and fell asleep in seconds.

A few minutes later, I awakened and felt the full effect of sleep deprivation and eating too much, too quickly. My stomach was bloated and hard, and I was wet with perspiration. Waves of dizzying nausea swept over me. With my right hand pressed against my upper stomach, I emerged from the cabin to get some fresh air.

Immediately, my son expressed concern about my health.

"It's just indigestion," I replied, as I stumbled along the deck toward the bow.

I flopped clumsily onto the spray-spattered foredeck. Someone called to me, but I couldn't be bothered answering and waved to indicate that I didn't want to talk. David, alertly interpreting my behaviour as a response to a heart attack, dialled 911 on his cell phone and reported our position to the N.Y.P.D.

With lights flashing and sirens wailing, the New York Fire Department's rescue boat arrived first. When it came alongside, the officer in charge insisted that I accompany him to shore where an ambulance was waiting. I was certain my heart was functioning normally, and was embarrassed by what I deemed unnecessary attention. Ultimately, when further protest appeared pointless, I acquiesced. I worried about leaving *Alice Rose* in someone else's hands and realized I hadn't properly prepared my crew for such an eventuality. I grabbed the ship's papers and my passport before directing my crew to motor in circles while I was gone. I made no provision for a scenario in which I didn't return. Everyone watched apprehensively as I stepped down into the oversized Zodiac.

Even before we reached the dock of a crumbling Yonkers smallboat marina, a New York City Police vessel arrived on the scene. In the midst of the marina's un-paved parking lot, an ambulance, a fire truck and various uniformed personnel awaited my arrival. I began worrying about the cost that my upset stomach was incurring in the form of man-hours and equipment.

The shabby marina was a carnival of flashing lights with curious locals standing in small groups, staring as I stepped out of the emergency-orange rescue boat onto the dock.

A blonde paramedic with a cheerful smile and an East European accent invited me into the ambulance. She began asking questions about my health, my age and my symptoms. The paramedic worked quickly and efficiently, sticking wired sensors to my chest as we conversed. Over the next few minutes, she gathered vital information from me and her electronic equipment simultaneously. My abdominal discomfort eased and soon disappeared completely. Her examination confirmed that I was perfectly healthy aside from a slightly elevated heart rate, so I was cleared to return to my anxious crew. I blamed my heart rate on her proximity and thanked her for her time and concern.

I was astonished and somewhat relieved to learn that no charge would be levied for any of the services provided.

The remainder of our upriver cruise proved routine by comparison.

Early that evening, we threaded our way through a twisting, narrow channel to gain access to Haverstraw Marina. Its shallow, silted bottom tugged at our keel on more than one occasion. At the gas dock, we replenished our fuel and water tanks before moving *Alice Rose* to a slip for the night. Then we languished in the showers for a few minutes and decompressed over a very expensive dinner at the riverside Bayview Club. The large dining room contained twenty-five or thirty oversized tables, surrounded by comfortable armchairs. It featured a wall of floor-to-ceiling glass overlooking the river. Perhaps because we arrived on a Monday, only two other tables were occupied, so Tony, the owner, visited with us for much of our stay. One of the highlights of going ashore had always been chatting with the locals. Invariably, they were curious to know where we had come from, where we were going, and why. Generally, they were equally willing to talk about themselves and their waterside communities.

On the morning of June 20, we awoke refreshed and set out with renewed enthusiasm, motoring northward in search of Catskill. At the mouth of the creek, with an hour of post-sunset twilight remaining, we snugged into a shallow berth at a floating dock though not without kissing the mud bottom a couple of times. Unable to determine who administered what appeared to be public docks, we walked to a nearby bar and grill.

When we entered through the Catskill Point Bar and Restaurant's creekside door, the attractive young barmaid greeted us with a smile. Sunni, a sophomore at an upper New York state university, was one of the local hangout's summertime bartenders. She immediately invited us to move *Alice Rose* to the bar's dock where we were welcome to spend the night.

Mark, David and I spent a couple of hours eating, drinking, and flirting with our youthful server. Sunni was friendly, smiled easily, and laughed—and occasionally scowled—at our jokes.

Cruising the inland river, far removed from the North Atlantic's penetrating chill, proved very relaxing. A hot meal and a couple of drinks helped a little too, and I found the evening to be a rather pleasant intermission. About ten o'clock, hours before David and Mark closed the pub, I left a generous tip on the bar and retired to my berth at the end of the wooden dock.

The evening was still and peaceful as I approached *Alice Rose* under a full moon. Only the soft thud of my footsteps against a backdrop of a thousand unseen croaking frogs disturbed the night. I adjusted my position in my berth two or three times, seeking that perfect comfort that immediately precedes sleep, and added yet another boating memory to my collection.

We put in at the Paul Castleton Boat Club on June 22, scrounged wood to build a cradle for *Alice Rose*'s aluminium mast, and paid fifty dollars for the use of the club's manual crane. Limited overhead clearance in parts of the Erie Canal forces sailboats to un-step their masts before entering the waterway. The crew and I lowered our forty-two foot spar in the mid-afternoon sun and secured it in the cradle we had constructed on deck.

It was after ten o'clock when we arrived at the Troy lock which was out of service until the following morning. In the dark we could see little of our surroundings aside from a random scattering of lights, their dancing reflections on the water, and a sign prohibiting us from tying to the lock wall overnight. I considered our options. We could circle for the next seven or eight hours, spend half the night exploring the dark waters for a suitable anchorage, or disregard the sign and risk an admonishment in the morning. I chose the latter without reservation and went to sleep.

Sleeping aboard a small boat for any length of time is a unique experience. While some prefer the security and stability of a shore-based Sealy or Simmons, most find a boat's motion relaxing. It's not surprising that the vast majority of skippers develop the ability to sleep without entirely relinquishing their senses; listening, feeling, even smelling subtle changes in their environment while they snore. Wind changes, betrayed by whispers and rattles in the rigging, the faint odours of a distant shore, and even variations in currents and wave characteristics will awaken most skippers. Together, these triggers seem to constitute a kind of sixth sense.

Shortly after 3 a.m., I awoke with an inexplicable, uncomfortable feeling. Someone snored softly in the coal-mine black of the cabin. I listened to the light breeze, felt the rhythmic bobbing of the hull, and inhaled the scent of oil emanating from some anonymous riverside factory. My conscious mind detected nothing unusual, yet the feeling persisted. Ultimately, I felt my way on deck as quietly as possible to check our mooring lines.

Fore and aft, the dock lines—as taut as guitar strings—angled down into the water between the hull and the lock wall. *Alice Rose* was listing slightly toward the timber wall, her starboard rail dragged down by the straining lines. The river's depth had increased three to four feet since we had tied up the previous evening, and now the knots were a couple of feet below the surface. It hadn't occurred to me that the tide would pursue us into the upper reaches of the Hudson, a full two day's cruise from New York City.

Feeling a bit foolish and a little desperate, I took a deep breath and plunged my head and shoulders into the cold water. Reaching down into the impenetrable darkness, I fumbled with the double half-hitches, and to my surprise, the knots released easily. Perhaps my weight on the rail had relieved the tension on the lines. I retied them higher up the wall, being sure to allow four feet of slack to accommodate low tide, and returned to my warm berth.

On the morning of June 23, *Alice Rose* transited Lock One at Troy and said farewell to the Hudson River. With the mast secured on deck, David, Mark and I tied to the concrete seawall at Waterford, New York. We had arrived at the entrance to the historic Erie Canal.

The 365-mile-long waterway had since 1825 linked Albany, at the head of the Hudson River, with Buffalo on Lake Erie. At a time when overland travel was still perilous and limited to a few miles per day, the canal opened up settlement and commercial development throughout Ohio, Indiana, Illinois and Michigan. The forty-foot wide by four-foot deep barge canal had a huge impact on westward migration and transport, reducing the cost of moving goods by as much as ninety per cent. Construction costs were recouped in less than a decade though, by the mid-twentieth century, most commercial traffic had been lost to railways, modern roads and the St. Lawrence Seaway. Nevertheless, recreational vessels continue to use the canal to reach destinations in upper New York state, the Great Lakes and beyond.

Mark and David's passage ended at Waterford because of work responsibilities. I couldn't continue through the canal's locks without crew, so we hired a car and drove five hours to Buffalo Airport where Trisha picked us up. I had only a few days respite to say goodbye to my crew-mates and prepare for the final leg of *Alice Rose*'s return to Hamilton.

Sleeping beside my wife in a queen-size bed—one that didn't move in response to the night breezes—was a welcome experience after living aboard my tiny sloop for three weeks.

CHAPTER TWENTY-ONE

Goodbye, *Alice Rose*

Trisha and I drove to Waterford, paid *Alice Rose*'s docking fees, re-provisioned, and spent the night aboard. Casting off the wall at 7 a.m. on the twenty-eighth of June, we began motoring through the Erie canal toward our destination on the southern shore of Lake Ontario. The community of Oswego, situated at the north end of a branch of the Erie Canal known as the Oswego Canal, was a four- or five-day cruise away. The port town was located on the site of Fort Oswego, established more than 200 years earlier by the British.

This segment of *Alice Rose*'s homeward passage would mark the first time Trisha had sailed on her since our arrival in Sydney, Nova Scotia the previous summer. From Oswego, we would drive home together, and I would return with a friend to step the mast at the Port of Oswego Marina before sailing across Lake Ontario to Cobourg on the north shore.

At Lock Two, we purchased a ten-day canal pass for $37.50 and continued our lock-to-lock westward passage. With her forty-two foot mast lying horizontal on deck, *Alice Rose* was about eleven feet longer than normal. As a result, I had to be vigilant when docking and particularly while entering and exiting locks.

On our approach to each of the twenty-nine locks that we encountered, Trisha armed herself with a boathook and took up a position at the forward end of the cabin, approximately twenty feet from where I stood at the wheel. Her job was to snag one of the slimy, vertical mooring lines that hung down the lock wall at twenty-foot intervals.

With Trisha standing by, I motored cautiously into the lock, keeping *Alice Rose* as close as possible to the starboard wall without touching it. Any contact with the lock wall was likely to redirect the vessel out into the lock and beyond the reach of the mooring lines. Once Trisha had hooked one of the hanging lines, I tried to slow *Alice Rose* as much as possible by momentarily reversing the engine. Then, having shifted into neutral, I quickly reached out with my boathook to grasp the second mooring line.

A problematic characteristic of the Alberg 29 is that it tends to yaw significantly to port when the propeller turns in reverse, a phenomenon known to mariners as "prop-walk" and something I have mentioned before. Consequently, my attempts to arrest the vessel's forward motion pushed the stern away from the wall, making my mooring line difficult to reach. Steering and slowing at

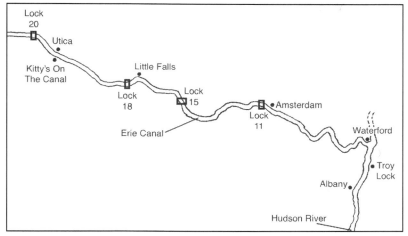

Map 17. Erie Canal, Eastern Section

precisely the right time while simultaneously hooking a mooring line—*before the distance to the wall exceeded my reach*—was always a challenge. The fact that we often shared the lock with one or more other vessels added an additional level of difficulty. Nevertheless, we invariably managed somehow, though I may have occasionally barked instructions a little louder than I intended.

With the greasy mooring lines firmly in our grasp, we were able to keep *Alice Rose* parallel to the wall while the lock filled with water. The huge volume of incoming liquid boiled and swirled around us. It tugged *Alice Rose*'s hull this way and that while we floated upward toward the top of the concrete box-like enclosure. Then we relinquished the mooring lines, passed through the opening gates, and continued westward.

With each lock, our teamwork improved and our confidence grew. By the end of our first day, *Alice Rose* had travelled forty-two miles into the canal and had been lifted 252 feet by the first ten locks. At the west end of Lock Eleven, in the town of Amsterdam, we came upon a municipal park and complimentary docking facility equipped with electrical outlets. We tied up for the night, ate dinner at a picnic table, and slept while our house batteries recharged.

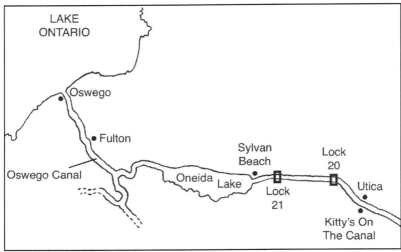

Map 18. Erie Canal, Western Section

Just after 8:30 on the morning of the twenty-ninth, with slightly less than a full tank of diesel fuel and a five-gallon jerry can in reserve, *Alice Rose* got underway again. Within five hours, we had cleared Lock Fifteen amid occasional afternoon thundershowers.

As long as we've had air conditioning, Trisha has avoided the worst of the summer heat by retreating indoors, but *Alice Rose* provided no such escape, and the rain did little to offset the day's oppressive heat and humidity. With no respite from the summer's worst, my wife's enthusiasm for boating waned as her hair curled into a tangle of frizz.

After tying up in Little Falls, New York toward the end of the day, we walked over a nearby bridge to the town centre. There, we found a small steakhouse on the main street and enjoyed a relaxing meal. Neither of us were looking forward to the long walk back to the boat, so I asked the waitress if Little Falls had a taxi service. To my surprise, she glanced at her watch and graciously offered to drive us back to the boat "in ten minutes" when her shift ended. It was one of those little things that leave an indelible impression on people—a kindness that we couldn't have anticipated. The words of the old song "Low Bridge, Everybody Down," which Bruce Springsteen covered in 2006, come to mind:

> Low bridge, everybody down
> Low bridge, 'cause we're coming to a town
> You'll always know your neighbour
> You'll always know your pal
> If ya ever navigated on the Erie Canal.

By June 30, we were about halfway to Oswego. First thing in the morning, as in countless marinas before, we had our waste tank pumped dry and paid our docking fee prior to setting out for Utica. I was glad to have my wife aboard again and wished I could have shared the experience of the first two weeks with her. Trisha's support, domestic skills, and especially her sailing experience proved invaluable as we plodded from lock to lock in the humid summer heat.

Within an hour we cleared Lock 18 at Jacksonburg where the Erie Canal temporarily diverges from the Mohawk River. Four hours later, we tied up at Kitty's On The Canal, a Utica restaurant that catered to canal traffic and provided overnight berths for small craft. We relaxed over lunch at Kitty's before walking to a nearby car rental agency. There, we selected a Ford Taurus with that new-car smell and drove to Waterford to retrieve our van. In separate vehicles, we returned to Little Falls to enjoy a second dinner at the friendly East End Steakhouse. It was almost midnight when we arrived at Oswego where Trisha's duties were scheduled to end three days later. We checked into the Days Inn, relishing a night ashore in the comfort of an air-conditioned hotel room.

Trisha and I awoke on Canada Day, ate breakfast, and parked our van in a lot near the canal's east wall where we anticipated berthing *Alice Rose* in a couple of days. Having arranged to leave it there until our return, we drove back to Utica in the rented Taurus. It was 2 p.m. by the time we returned the rental car and sat down to our second lunch at Kitty's.

Lock 20 was located an hour west of the restaurant, and by the time we cleared the lock it was rather late in the day. The idea of continuing another eighteen miles to Lock 21 simply lacked appeal, so we secured to a floating dock above Lock 20 for the night. The dock gave us access to a quiet, treed park equipped with picnic tables. Trisha prepared dinner and served it at one of the weathered tables, but with twilight came hordes of pesky mosquitos. Our Canada Day evening meal was less than leisurely as we hurried to regain the bug-free security of the cabin.

Alice Rose's homeward progress lacked the anticipation and excitement of the outbound journey a year earlier. It was instead routine and slightly tedious.

Though refitting and maintaining a boat had been a drain on our finances, my plan to explore the world had justified the cost. But with my dream now abandoned, the expense seemed extravagant and unwarranted. I simply couldn't justify keeping *Alice Rose* another year to sail to and from a Hamilton dock. Though committed to selling my dream once we arrived in Hamilton, during those final days on the canal I couldn't help feeling from time to time that we were cruising in the wrong direction.

Trisha and I were already underway by 6:50 a.m. on the second of July. To alleviate the boredom of steering for hours at a time, I engaged the electric auto-helm whenever possible. The device relied on a magnetic compass to maintain a constant heading, so I could simply set a course and occupy myself with another task while Otto kept us moving in a straight line. After a few hours of use, the device lured us into trusting it without reservation. Of course, neither life nor electronic equipment are entirely predictable. As we passed under a railway bridge on our approach to Oneida Lake, I noted a brief though significant course deviation, undoubtedly due to the proximity of the bridge's iron girders. Because the mechanism re-acquired the appropriate heading before I could assume manual control, the incident didn't constitute a navigational risk. Nevertheless, it was worthy of a note in the ship's log and demonstrated the importance of adequately monitoring automation.

I topped up our fuel at Sylvan Beach before entering Oneida Lake. The southwest wind conspired with the morning sun, turning the ten-mile-long lake's surface to dancing silver. The resulting glare rendered my sunglasses ineffective.

The shallow, sweet-water lake was our first exposure to open water since leaving Long Island Sound a couple of weeks earlier, and the steep, wind-driven waves caught me off guard. Accustomed to the long swells of the Atlantic, I had forgotten how the ragged chop of a wind-blown, inland lake can jar a vessel. I wished we could raise the sails to steady *Alice Rose* as she banged her way westward, but her aluminium mast lay in a hastily constructed cradle, a mere piece of useless deck cargo. With the deck bucking and yawing beneath my feet, I inspected and tightened its bindings. Trisha and I ducked under the dodger as bow-spray rained down on the deck and splashed into the cockpit. The lake was alive with mid-summer boaters, water skiers, jet skis, and even a distant parasailer.

Shortly after exiting the west end of Oneida Lake, we turned north into the Oswego Canal and continued to the Canal Landing Marina at Fulton where we spent the night. Now, less than three hours from the Oswego Terminal, Trisha began gathering her things for the drive home.

Since reaching the upper Hudson River, *Alice Rose* had been lifted through twenty-two locks and lowered through five. Three more locks awaited her at Oswego before she could again sail out into the open waters of Lake Ontario.

We left Fulton at 9:15 on July 3, and tied to the wall in Oswego at twelve minutes after noon—exactly as planned. Aside from the summer heat that Trisha had grudgingly endured over the past week, the passage had gone well. I felt comfortable and at ease in the warm, familiar environment of the Great Lakes.

Now we faced the formidable task of cleaning and reorganizing our temporary home, and preparing her for the upcoming lake crossing. Trisha loaded her belongings into the van while I secured the ports and hatches. Then we began the long drive to Hamilton where I would be able to relax and regroup for a couple of days.

A few days later, Brian Perro, a colleague and longtime friend, accompanied me to Oswego to help step the mast and prepare *Alice Rose* for our seventy-seven nautical mile crossing of Lake Ontario. I recalled the last time we had sailed together, an adventure that ended abruptly when Brian informed me that the Canadian Coast Guard had just called *Alice Rose* on the VHF.

We had been motoring through a narrow, rocky channel in late September 1997, having set out from Penetanguishene to explore the islands of Georgian Bay's eastern shore. I was below, enveloped in engine noise, when the call came through the cockpit speaker. Familiar with Brian's irrepressible sense of humour, I looked about for a Coast Guard vessel but saw none. I doubted my friend was serious, and I didn't want to fall for whatever scam he was perpetrating. I couldn't imagine why the Coast Guard would be calling *Alice Rose*, but a few seconds later, I heard the call repeated and hurriedly responded with, "Thunder Bay Radio, Thunder Bay Radio, this is *Alice Rose*. Over."

When I was advised to "call home on an urgent family matter," I felt a sickening surge of adrenaline and requested additional information, but none had been provided to the radio operator. Heart pounding in my chest, I thanked him and terminated the call. I increased the engine's RPM to maximum cruising speed, but we were far from any known community and neither of us had yet purchased our first cell phone. In fact, in 1997, cell phones were neither common nor particularly reliable in lightly populated areas. We eventually anchored in King Bay, immediately north of Big David Bay, and went ashore in the dinghy to locate a pay phone. I checked my watch as I made the call. Forty minutes had passed since the Coast Guard's notification; my mind was whirring in anguish. When Trisha answered, she explained that, while babysitting our daughter's children, she had fallen down the stairs and broken her leg. Though a close friend had temporarily come to her rescue, she needed my help to care for our grandchildren until our daughter and her husband returned from their vacation. Brian's weekend adventure thus ended abruptly.

The upcoming passage from Oswego to Cobourg would be Brian's make-up cruise. With time to spare before our scheduled departure, we walked to a harbourside restaurant where we enjoyed a leisurely lunch at an outside table. My sailing plan called for a daylight approach to Cobourg which, in turn, required a late afternoon departure. When the server asked if we'd like another beer, we didn't hesitate for a moment and readily lounged for another thirty minutes in the shade of a bright green Carlsberg umbrella. Uncharacteristically, we left the dock on time and soon found ourselves ahead of schedule.

When, in the afternoon, we entered Oswego's outer harbour amid a chaotic fleet of marine traffic, I was surprised to see how rough the water appeared. The prevailing westerly wind blew at a steady fifteen knots, and I noted no other vessels were venturing out onto the lake. Nevertheless, we had a date with Trisha the following day, and *Alice Rose* had endured much worse on several occasions. With a fetch of 180 miles, the wind provided an endless supply of steep, two-metre waves; however, the steady blow enabled us to sail close to a beam reach throughout the crossing. That being a sloop's fastest point of sail, we figuratively shot out of the harbour toward our north-shore destination.

Under a clear blue sky, and later a black canopy of twinkling stars, *Alice Rose* skimmed over the furrowed surface at hull speed, reducing the planned twenty-hour crossing to just sixteen hours. Brian and I sat together in the cockpit much of the night, looking up at the stars and enjoying our last sail together. In the first faint light of July 7, we approached the Canadian shore. My last sailing adventure was quietly slipping away.

Once tied to the dock in the sheltered Cobourg Marina, Brian and I checked in with the office, wolfed down a bowl of cereal, and tidied the cabin before closing up the boat. Then, we wandered into town and looked around for a while before stumbling on the Buttermilk Café. With time to kill until our planned rendezvous, we ate an early lunch there and returned to lounge in the cockpit until Trisha's mid-afternoon arrival.

Two days later, Trisha and I returned to Cobourg to sail *Alice Rose* home, motoring against the prevailing west wind for most of the 100-mile passage. We moored overnight at the Whitby Yacht Club and got an early start at 7 a.m. on the tenth, with just over half of the distance covered. My wife and I watched the skyline of Toronto glide by as we shared our final cruise together. A few hours later, I watched the masthead slip beneath the Burlington Canal lift bridge as we entered Hamilton harbour on July 10. The return of *Alice Rose* to her home port elicited a stew of emotions, including elation, resignation, relief and frustration. My dream of a trans-Atlantic crossing and a potential circumnavigation of the globe had been slipping irrevocably beyond my reach for eleven months.

Tying up in Hamilton was, for me, the moment of final acceptance. I would never know what it was to sail in isolation amid the waves of the mid-Atlantic though, admittedly, I had enjoyed a wonderful series of adventures on sweet and blue water over the past decade.

I had *Alice Rose* hauled and cradled in the boatyard where I spent a few weeks preparing her for her new owner. Scrubbed and dressed in a fresh coat of grey anti-fouling paint, she looked shiny and new when I was finished. All she needed now was someone with a dream.

Alice Rose had, in recent years, been lovingly fitted with essential equipment and lots of ancillary devices and comforts. She had survived rigorous offshore testing, and, apart from the wealthiest adventurers for whom size (and cost) were not an issue, buyers would undoubtedly find her appealing. I composed a detailed advertisement, listing thousands of dollars of recently installed accessories. Not at all anxious to part with my little sloop, I priced her a little high for the market.

On the nineteenth of September, I accepted a certified cheque from Jack Nye as payment for my beloved *Alice Rose*. She has since crossed the North Atlantic from Newfoundland to Ireland twice. I think of her often.

I never regretted pursuing my dream, though regret has pursued me like a shadow since *Alice Rose* and I parted ways.

Glossary of Marine Terminology

abeam: seen to be on a line at right angles to the centreline of a boat
aft: toward the stern
amidships: the widest portion of a boat between the bow and stern
antifouling: hull paint designed to shed or repel marine growths (e.g., barnacles).
astern: behind a vessel; beyond the stern
backstay: wire rope between the masthead and stern to support the mast
ballast: weight carried low in a vessel to provide vertical stability
beam: the width of a boat
beam ends: the side of a vessel (where lateral deck beams terminate)
beam reach: sailing at right angles to the wind; a rigging configuration
berth: a place where a vessel is secured; a sleeping place aboard a boat
bilge: a cavity located beneath the cabin or cockpit sole (floor) of a boat
bimini: an open front canvas to shade a cockpit and its occupants
block: assembly of sheaves or pulleys used to gain mechanical advantage
blue-water: a body of salt water; sea water
boathook: pole fitted with a hook to retrieve lines from docks and locks
bollard: squat post on a pier to which a ship's dock line may be secured
boom: a horizontal spar attached, at the forward end, to the mast
bow: the forward end of a boat
bowsprit: narrow extension of the deck that extends beyond the bow
bow-stem: structural member between the deck and the keel at the bow
bridge deck: raised area at the forward end of the cockpit to prevent water entering the cabin
broad reach: sailing downwind, about forty-five degrees off the wind
bulkhead: partition within the hull; adds strength and divides cabins or holds
cat-rigged: a single sail attached to a mast located at a vessel's bow
centre of effort: a sail's or a set of sails' balance point with respect to wind force
chain locker: a deck locker located at the bow for stowing the anchor rode
chain plate: metal plate built into a hull as an attachment point for a shroud
chock: a deck fitting with a gap at the top through which a line or rope runs
close hauled: sailing into the wind at an angle of about thirty degrees; sail configuration
close reach: sailing slightly into the wind at an angle of about sixty degrees
coastal navigation: fixing one's position from known data and visible reference
collier: coal-carrying ship

collision blanket: canvas used to cover hull damage and reduce the inflow of water
come about: turn into the wind in order to sail in a different direction
companionway: a stairway or ladder between deck levels on a boat
CQR (based on the word "secure"): a plow-like anchor design
cradle: metal or wooden framework used to store a boat upright on land
cutter: a single-masted sailing vessel featuring multiple foresails
davits: crane booms on a ship or yacht for suspending or lowering a lifeboat or dinghy
deck combing: a raised edge around a boat's deck; see *toe-rail*
deck stepped: as in a mast mounted on a boat's deck; see *keel-stepped*
depth sounder: electronic device to measure water depth under a boat
deviation: compass error due to the influence of nearby metal objects
dinghy: small boat used to commute to a vessel anchored offshore
displacement hull: hull designed to move *through* water, not over it
dodger: shelter incorporating a windshield to protect the cockpit from sun and rain
draft: the distance a boat's keel protrudes into the water
fender: air-filled rubber cylinders hung at intervals along the hull to prevent damage
fender baskets: stainless wire enclosures for storing fenders
fender boards: wooden planks hung horizontally along the hull to prevent damage
foredeck: the forward portion of a vessel's weather deck
forefoot: point where the bow-stem meets the forward end of the keel
forestay: mast-supporting wire rope fitted between the masthead and bow
forward: toward the bow
full keel: a keel which extends throughout the length of the vessel
genoa: a sail that fills or exceeds the area between the forestay and the mast
gooseneck: flexible fitting (universal joint) connecting a boom to a mast
ground tackle: a combination of chain, rope and anchor
halyard: a line or wire rope used to raise sails
hank: a spring loaded piston closure; *verb* to attach with a fitting known as a hank
hatch: a hinged closure over an opening in a deck or a bulkhead
hawse pipe: a grommet-like deck or hull fitting through which the anchor chain slides
head: mariners' term for a toilet or a room to house a toilet on a boat
helm: a tiller or wheel and any associated equipment for the directional control of a boat
helm's alee: a shouted warning that the tiller is being pushed downwind
hove-to: setting the headsail and rudder in opposition to arrest a boat's progress
hull: the outer shell of a boat below the weather deck

hull speed: a theoretic maximum speed for a given hull design
jack lines: lines secured along the deck to which safety tethers are clipped
jenny: slang for genoa; sail that fits or exceeds the area between the forestay and the mast
jib: a relatively small foresail that is clipped (or hanked) to the forestay
jib sheet: a line attached to the rear-most, bottom corner of a foresail
jibe: swing a fore and aft sail across a following wind to change course
keel: a blade protruding beneath a boat's hull to directionally stabilize it
keel-stepped: as in a mast set on the keel at the bottom of a boat's hull
ketch: a boat with a short mast between the main mast and the rudder
knot: unit of speed (1.15 mph) or unit of distance (1.15 statute miles)
lazaret: a deck-accessible storage locker located at the aft end of a boat
lazy jacks: webbing between a mast and boom to catch a lowered sail
lee cloth: vertical cloth barrier fixed to a berth to prevent its occupant from falling out
leech: the rear-most edge of a sail
leeward: down wind of a vessel or geographic feature
life-line: cable strung around a deck's perimeter for the safety of the crew
line: most ropes on boats are referred to as "lines" (see also *sheet*)
loom: the visible glow of an unseen light, as from a lighthouse just beyond the horizon.
loran: long-range navigation system using transmitters at known sites
mainsheet: a line attached to the aft end of the mainsail
mast: a vertical spar to which a sail is attached
mast boot: weatherproof covering surrounding a mast's base on the deck
masthead sloop: a sloop with its forward stay fastened to the top of the mast
mid-ship: the centre portion of a vessel between the bow and stern
mizzen: a mast or sail located aft of the mainmast
mooring buoy: an anchored float to which a vessel can be secured
painter: line attached to the bow of a small boat for towing and securing to a dock
parallel rules: device to facilitate drawing a line parallel to another line
point of sail: a sailboat's relationship to wind direction; a sail arrangement
port: the left side of a vessel; to the left of a vessel
prop-walk: tendency for reversed propellers to draw a stern to one side
prow: that portion of a ship's bow which is above the water
quarter: either of the rear corners of a vessel
quarter-berth: sleeping accommodation on either side of a vessel's stern
range lights: lights aligned at different heights to guide vessels into narrow channels
reef: verb reduce a sail's size by lowering it and securing the excess to the boom
riding sail: small sail used to directionally stabilize a boat at anchor
rode: a line to which an anchor is attached (often includes a length of chain)

rope clutch: a locking device to secure one end of a line or sheet
rudder: a submerged, vertically hinged blade used to steer a boat
salon: a living or dining area within the cabin of a boat
sea-anchor: a submergible, funnel-like device used to minimize drifting in high winds
screw: colloquial term for propeller on a boat or ship
sheet: a line (or rope) attached to the aft end of a sail
shroud: wire rope support between the mast and deck amidships
sloop: a sailboat with a single mast amidships
sole: floor; as in cabin *sole* or cockpit *sole*
spreaders: horizontal spars attached to a mast to spread the shrouds and stabilize the mast
stanchion: a post fixed to a deck's perimeter to support a life-line
standing rigging: hardware, lines and sails used to propel a vessel by wind power
starboard: the right side of a vessel; to the right of a vessel
stay: wire rope connecting masthead to bow or stern to stabilize the mast
stern: the rear (aft) end of a boat
storm jib: a small jib of heavier than normal material
sweet-water: inland bodies of fresh water; lake water
tack: one leg of a zig-zag course that enables sailing into the wind
tacking: alternately sailing to port and to starboard into the wind
tender: small boat or dinghy used to reach a vessel moored offshore
tether: line attached to a mariner to prevent falling overboard
tickle: a narrow salt-water strait, as in an entrance to a harbour (Newfoundland 1870)
tiller: lever connected to a boat's rudder to facilitate steering
thru-hull: fitting through a boat's hull to accommodate a discharge or intake pipe
toe rail: raised edge surrounding a boat's deck; see *deck combing*
transducer: depth sounder's transmitter-receiver usually installed through a boat's hull
transom: the portion of a boat's hull that closes the aft end of the vessel
travel-lift: purpose-built vehicle for moving boats within a boatyard
trimaran: boat consisting of a primary hull fitted with two outrigger hulls
un-stayed: describes a mast that is not supported by stays or shrouds
V-berth: V-shaped double sleeping berth located in a vessel's bow
variation: directional difference between true and magnetic north
VHF: short-range marine radio using very high frequency radio waves
wake: an often visible trail of disturbed water left by a moving vessel
washboard: rigid, weather-proof covering installed over a boat's companionway
weather boards: canvas panels fixed between stanchions to deflect wind and sea spray

wet-locker: an area specifically designed to house wet clothes and rain gear
working jib: most commonly used moderate-weather foresail
winch: a vertical drum around which a line can be wrapped for mechanical advantage
yawl: a sailing vessel with a second mast aft of the rudder post
Zodiac: a brand name inflatable rubber boat

Made in the USA
Charleston, SC
29 October 2016